"I'LL SEE YOU IN COURT"

"I'LL SEE YOU IN COURT"

GODFREY ISAAC

Contemporary Books, Inc.
Chicago

Library of Congress Cataloging in Publication Data

Isaac, Godfrey.
  I'll see you in court.

  1. Isaac, Godfrey.   2. Lawyers—United States—Biography.
  3. Trials—United States.   I. Title.
KF373.I78A34   345'73'00924 [B]   79-51021
ISBN 0-8092-7399-3

Published by Contemporary Books, Inc.
180 North Michigan Avenue, Chicago, Illinois 60601
Manufactured in the United States of America
Library of Congress Catalog Card Number: 79-51021
International Standard Book Number: 0-8092-7399-3

Published simultaneously in Canada by
Beaverbooks
953 Dillingham Road
Pickering, Ontario L1W 1Z7
Canada

Under certain circumstances the names of persons involved in the cases related herein have been fictionalized.

"I'LL SEE YOU IN COURT"

Chapter One

As a trial lawyer, and a trial lawyer with a good reputation and a lot of experience, I have the knack of asking the right question at the right time. The zinger.

So I asked the zinger of myself as I walked across the yard in San Quentin. It was a one-question cross-examination.

"Godfrey," I said, "what the hell are you doing here?"

I almost laughed, but it wasn't the place for laughter. I almost laughed because there was no rational, sensible answer to that question. I was on an errand which I doubted could result in a significant victory and might, indeed, prove detrimental to my practice.

I was on my way to interview Sirhan Bishara Sirhan, the infamous Palestinian who had been convicted of murdering Senator Robert Kennedy in the Ambassador Hotel in Los Angeles. As the convicted murderer of Bobby Kennedy, he was one of the most passionately hated men in the world. It stood to reason that his lawyer might have some of that hatred

1

transfer to him. I was not yet his lawyer, but there was tremendous pressure on me to take the case.

The yard at San Quentin Prison in those days was a snakepit. The system made visitors to Death Row, where Sirhan was in residence, walk through the yard. I do not know if that is a deliberate step, but it does serve to make Death Row visitors stop and think—is this trip really necessary? En route to your destination, you pass dozens of inmates, all shapes, sizes, and colors, but all with one common denominator—each is a convicted felon. You don't know whether, as your eye catches theirs, you should look away or hazard a smile or try to out-stare them. I tried all three tactics that hot day in 1970, and none of them was satisfactory. I walked briskly, or as briskly as I could without breaking into an unseemly gallop.

Once again that question echoed in my brain—"Godfrey, what the hell are you doing here?"

I had been involved in the assassination inquiry for about a year already, representing Teddy Charach, perhaps the first journalist in the country to uncover evidence of the possible second gun in the Kennedy assassination. Teddy was flamboyant, tenacious, and often pigheaded. He had convinced himself and me, too, that Sirhan Bishara Sirhan may not have been the assassin. He could not be called innocent, of course—you can't call a man who shot off a pistol in the presence of a presidential candidate innocent. There was no doubt that Sirhan did do that—the pistol was wrested from his hand and it had been fired. No, he was hardly an innocent. But that did not necessarily make him a murderer, either. Charach and his associates had uncovered a wealth of seemingly irrefutable evidence indicating that somebody else was in that kitchen at that hotel that night, firing a revolver, and there was much evidence pointing to the fact that someone else was in a much better physical position to have fired the fatal bullets than Sirhan was.

So, I had been involved in the case for a while, but it is one thing representing an outsider and it is another thing representing a man convicted of having assassinated one of the most popular figures in American public life. Pinpricks of anticipation tickled my spine. Yet, the anticipation was tempered with determination. I was determined to do what I considered right, no matter what the consequences.

I kept walking across the San Quentin yard, thinking of the legal issues so hard that it took my mind off the ominous-looking men. The sky was cloudy, gray, forbidding. Was that symbolic? I kept on walking.

I knew that should I decide to take the case—that is, of course, always assuming that Sirhan decided to retain me—I would be in for a rough time. Already, I could feel it even before I made the trip north from my Los Angeles home to the monstrous, cold, impersonal mass of stone that is San Quentin. There were intimations of what would lie in store for me in the press, even before the trip. There had been hints that I might become Sirhan's attorney, and that had brought forth a rash of stories speculating on my motives.

The sum of most of them was that the only reason I—or any attorney—would possibly elect to represent Sirhan would be for the publicity which would accrue. I knew that, in my case at least, that was obviously untrue. I didn't need it. I was already successful, thanks to several factors, not the least of which was my successful defense the year before of Dr. Thomas T. Noguchi, the beleaguered Los Angeles medical examiner and coroner. That trial made me popular and in demand throughout Southern California. I didn't need any more publicity; I had had all I needed, and, because of that, I had more cases than I could possibly handle. Besides, any publicity would probably be negative.

What, then, were my motives?

At first it was simply because the case was interesting. More than that, fascinating.

It hadn't been an easy affair, representing Teddy Charach as he tried to force action about his theory that a second gun—

presumably fired by a second trigger finger and, thus, a second gunman—had, indeed, shot and killed Senator Kennedy.

There had been death threats, nasty phone calls, and the like. Lawyers, if they get involved with any sort of controversial case, become familiar with the fine art of receiving threats over the phone. It seems to be part and parcel of the profession. Everybody knows, or should know, that every criminal, no matter how heinous and reprehensible his crime, is entitled to adequate legal representation; yet there are still some segments of the public who cannot separate the lawyer from the criminal he represents. I had had threats before, as every lawyer has had, and I simply would hang up the phone and go on with whatever it was I was doing. I knew that people who make threatening phone calls generally do nothing else. Moreover, I had made up my mind long ago that harassment would not control my actions.

While representing Charach I became more and more familiar with the facts surrounding the killing of Senator Kennedy, and a sense of history began to dominate my thinking. The case did after all concern the assassination of a United States Senator, a member of the Kennedy family and a man believed to be the front-running candidate for President of the United States. A bullet from a gun held in the hand of an assassin had outweighed millions of votes. Ballot boxes all over the country had shrunk into the size of a .22 caliber automatic. History had already been written, but I suddenly realized that perhaps there was another paragraph still to be recorded. What lawyer would not break his ass to be instrumental in correcting an historical error?

Finally, I arrived at the Death Row door. A guard inspected the pass I had been given, opened the door, locked it behind me, escorted me to a small office. Again, my pass was examined. Another guard asked me to follow him and we went up a stairway.

Death Row!

I was first struck by the silence. The absence of any sound

was so strong it was almost like a physical presence. It occurred to me, as I sensed the utter despair of the place, that there was something wrong with our system if human beings ended up like this. You could almost smell the terror. Suddenly and unexpectedly, I heard laughter.

The guard stopped before one of the doors, opened a small aperture, and looked in.

"Visitor, Sirhan," he said.

He didn't wait for a reply, but shoved his huge key into the lock and opened the door.

"Let me know when you're through, Mr. Isaac," the guard said, and held the door wide for me to go in.

Sirhan was seated, but he jumped up to greet me.

I don't know what I had expected when I first met Sirhan Bishara Sirhan, but this wasn't it. I assumed that an assassin (or, at least, someone who had fired a gun in the vicinity of a presidential candidate) would look like an assassin. Brutal. Evil. Cruel. But no. Not Sirhan. He was a small, dark-eyed, dark-haired man, a sensitive, seemingly caring man. There was no hostility. Instead, an attitude of friendly anticipation. He gave off an air of warmth and appreciation. I had been prepared to dislike him, but, after I spent three hours with him that day, I wound up finding him likable—and that feeling continues to this day.

I deplore violence and have never condoned the use of a gun. I can, however, separate the person from the act. And Sirhan Sirhan, I know, is bright, intelligent, well-informed, and shows no signs of being psychopathic. He has a well-developed sense of humor. He is polite and charming, and if I hadn't known about his alleged crime, I would say he would be the kind of person I would enjoy talking to at a friendly cocktail party.

We talked for a few hours about this and that, but mostly about his involvement in the assassination of Senator Kennedy. His position then—and now—is that he doesn't remember shooting his gun. They told him he did, and he accepted that. They told him he was the one who killed Kennedy, and because so many of them said it and seemed so sure of it, he accepted that, too. He can't remember it. I believed him then, I still believe him. I am not saying I believe he did not kill Bobby Kennedy, because Sirhan doesn't say that. All Sirhan says is that he cannot remember what happened that terrible night. I believe that when he says he cannot remember, he is telling the truth.

It is not my intention to throw more oil on the fires of controversy raging around the Robert Kennedy killing. As far as I am concerned, the case is now closed. Sirhan Sirhan was tried and convicted and his conviction stands. The appeals and motions I brought have, I believe, added some enlightenment to the matter, but have not altered the ultimate fact. I am still Sirhan's attorney as this is being written, and my professional obligation and my goal at this point is to assist where I can and advise when requested. Sirhan looks forward to his eventual release from prison, and I believe that will come. He has become reconciled to the cold, hard fact that, despite all the doubts, the verdict is in and will probably never be changed.

I suppose that all lawyers have a continuing concern over the effects of becoming involved in an emotionally charged representation such as the one in which I found myself. In the years that I have been Sirhan's attorney, the case has affected my marriage, my business, and even some friendships. Everything we do, of course, affects us to some extent, but a case like this really exacerbates emotional reactions.

In legal life one thing leads to another and we often find that an involvement in one case leads to new and varied experiences. In 1969, my representation of Dr. Thomas Noguchi (see Chapter 3) led me to new frontiers of legal representation. One of the cases to which it led was that of Sirhan.

During the highly publicized Noguchi hearing, I was approached one day by a man who identified himself as Theodore Charach. He was an investigative journalist, deeply involved in his inquiry into the Kennedy assassination.

"Mr. Isaac," he said to me, "you have to listen to me. I can prove that Sirhan Sirhan didn't kill Robert Kennedy."

Another of those nuts, I thought.

"Mr. Charach," I said, "I'm sure you are very sincere and I am sure you believe what you are saying. But I am involved right now in the Noguchi case and I have no time . . . "

"This is the most important case in the world I'm talking about. There's a man on Death Row in San Quentin who didn't do it."

"Look, I know it's important. But I can't do anything about it right now and, besides . . . "

I kept trying to get rid of him, to shake him off for several weeks. He was insistent. He was often in my reception room in the office. He was frequently on the phone. He shoved documents under my nose which he wanted me to read. I kept turning him down; everyone knew Sirhan was guilty. Finally, after what must have been six or seven months of this, he persuaded me to listen to some tapes he had made which, he said, would convince me to take his case.

The tapes he played included an interview he had had with a man named Thane Eugene Cesar.

Cesar had been a part-time security guard, hired to be at the Ambassador Hotel on the night of June 4, 1968, to help protect the person of Senator Robert F. Kennedy. He was moonlighting on that job, because his full-time job was as a worker at the Lockheed plant in Burbank. He had been hired by the Ace Security Guard Service, which had been contracted to supply the security at the hotel that night, and he had carried a revolver and had been assigned to the kitchen area.

On the tapes that Charach made, Cesar seemed to be something of a right-wing fanatic. He said things about how he felt the world would be a better place without the Kennedys, how the blacks were taking over the world and the Kennedys were handing the U.S. to them on a silver platter. Charach asked him who he supported for president and he answered, without any hesitation, "George Wallace, of course."

Being a right-wing fanatic does not necessarily make him appear to be a murderer, or even a potential murderer, but there was more. Charach had done his work well.

"I can prove," he said to me, "that Thane Eugene Cesar drew his gun."

If he could prove that, I knew that would be a startling fact. After the trial, Evelle Younger, the district attorney of Los Angeles County at the time of the shooting, stated flatly that only one gun was drawn in the Ambassador kitchen that night—and that one gun belonged to Sirhan. Charach, admittedly something of a fanatic on the subject, came to the conclusion that Cesar had fired a gun that night. It might have been in the line of duty. Perhaps, when he saw Sirhan draw his gun, Charach speculated, Cesar acted on the spur of the moment, drew his own gun, and fired, hitting the man he admittedly hated. According to Charach, the position of the wounds and the ballistic information clearly indicate that Sirhan could not have fired the fatal shot, or the others that entered Kennedy's body, but Cesar, according to Charach, was in a position from which those shots could have been fired.

Later, when I petitioned the California Supreme Court, on Sirhan's behalf, to issue a writ of habeas corpus, my petition included the following section, which, in essence, was the gist of Charach's argument:

"At the time SIRHAN BISHARA SIRHAN commenced firing of his pistol, DONALD SCHULMAN, an employee of Los Angeles Television Station KNXT, was directly behind SENATOR KENNEDY and saw a uniformed security guard fire his hand gun and said DONALD SCHULMAN saw SENATOR KENNEDY hit by three bullets. The District Attorney never called SCHULMAN to testify before the Grand Jury or at the trial of SIRHAN BISHARA SIRHAN, nor did he mention SCHULMAN in his report to the people of the State at his press conference reporting on the KENNEDY

MURDER. However, SCHULMAN had been interviewed by television newsmen within minutes of the shooting and reported the firing by a security guard, which interview was both broadcast on television and reported in numerous newspapers. The significance of this is not that he was necessarily correct, but that he was deliberately ignored by the police to avoid any conflict in their pre-supposed theory of one gunman."

And, then, in the next paragraph of the petition:

"The security guard, referred to above, was THANE EUGENE CESAR, a part-time employee of ACE SECURITY GUARD SERVICE, and was assigned to the Ambassador Hotel to augment the hotel's security staff. He was accompanying SENATOR KENNEDY AND KARL UECKER through the kitchen after waiting at the swinging doors leading into the room where the SENATOR was shot. CESAR admits drawing his gun at the time that SIRHAN BISHARA SIRHAN began firing and being near the floor with his back against the ice machine behind and below and to the right of SENATOR KENNEDY, close enough to, and he did receive powder burns. For reasons known only to the Police Department, CESAR'S gun was never examined to determine if it had been fired, nor did the prosecution call CESAR to testify before the Grand Jury or at the trial of SIRHAN BISHARA SIRHAN. Furthermore, Cesar had owned a nine shot .22 caliber cadet revolver, serial number Y13332, which he sold on September 6, 1968 to a JIM YODER in Arkansas. Shortly thereafter, the gun was reportedly stolen from YODER'S home and has never been recovered. Thus, it was not and now cannot be examined or tested for ballistic comparison purposes in the instant matter."

That was the gist of what Charach told me along with showing me the autopsy report. The autopsy had been performed by my then client, Dr. Thomas T. Noguchi, the Chief Medical Examiner-Coroner of Los Angeles. I knew that Noguchi was tremendously capable in his field—so capable that many of his colleagues considered him a genius—and I also knew that Noguchi considered the Kennedy autopsy his master work, if any autopsy can warrant that designation. Noguchi had been very much aware that the eyes of the world would be on that autopsy, and he also had been very much aware that the autopsy on President John F. Kennedy, in Dallas, was considered widely to have been badly botched. Therefore, he was meticulous about the post mortem examination he did on Bobby Kennedy. I was confident that if there was anything that could be said for certain about the case it was this: Noguchi's autopsy had to be as close to perfection as anything could be.

Noguchi's autopsy seemed to support Charach. The shots that entered Senator Kennedy's body, including the fatal one, had all come from behind him, right to left, and had entered his body on an upward trajectory. More importantly, they had been fired from near point-blank range. At the most, the muzzle of the murder weapon was no more than six inches away.

OK. Now, where was Sirhan Bishara Sirhan? That had been established. He was in front of Senator Kennedy. He had been standing near the steam table. As Kennedy passed the ice machine, Sirhan stepped out and fired directly at Senator Kennedy as the two men faced each other. Not from behind him.

Later, a noted criminalist told me there was another firing position. That was the position at or near where Thane Eugene Cesar was reported to be standing, as observed by a competent observer, television newsman Don Schulman. Cesar was behind Kennedy. According to the reports he had fallen and was in a seated position when he drew his gun, so he was obviously at a point below Kennedy.

Charach made a persuasive case. If Noguchi's autopsy was to be believed, and if Schulman's eyewitness testimony was accurate, then Charach felt there could be only one conclusion.

That conclusion: Sirhan didn't kill Kennedy. He shot at him, yes; but his shots went wide and hit and injured several people in the Kennedy entourage. However, his were not the bullets that killed Kennedy. Those lethal shots came from another gun. That was what I came to believe after I listened to Teddy Charach, examined his evidence, and heard the tapes that he played for me. At least, I felt, serious questions had been raised and the public was entitled to serious answers. But Charach and his persuasive material were not sufficient for me. I needed more, so I went to see Joe Busch.

Joseph Busch, who has since died, was then the district attorney of Los Angeles County. We had gone to law school together, at Loyola, and had been good friends for some twenty years. I wanted to talk to someone on the inside, to get some corroboration of the Charach charges. Charach was convincing, but I knew he had a vested interest in the inquiry. He is a nice-looking man who was, in those days, somewhat down on his luck; his clothes were worn and the total impression was not inspiring. I made an appointment to talk to Busch, just to get another view.

"Joe," I said to Busch, "tell me something. Where was Sirhan Sirhan in relationship to Senator Kennedy? And how close were they?"

Busch picked up the phone and asked his associate, John Howard, to step in. Howard had been one of the attorneys who prosecuted Sirhan. He was intimately familiar with the facts. I repeated my question to Howard, about where Sirhan was at the time of the shooting.

"Sirhan was in front of Kennedy," John Howard said, "and I place him about eleven feet from Kennedy."

"All right, then," I asked, "how in the hell can a man who is eleven feet in front of Kennedy shoot him point-blank from the rear?"

Howard and Busch looked at each other a moment, as though that simple question had never occurred to them.

"That," Busch said, "is a good question."

It was a good question. A damned good question. To this day, I have never gotten a satisfactory answer to that good question, either. In fact, as the years go by, they keep moving Sirhan closer and closer to Kennedy.

"Yeah," Howard said. "That's a good question."

"Absolutely," Busch said. "And, you know something, Godfrey? You and I, we'll have to get together sometime and bullshit about it."

I stood up and looked him in the eye.

"Joe," I said, "I'm going to get into this case."

"That's great, Godfrey," said the district attorney. "You do that. And we'll have some fun with the case."

I don't exactly get into cases to have fun with them. I enjoy the legal maneuvering sometimes, and I must admit that cross-examining a hostile witness, when I know I have the equipment to get at the truth, can be a high—but fun is not precisely what I had in mind when I became a lawyer. In this matter, I felt that the Kennedy assassination was too deadly serious to be fun and games.

All the information I have mentioned in this chapter—all the facts about the possibility of a second gun—were not brought out by the defense in Sirhan's trial.

The lawyers who represented Sirhan, though eminently competent, never elicited in court any facts raising a doubt that Sirhan had fired the fatal shot.

When I looked back over the transcript of Sirhan's trial, I kept looking for some reference to the possibility that a second gunman had been in the Ambassador Hotel kitchen. I searched for a mention of Thane Eugene Cesar and his drawn pistol. I scoured the testimony for an explanatory word about Sirhan's position relative to the path of that fatal bullet.

Nothing.

After studying the transcript of the trial, and contrasting it with what I had learned, I made my decision to enter the case. That decision was based on my growing concern that justice had not been done and that expediency may have dictated the result of the Sirhan trial. I respected the verdict, and had no criticism of the prosecution or the jury. I merely felt that there was more to know. I took the case.

It was not an obsession with me. It was not a cause. It was nothing that would have me carrying banners or affixing bumper stickers to my car. The assassination buffs, many of whom are wild-eyed folks who see conspiracies behind every political murder, jumped on the fact that Godfrey Isaac had become involved on the side of Sirhan Bishara Sirhan and the second gun theory. When that news got out, I was besieged. Every nut in the Far West was on my trail. I am not generalizing all of the conspiracy fans as automatically "nuts," because I know many who are intelligent and sincere in their belief that Oswald was not alone in killing John Kennedy, that Ray was not alone in killing Martin Luther King, and that Sirhan was not alone in killing Robert Kennedy. But, for every one of those sincere believers, there are dozens of kooks—people who see conspiracies behind everything.

They wrote me letters, full of misspellings and references to Communism and atheism and anarchism and every sort of ism that made the particular correspondent angry. There were phone calls of the same sort, ranting and raving and saying that before I was done with the case, I had to prove that the Bobby Kennedy assassination was part of the international plot to (a) kill all Catholics in public office; (b) have the oil cartel take over Washington; (c) elect George Wallace President; (d) kill everybody who was involved in the Jimmy Hoffa prosecution. And on and on.

My client, then, was Teddy Charach. I must say that he was a benevolent fanatic. The case had become a total obsession with him. Not me. I tried hard to maintain my cool, my perspective, and I think I succeeded. The thing was all very emotional and there were nuts on both sides of the fence. For all the assassination buffs who welcomed my participation, there were an equal number of Sirhan-haters who decried that self-same participation.

I had many Jewish clients who were angry with me. They

felt that Sirhan's motives had to do with Kennedy's defense of Israel, and, therefore, I was being anti-Israel and anti-Semitic in working on his behalf. (I wasn't precisely working on his behalf, at least not yet, but that was splitting hairs to those people.)

I told them that a lawyer sometimes defends unpopular clients, and repeated the old legal truism that every person, no matter who he is or what he is, has a right to the best legal help available. My appearing on the side of Sirhan did not in any way mean that I approved of his politics or his philosophy. It was simply that he and his supporters had a perfect right to adequate legal counsel, and, for the present at least, that was going to be me.

The first thing Charach did was to go out and retain a criminalist to investigate thoroughly the scientific and criminological aspects of our case. I felt we needed more authenticating support about all the elements—the ballistics, the wounds, the firing positions—before we could do anything legally. I have always felt that you can never have too much evidence. I like to buttress my cases with expert upon expert, affidavit upon affidavit, exhibit upon exhibit. Sometimes, the sheer weight of evidence can be impressive and convincing in itself. I must admit that sometimes when the facts are not too precise, merely having a great number of experts can give those facts weight. If you have many people testifying to your fact, it may gradually appear to be stronger than it is.

In this case, I felt the facts were solid. But my habits were hard to break.

"Teddy," I said to Charach, "we have to get somebody else to probe this. I want the best there is."

Charach discussed this with Grant Cooper, the renowned lawyer who defended Sirhan during the murder trial. He immediately suggested that we contact Bill Harper. That turned out to be an excellent choice.

William W. Harper was a consulting criminalist to the Pasadena Police Department, a former Navy Intelligence officer, a consultant with a long and distinguished record. Teddy contacted him and retained him to look into every aspect of the case for us. After more than seven months of investigation, he turned in his report. His affidavit, part of the same petition for habeas corpus filed on Sirhan's behalf later, sums up his findings:

"An analysis of the physical circumstances at the scene of the assassination discloses that Senator Kennedy was fired upon from two distinct firing positions while he was walking through the kitchen pantry at the Ambassador Hotel. FIRING POSITION A, the position of Sirhan, was located directly in front of the Senator, with Sirhan face-to-face with the Senator. This position is well established by more than a dozen eyewitnesses. A second firing position, FIRING POSITION B, is clearly established by the autopsy report, and was located in close proximity to the Senator, immediately to the right and rear. It was from this position that 4 (four) shots were fired, three of which entered the Senator's body. One of these shots made a fatal penetration of the Senator's brain. A fourth shot passed through the right shoulder pad of the Senator's coat. These four shots from Firing Position B all produced powder residue patterns, indicating they were fired from a distance of only a few inches. They were closely grouped within a 12-inch circle.

"In marked contrast, the shots from FIRING POSITION A produced no powder residue patterns on the bodies or clothing of any of the surviving victims, all of whom were walking behind the Senator. These shots were widely dispersed.

"Senator Kennedy suffered no frontal wounds. The three wounds suffered by him were fired from behind and had entrance wounds in the posterior portions of his body.

"It is evident that a strong conflict exists between the eyewitness accounts and the autopsy findings. This conflict is totally irreconcilable with the hypothesis that only Sirhan's gun was involved in the assassination. The conflict can be eliminated if we consider that a second gun was being fired from FIRING POSITION B concurrently with the firing of the Sirhan gun from FIRING POSITION A. It is self-evident that within the brief period of the shooting (roughly 15 seconds) Sirhan could not have been in both firing positions at the same time. No eyewitnesses saw Sirhan at any position other than FIRING POSITION A, where he was quickly restrained by citizens present at that time and place.

"It is my opinion that these circumstances, in conjunction with the autopsy report (without for the moment considering additional evidence), firmly establish that two guns were fired in the kitchen pantry concurrently."

There was more. Harper had gone to exhaustive lengths and there was evidence about the total number of shots fired vs. bullets recovered; about the angle of the bullets that hit the other victims; about the serial numbers of Sirhan's gun and a second gun, which mysteriously popped up; about the ballistics on the bullets fired from the two guns.

Harper's conclusions:

(1) Two .22 caliber guns were involved in the assassination.
(2) Senator Kennedy was killed by one of the shots fired from FIRING POSITION B, fired by a second gunman.
(3) The five surviving victims were wounded by Sirhan shooting from FIRING POSITION A.
(4) It is extremely unlikely that any of the bullets fired by the Sirhan gun ever struck the body of Senator Kennedy.

Harper told us that he had even more conclusive evidence, involving the science of ballistics. He had taken a special camera and photographed the bullets—a bullet taken from Kennedy's body and bullets fired from the second gun that had mysteriously appeared in the case. He found, first, that the rifling angles were markedly different in the Kennedy bullet and the Sirhan gun bullets.

"The bullets that hit Kennedy," Harper told us, "were not fired from the gun Sirhan was carrying."

Then he got into the question of cannelures—the gnarled grooves that bullet manufacturers place on the bullets. He found the Sirhan gun bullets had two cannelures. The bullets taken from Kennedy's body had one cannelure. To him, that was proof that not only were the bullets not from the same gun, but they were even from different manufacturers.

"The bullets that hit Kennedy," Harper said again, this time with more conviction, "were not fired from the gun that Sirhan was carrying."

Meanwhile, Charach had been doing some investigating on his own. He had gone to the County Clerk, found the evidence envelope where the Sirhan gun test bullets were stored, and studied them. He found that they bore a number on them that was different from the registered number of Sirhan's gun. Here was another puzzle, without an explanation or an answer.

When Harper finished his work and turned in his report, Charach and I were excited. We now felt that we had a solid case, because Harper seemed positive and Harper was a man who was tremendously well regarded and respected in criminology circles. We knew that we now had a solid position from which to take action. The problem was—what sort of action could be taken? Charach turned to me. That was obviously my department, as the lawyer. What should we do now?

I had, of course, been thinking about that question for some time. All those months that Harper and Charach had been doing their probing and researching and studying, I had been doing my homework, too, trying to find a way, an opening, a chink in the legal armor.

Many laymen have little concept of the complexity of the law. Practicing law is far from being simple. There are myriad ways to sue, many ways to defend against a suit. Sometimes there doesn't seem to be any remedy at all for a particular situation.

That was the problem when I represented Teddy Charach.

On what possible grounds could I use the report Bill Harper had made? Charach wasn't legally involved. He was neither the accused nor the accuser, not even a victim, not even related to a victim.

My idea, which I had been examining during the months that Harper and Charach had been working, was to bring an action under the Brown Act—the public's right to know. The Brown Act (the Brown was Governor Edmund "Pat" Brown, Sr., the father of California's present governor) was new and in this regard untested in the courts, but I felt I could make a good argument that "the public's right to know" should most certainly include the facts about the Sirhan-Kennedy case our investigation had unearthed and should require disclosure by the police of all their evidence. These facts should have been presented during the original trial, I felt, but better now than never.

Finally, on behalf of my then client, Teddy Charach, I brought an action under the Brown Act. I sued Mayor Sam Yorty of Los Angeles, District Attorney Evelle Younger, the Los Angeles Police Department, and others.

Charach called a press conference; he had high hopes of a major news breakthrough. But it was not a rousing success.

The press was skeptical and unflattering. They doubted Charach's sincerity. They knew that my reputation was good but wondered about my motives in this case. They accepted Harper's credentials but cast aspersions on his research capabilities.

It degenerated into a shouting match, even though only a few media representatives attended. I tried to keep order and hold it in check, but Charach lost his temper and began yelling at some of the reporters. That was, of course, the worst thing that he could have done. Even worse, from Charach's standpoint, was that there was practically no coverage—and most of what there was was negative.

The suit I had brought had actually been intended to force the state to disclose certain records to Charach, records which

we contended would show positively that Sirhan Bishara
Sirhan could not have killed Senator Robert Kennedy. It was,
I felt, a legal and proper action under the terms of the Brown
Act, and might establish a very important legal precedent. The
Brown Act, heretofore to my knowledge, had not been used as
the basis of this sort of legal action.

Wide press coverage would have been a bonanza for Teddy
Charach, of course. I knew that and knew that everybody
else—the press included—knew that, and that was one reason
they were so antagonistic toward him. In a sense, I understood
that. They perceived him (Charach) as being wild-eyed and
bushy-haired and felt there had to be something wrong with
him. The gravest sin of all was that he was poor. Obviously,
to those on the outside, he was only involved in the case for
the money he might make out of it. There was, I believe, a
grain of truth in that allegation. Charach's motives included
money, I believe, but he was also influenced by public-
spiritedness, curiosity, and a sense of history.

He wanted to become rich and famous. I think he also
wanted to get at the truth in the process. Somehow, those
goals became intertwined. It happened that he had latched on
to a cause where it served him to be on the side of disclosing
truth, so that was what he espoused. And he espoused it with
vigor, tenacity, and a determination I have rarely seen.

The reporters, who were certainly no dummies, sniffed out
his desire for publicity. I am afraid that, because Charach and
I were joined together, they may have labeled me a publicity
seeker, too. As I have said, all too often the lawyer finds
himself tarred with the same brush as the client. It is hard for
the lay public—even an informed lay public, such as the
press—to distinguish between the two.

So the press conference degenerated into a contest between
Charach and the press, with me trying to maintain some
semblance of order in all that chaos.

The upshot was that the press reports were bad. Bad? They
were dreadful. They impugned Charach's motives and

Harper's motives and my motives. And, thus, they impugned the motives of the legal action we had been bringing.

That was when the death threats began, too. They got so bad that no one in my family—my children included—wanted to pick up the phone. It was always a relief when our home phone rang and it turned out to be someone we knew.

I recognized the signs of an impending legal disaster. That is one thing an experienced lawyer can usually tell quickly—when the case he is involved with is a definite winner or a definite loser. There are many in that gray in-between area, cases that could go either way, but there are more that are obviously good or bad. And this one had apparent problems. The way the press felt was obvious. They suspected Charach of the basest of motives and, therefore, they were totally unsympathetic to the action he was bringing. I felt that any judge might feel the same way.

Before reaching my final conclusions, however, I went back over all the evidence.

First, there was the Noguchi autopsy.

I must say, again, that this was the clincher for me—the main reason, the deciding factor for my decision to enter the case. Noguchi was a man I respected. And he had done his best on the Bobby Kennedy autopsy. Noguchi had been perceptive enough not to do it all himself. He had called in some of the greats in the fields of forensic medicine and pathology and related sciences—men such as Dr. Cyril Wecht, the distinguished Pittsburgh coroner; the brilliant William Eckert of Wichita; and several other outstanding scientists.

During the Noguchi trial, one of my key witnesses was Dr. Victor Rosen, a brilliant and honorable pathologist who, at the time, was a pathologist at Cedars of Lebanon Hospital in Los Angeles. It was Rosen who called Noguchi's Kennedy autopsy "the most perfect medical examination in history."

I was certain that when Noguchi said that the fatal bullets had been fired from behind, below, right to left, and from a distance of not more than six inches, then the fatal bullets had been fired from behind, below, right to left, and from a distance of not more than six inches. I started with that assurance, that the autopsy was gospel.

Noguchi, incidentally, had found other wounds, and I felt one of those was curious. That was a contact wound under the right arm, the bullet having been fired into the armpit. Noguchi said the gun must have been held against the body for that wound to have occurred the way it did. I remembered hearing that that tactic, holding the gun under the arm and firing into the armpit, had been a favorite Mafia method. It muffled the sound that way. I remembered how Robert Kennedy had fought the Mafia so vigorously and wondered about the possibility that the killing might have been an underworld affair.

In addition, there was the testimony of witnesses, all of them placing Sirhan in front of Kennedy, and many placing him around eleven feet from Kennedy at the time of the shooting. A few witnesses had Sirhan somewhat closer, but none close enough.

The two facts were plainly and clearly contradictory. Again, I asked myself the unanswerable question—if Kennedy was killed by shots fired at point-blank range from behind and below him, how could Sirhan be the assassin if he was in front of, on a level with, and eleven feet or eight feet or even four feet away?

The icing on the legal cake was Bill Harper's report, which corroborated many of Charach's discoveries.

At that time, as I reviewed what I had learned and what was in evidence, I was convinced. Sirhan Bishara Sirhan did not kill Robert Kennedy. He may have intended to kill him—I never questioned that—but he missed and had, instead, wounded five other people. But you can't—or shouldn't—convict a man for murder on the basis of intent or on mistaken facts alone. The law, which I love and respect, was crystal clear on that point. Except in certain unrelated circumstances, you have to prove that the deed has been done by the accused, beyond a reasonable doubt. I doubted that the prosecution could prove that now, not with the evidence we had amassed. Unfortunately, that issue had already been resolved in court.

The more I thought about it, the more I realized that the Charach case could not win. I called him into my office for a consultation, and I told him that, flat out.

"Teddy," I said, "I want you to withdraw the suit. We are going to take a beating if we persist."

"But, Godfrey, after all we've done? After all the facts we've gotten? We just can't quit."

"Who said anything about quitting? I just said withdraw this suit, the Brown Act thing. I have another idea. The suit won't work, but maybe this will."

My idea was to turn the antagonism of the press to our advantage. If you can't beat 'em, at least try to get 'em to join you. My thought was that we call the press in, the newspapermen, radio and television men, and public officials, as well, and tell them what we know about the case. They had long harbored some doubts about it all. Tell them the facts we have. Tell them of Harper's conclusions. Pose the questions we have asked ourselves.

"Then," I continued, "we suggest to them that they appoint a committee to investigate the whole case impartially. That way, nobody will be out to benefit from the disclosures. You know, Teddy, that they suspect you of planning to gain from all this."

"Who, me?" Charach said, all innocence. I had to laugh, because we both knew that he was Mr. Ambition personified.

But that idea didn't work either. I called a few of my press friends and sounded them out on it, and they told me that they doubted it would work. The press couldn't be used to form a committee like that, they said, because it would hurt their impartiality. They were supposed to report the news, they said, not make it. They said that perhaps a committee could be formed from other aspects of society, and, if that happened, they would be delighted to report on their activities. But, no, the press itself would have no part of it.

Public officials, too, refused. They would not, or could not, cooperate, and so such a committee was never formed. Shortly after, I abandoned that idea, however, something happened which changed my whole relationship to the case.

Teddy Charach called me.

"Godfrey," he said, "I was just with Mary Sirhan." I knew that Mary Sirhan was Sirhan's mother. "She wants to see you."

"What about?"

"She wants to talk to you about representing her son."

Chapter Two

I TALKED TO MARY SIRHAN. If ever there was a Jewish mother type, it was that little Arab lady. I guess all that proves is that a mother is a mother is a mother, regardless of race, creed, or religion. In fact, here is an incident to illustrate that contention:

On the Fourth of July, in 1972, my wife, Roena, died. Roena will play a very definite role in my life, so it may seem strange to introduce her with her death. But she was an unusual lady, as you will learn, and perhaps this is the best way for you to get to meet her. Roena died in Monterey on the Fourth of July. Anyhow, I made all the arrangements, those terrifying and difficult arrangements, and then came home to the house we had in the Cheviot Hills section of Los Angeles. I was "at home" as our friends and relatives trooped in to pay their condolence calls. There were so many of them that I realized I would have to run out to the store to replenish my supply of food and drinks for the callers to eat and drink. So I ducked out, hopped in the car, went to the supermarket, and bought a whole mess of things.

When I got back, my father-in-law, Douglas Potts, said that a gift had arrived while I was away. He pointed to a package on the table. I unwrapped it and there was a lovely slab of baklava, the exquisite Middle Eastern pastry.

"Where did that come from?" I asked.

"A woman brought it," Potts said.

"Did she give a name?"

"No, I don't know who she was, but I'll tell you this—I think she was Jewish."

I couldn't figure out who it could possibly be until a little while later when the phone rang and it was Mary Sirhan; she asked me if I had gotten the baklava. I couldn't help it—I started to laugh. I could see all the sorrowful people turn and stare at me, the bereaved widower, laughing into the phone. Mary asked me why I was laughing. I guess it was just the release from the tension of the past few days, but I couldn't stop. I kept right on laughing. Potts, who was a nice man, came over to me and asked me what I was laughing about. I managed, then, to get control of myself sufficiently so I could gasp out an answer to him.

"That typical Jewish mother who you said left the baklava. You know who that was?"

"No."

"That was Sirhan Sirhan's mother, Mary."

It was then that I realized what I already had known, and what we all should know—there is little difference between people. Mary Sirhan, a very good Arab lady, looked and acted just like a very good Jewish lady would look and act. When her friend had died—she and Roena had gotten on famously— she had rushed over with her masterpiece, a baklava, as a gesture of sympathy and concern.

At any rate, Mary Sirhan was a mother and had a mother's total concern about her son's fate. As any mother in her situation might, she lived only for one purpose—to see her son freed from prison. She had read all the evidence, heard all the testimony, but nothing could ever convince her that her little boy had done wrong. He couldn't. To her, he was a good boy, he had always been a good boy, he always would be a good boy. Mary Sirhan was a woman with a mission, and that was purely and simply the release and, if possible, the clearing of her son.

She was an articulate woman. She can be very eloquent and passionate when on the subject of Sirhan. She felt that he had been wrongly convicted, unjustly imprisoned. The first time we met, she almost had me in tears. I knew that Sirhan would have to spend many years in prison, and rightfully so, because he did shoot at Kennedy and, at the least, he did injure several people with those shots. He may not have killed Kennedy, but he was hardly the innocent his mother believed. Too many eyewitnesses and too much factual evidence proved otherwise. Still, when she began talking about him and began her emotionally supercharged talk, she moved me.

Over the months that I represented Teddy Charach, Mary and Teddy had frequent conversations about me. She felt she detected a sympathy for her son in me. At the time, I was becoming increasingly sympathetic with the fact that not all the truth had been told. Since I was working on a case that might be of advantage to her son, Mary Sirhan seized on that as proof that I was on her side, and her son's side. She approached me, through Charach, to represent her son.

We met. I held out no unrealistic hope. I made no pie-in-the-sky promises. I merely said that, if her son wanted me to represent him, and if I ultimately decided that I would represent him, then I would certainly do my best for him, and I thought there were things that could be done.

However, first there was a major stumbling block. I was still Teddy Charach's attorney-of-record, and the Brown Act litigation was still on file. I felt that I could not, under those circumstances, also undertake to represent Sirhan Sirhan. That would be a distinct conflict of interest.

I called Charach and said that, before I could even talk to Sirhan, he would have to release me. He would have to sign a letter saying, in effect, that I was no longer his attorney and that I was no longer involved in litigation in his behalf. He was very willing to sign such a letter because, he said, he was anxious for me to represent Sirhan. He felt that I might be able to clear Sirhan of the assassination charge if I were to represent him individually. So I dictated the letter, and Teddy came in and signed it. It clearly stated that my primary legal duty was to Sirhan. He agreed.

That cleared the way for me to talk to Sirhan. After that, it would be up to the two of us—how we hit it off, if he wanted me to represent him, if I were willing to do so. That aspect of the lawyer-client relationship is something you never study in law school, yet it is vital to the legal business. You and your client must establish a working rapport, certainly in cases that come to court, or else you are doomed to failure.

Before I could go to San Quentin, however, there was another formality to attend to. Sirhan did have an attorney, a criminal attorney named Luke McKissick, handling his case at that point. He had gone through several lawyers since his trial. McKissick was a specialist in appellate law, and had been handling his appeal. Understandably, McKissick did not particularly relish the idea of another lawyer coming into the case at this point. I could not blame him.

The procedure in such a situation, when you, as a lawyer, are asked to see a potential client who already has a lawyer of record, is to get a formal letter requesting you to see the client. I got such a letter from Sirhan, in which he stated that he desired me to consult with him. Then I took that letter to a Superior Court judge and had him, in turn, issue an order to the warden of San Quentin Prison to allow me to see and talk with Sirhan. At that point, I did not officially contact Luke McKissick, in case my meeting with Sirhan turned out to be fruitless. If Sirhan didn't want me, or I didn't want him, there was no point in causing prejudice to Sirhan by having told

McKissick about the meeting. If, on the other hand, my meeting with Sirhan turned out well, there would be ample time later to inform the other lawyer.

In the meantime, there was Roena. My wife had a sense of mission. She felt that someday, sometime, somewhere, she would be involved in something very big, very important. History was waiting to embrace her. She thought that maybe this case, the Sirhan case, was her moment.

During the few weeks between Charach's first telling me that Mary Sirhan wanted me to represent her son, and my first full-scale conference with Sirhan in San Quentin, she was after me all the time to take the case.

"Godfrey," she would say, "you *must* take this case. It's your destiny, your fate."

And so it went, day after day, night after night. Roena could be very persuasive, very stubborn. When she went after something she generally got it. She was bound and determined that I would take the Sirhan Sirhan case. I understand her thinking, too, and I must say that in some way I shared her desire to have a role in something historic. But there were other considerations—the evidence, the available legal avenues, balancing the pros and cons, and reaching a rational decision. Where she was emotional, I was trying to be logical.

I promised her that, before my final decision, I would meet Sirhan and then make my determination.

Finally, the day arrived. We flew to San Francisco. Roena went with me, and all the while we were airborne she was pumping me full of her own brand of enthusiasm for taking the case. She kept saying that I should keep an open mind, because she suspected I was tending toward not representing him. I realized then that Roena's ambition was totally boundless and, thus, not reasonable.

I rented a car and we drove to San Quentin. While I went in, Roena sat in the car in the prison parking lot. She could not come in. But she would not stay home, nor would she let me drop her off at a hotel or a park or even a motion picture theater. She wanted to be as close to the scene of action as possible. I think she felt she could exert some influence on me if she was close enough. So she sat in the car in the parking lot for the three hours I was in Sirhan's cell. I am sure that, for those entire three hours, she kept thinking positive thoughts, kept directing vibrations my way.

She never did meet Sirhan, and I think that was one of the big regrets of her life. She was absolutely voracious in her curiosity about him, reading everything she could read, asking questions of me and Mary and anybody else who knew him. It got so that I think she became probably the world's leading Sirhan Sirhan expert. She and Mary Sirhan were very close, and Mary raved about what a great person Roena Isaac was; and Mary told Sirhan about her, so that Sirhan would ask me about Roena whenever we met. Once he told me that he felt he knew her. Sirhan seemed as fascinated with Roena as Roena was with him.

But that was later. The first day, I don't think I mentioned Roena to Sirhan. That first day, I must confess, was a revelation to me. As I said, I was expecting an ogre, a monster, something horrible. I didn't expect this slim, smiling, soft-spoken, witty, intelligent young man.

We did talk for those three hours. We talked about the case, primarily. He told me how he had gone to the Ambassador Hotel that night and that he had been angry with Bobby Kennedy. I was amazed to learn that Robert Kennedy had been his choice for President. He read in the newspapers, however, that, if elected, Kennedy intended to send planes to Israel. This infuriated him; he felt betrayed. Sirhan's family had been expelled from their home in the Israeli war and he had strong nationalistic feelings. He was emotionally distraught, believing Kennedy was willing to do harm to the Arab cause. He did not remember shooting him. He remembered nothing from the moment he came into the kitchen until later, when he was being mauled by the police and the security guards and everybody else in the Kennedy entourage. He was sorry, but that is all he could say. He just didn't remember.

He said that everybody told him he shot the Senator. He supposed he had, because they were good people and they said they had seen him shoot so he guessed they were right about it. Why would they lie? No, he supposed he was guilty.

I told him of the evidence we had found, of the conflict between what all those people had told him and the facts that we had learned. I told him about the autopsy and what it said, and about Harper's research, and about all the other facts that indicated to me that it wasn't Sirhan who had killed Kennedy.

He sat quietly and seemed to be interested, but hardly excited. I am sure he had read it all before in the papers when we had presented our case for Charach, or had discussed it all with his mother.

Finally, as we were talking, he held up his hand and he said, "Mr. Isaac, I want you to be my lawyer."

It was the moment I had been anticipating, with mixed feelings. I now had to make a decision. But, first, there was something I felt I had to clear up with Sirhan.

"I appreciate that, Sirhan," I said. "But before you decide I want to tell you something, I want you to know that I am Jewish."

He looked at me as though I was crazy.

"What the hell difference does that make?" he asked.

"It might be important," I said. "There are many things that we may agree on, but we are undoubtedly in total disagreement about the Middle East."

"Mr. Isaac," Sirhan said. "Let me ask you something. Do you require that I agree with all your views before you'll represent me?"

"Of course not."

"All right, then. Neither do I."

And after a few more minutes of conversation, we shook hands on it. I agreed to represent Sirhan Sirhan.

When I came out of the prison, Roena leaped out of the car and ran across the parking lot to meet me.

"What happened?" she yelled, before we were even close.

I gave her a big smile and a thumb's up sign; she shrieked with delight and ran to me and threw her arms around me in the biggest demonstration of emotion I had had from her in years.

From then on, I had many meetings with Sirhan. I saw him frequently, and never lost my feeling of surprise about him. Each visit reinforced my respect for his command of the language, his humor, and sometimes even his wisdom.

He also often exhibited an incredible street sense. One day, Mary Sirhan called me, very excited. She wanted to see me immediately. She rushed to my office with a letter. It was, she said, a copy of a letter that Sirhan had written to the warden.

In essence, his letter to the warden of San Quentin read:

"Warden: I'm not getting any exercise. My body is atrophying. Don't fuck around with me. I'm not taking any more of your shit."

I was stunned. I wondered what had motivated him to write such a letter. He sometimes used that kind of language, but not in a letter to the warden. It seemed as though he was looking for trouble. I went up to see him at the prison as soon as I could. I found him in handcuffs with his legs manacled, but he was happy.

"They let me out to exercise now," he said.

"Why didn't you just ask them, politely, to let you exercise?"

"Godfrey, you don't understand the mentality of these people, but I do. If I had asked politely, nothing would have happened. I had to do it the way I did it to get any results. The proof is that I am now exercising."

He established an excellent relationship with his guards. They seemed to have a high regard for him and he for them. He has never been a problem prisoner and he has accepted the prison regimen.

Sirhan took a great interest in me and my work and the things I began to try to do for him.

It wasn't an easy situation for a lawyer. The great weight of public opinion—and the courts are very responsive to public opinion, in the long run—was against my client. In fact, I think if the public had its way, Sirhan Sirhan would have been executed on the next clear morning. They certainly did not want to see him released. There was a small but vocal knot of people, such as Teddy Charach, who actually felt he had not killed Kennedy. Even so, he had committed several crimes that fateful night.

My immediate goal was not Sirhan's release. I did feel, however, that the evidence we had found, as a result of the autopsy and the Harper investigation, was enough to warrant a reopening of the case. Perhaps even a new trial. That was, I felt, the most I could possibly strive for. Anything more would be unrealistic. Yet anything less I was certain, would be unjust.

What finally did develop was something unique in American jurisprudence. As a result of my efforts, and those of part of the media and Paul Schrade, one of Sirhan's alleged victims, the court reopened the evidentiary aspect of the case—seven years after the crime had been committed and six years after my client had been convicted of that crime. That was unheard of in legal history. The court said it did so "in the interest of justice and history." Whatever the reason, it was a fantastic coup. Later, moreover, there would be more. The Los Angeles County Board of Supervisors, a body that is certainly nonjudicial, got into the case to conduct its own investigation into the whole Sirhan-Kennedy situation. That, too, was unique.

I presented my arguments to the California Supreme Court in a lengthy brief, full of documentation, full of exhibits, and, I felt, full of facts. I had thoroughly convinced myself that a court, reading the brief I had written, would grant some relief. I was hopeful for an evidentiary hearing at the very least.

I didn't quite get that, but I certainly didn't come away empty-handed either. Judge Robert Wenke, presiding judge of the Superior Court of Los Angeles County, the largest court of its type in the world, reopened that part of the case dealing with the ballistics evidence. He said he wanted to find out if, based on firearm identification and ballistics information, Sirhan had or had not fired the fatal shot. In effect, he was reopening the case to ascertain whether or not there had been a second gun and a second gunman. That, obviously, was exactly what I wanted. I was jubilant and raced to San Quentin to tell Sirhan the good news.

Judge Wenke ordered that the evidence be developed in a unique way. Rather than the usual order of proof, he suggested a novel approach.

His order stipulated that there be six experts appointed. One expert could be appointed by each of the six interested parties in the case—among them were Sirhan Sirhan, the Los Angeles County district attorney, the California attorney general, Paul Schrade, CBS—and that these six name one more, a seventh. He further ordered that all the ballistics evidence be examined by the seven experts who would then report to the court. On the basis of that report, the court would rule on whether or not to grant further relief.

It wasn't totally what I wanted, but I was not unhappy. I felt hopeful that the evidence was such that the experts would have to agree that there was, at the very least, reasonable doubt that Sirhan was the sole gunman and, thus, he was eminently deserving of further consideration.

I felt the evidence would demonstrate there were two guns involved. Yet I knew there were plenty of experts who had tried to negate every point we had developed. For example, when we stated that Sirhan was in front of, and more than three feet away from the Senator, others claimed that as Sirhan fired, Kennedy turned to greet someone else and hence his back was toward Sirhan. Some said that while Sirhan may have been some distance away from the Senator when he first jumped up with his gun, he also lunged toward the Senator and, at the moment he fired, he was considerably closer.

Still, it seemed to me those arguments pitted one group of eyewitnesses against another group of eyewitnesses. Most lawyers feel that eyewitness testimony is chancy at best. The seven experts would be examining hard evidence, not eyewitness evidence. They would be considering firearm identification and ballistics, and I felt that the cannelure differences and the bullet differences noted by Harper would be corroborated by the experts.

However, when the seven experts reported back, a portion of their report was unanimous. They found that there was no demonstrable evidence that there was a second gun. I listened in disbelief, but I recognized the finality of it at once. That report effectively laid the second gun theory to rest. All seven experts signed it, and they were the best in their fields. There could be no realistic probablity of resurrecting that second gun theory, ever again.

There was one ray of hope for the assassination buffs, however. The report contained no positive finding that it was Sirhan's gun that fired the fatal bullet. Thus, the seven experts left the door slightly ajar for future theorists.

But, I am practical. What's done is done, and that second gun theory was done.

I was the first one out of the hearing room. There were dozens of reporters, TV and radio newsmen, lights, cameras, the works.

"Mr. Isaac, as Sirhan's attorney, what did this decision do to the second gun theory?"

I knew it had to be said, and this was as good a time as any to say it.

"In my opinion, the second gun theory is dead."

I went on to explain that because these seven leading experts could find no concrete evidence that there was a second gun, then there was no way to prove the theory of that second gun. Hence, if it could not be proven, it was of no legal value. Ergo, it was dead.

The assassination buffs were now the ones calling me,

heaping invective on me. They had been fans when I led the fight for a new trial, when I was a big second gun proponent. But now that I faced what I perceived to be the truth, they turned against me. Some reasonable people on their side recognized that it was over, but the fanatics swallowed their disappointment as though it had never happened and continued believing the same old theories. But a lawyer cannot be a dreamer; a lawyer must face up to reality and, in this case, bitter though it was, I did just that. I told Sirhan that that phase was finished. It hadn't helped him. We would have to do something else.

I must say that he took it well. Stoically. Calmly. He just shrugged and said, "Whatever you say, Godfrey."

The next few times I saw him, he was downhearted. Not to the point of irrationality. He was never anywhere near suicidal. But he had been up, riding on a cloud of hope. I thought there was good reason to be hopeful—with legal processes, there is never a guarantee—and it was hard to tell him that his hopes had been permanently dashed.

Sirhan bounced back. Pretty soon he was full of plans, looking ahead. He never again mentioned the second gun theory or alluded in any way to that phase of our relationship. Now he was gung ho for what I might do next.

The court had turned me down on my petition for habeas corpus. The fact that the seven experts had found no evidence of a second gun effectively killed that avenue. There really was no practical legal maneuver left to me. Sirhan's appeals had been exhausted long before. The reopening of the evidentiary hearing was now history, so there was nothing more I could do in that connection.

It was on to another arena. There was still the arena of public opinion.

Initially, public opinion had been heavily against Sirhan. He was considered by many to be a villain, an agent of the devil. I doubt if there has ever been a criminal so thoroughly and universally hated as this man.

I decided my next step had to be to try and turn public opinion around. I felt it was essential. Sirhan would be coming up for parole some year—probably 1985—and, if public opinion then was still as violently opposed to him, he would stand little chance of gaining his freedom at that time. So my effort to alter the world's feelings about him would be designed, at the least, to give him a better chance at parole a decade later. Perhaps, if I could help to make a significant shift in public opinion, there might be some help sooner, as well. You never can tell.

The way to change public opinion is to give the public a new, different and, if you possibly can, more favorable impression of the person you represent. That must be accomplished via the press. Probably the best way to do it is through television. Today, at least, that is the most widely disseminated medium with the largest total audience and, hence, the greatest and swiftest impact. So TV was the key.

But Sirhan was dead set against any interviews, any exposure in the press in any shape or form. I respected his feelings, although I really don't know why he was so firmly against interviews. He told me he didn't like reporters, but although I have a feeling there was another deeper reason, I honestly don't know what it was. Maybe it was simply that most of the things written about him had been unsympathetic, and so he had naturally developed an aversion to reporters in general.

At one point I got a call from CBS in New York. They told me they were planning a series of specials on the major assassinations—the two Kennedy killings, the Martin Luther King murder, the attempt on the life of George Wallace. And they said that Dan Rather wanted to interview Sirhan Sirhan in prison, and use that interview as the heart of a special.

As the CBS person spoke, I knew this might be a golden opportunity. Rather was a tough interviewer, but I believed that if he could meet the Sirhan I knew—the bright and witty and intelligent Sirhan—he would be captivated and he would convey a favorable impression to his vast public, and perhaps

I could begin to achieve our goal of changing public opinion about my client.

Sirhan was still the stumbling block. He had not spoken to a reporter in eight years. He had turned down very exciting monetary offers. Certain periodicals had offered him thousands of dollars for interviews. He had turned those offers down, and he showed no sign of changing his mind.

CBS made it clear they were offering nothing, not a dime. The only thing they offered was Dan Rather.

I thought that might be enough. I knew Rather, as a TV viewer knows him—a handsome man, smart as a whip, a droll sense of humor. I knew, too, that he had a book just published, a book about the men around Nixon called *The Palace Guard*. I knew that—except with ex-President Nixon—Rather had an impeccable reputation. To me, he was just the man I wanted to talk to Sirhan.

I went out and bought a copy of *The Palace Guard* and read it through. As I expected, it was a fine work. I enjoyed what Rather had to say, and the way he said it.

Then I went up to Soledad Prison. (After death sentences had been ruled unconstitutional, the Death Row at San Quentin had been abolished and the prisoners scattered; Sirhan wound up at Soledad.) I told Sirhan about Rather's wish to see him and interview him. As I expected, he said no.

"You know that, Godfrey. You know I don't want to do any interviews."

"But, Sirhan, this man is different. He is one of the most popular men on TV. You've probably seen him a hundred times yourself."

"It doesn't matter. I have a rule. No interviews."

Nothing I could say would change his mind. But he finally did agree at least to read Rather's book, which I sent to him. I just had a hunch that Sirhan, who had developed into a rabid reader, would find Rather's work to his liking.

I was right. On my next visit, he said, enthusiastically, "Godfrey, that book you sent to me, that was a very good book. That Mr. Rather has a fine grasp of history and a wonderful way of expressing himself."

"I thought you would like it, Sirhan," I said. "And I think you will like him, too. How about it? How about letting him come up here and interview you?"

He seemed to hate to say yes, but he had, apparently, come to the conclusion that he would say yes. And so, in a small, reluctant voice, he said, "OK."

But then, louder and firmer—"but no cameras!"

I tried, but I couldn't change his mind. No cameras. I knew Rather and CBS would not be too happy about that—a TV interview without cameras is something like a strawberry shortcake without strawberries. But at least Sirhan was the shortcake and maybe that would be enough to whet Rather's appetite.

I called CBS in New York as soon as I returned to my office, and I told them my "good news." They were only half-happy about it, as I expected, but that was better than nothing at all. They said OK, they would send Rather and a sound crew out to see him.

The arrangements were that, on a certain day, Rather and his team would fly to San Francisco. I arranged for them to stay at the Stanford Court Hotel, my favorite in the Bay City.

At the appointed hour, I picked Rather up and took him to my favorite San Francisco restaurant, the Empress of China. We hit it off well, although he seemed very skeptical when I told him that he would like Sirhan.

"I like him," I said.

"You actually, literally like him?" Rather asked.

"Yes. I like him. And you know something? You are going to like him, too."

Rather looked at me dubiously. I could almost hear him say to himself, "I doubt that, my friend, I doubt that." I didn't press the issue, because I knew that once Rather had a chance to talk to Sirhan for any length of time, he would like him. He wouldn't be able to help himself.

The next morning, I picked Rather up, and we drove to the San Francisco airport, where we were to board a flight for Monterey, the nearest airport to the Soledad Prison. The planes that fly those small, feeder routes around California can sometimes be relics, and the one that was out on the tarmac that morning was one of those.

"Where did they unearth that antique?" Rather asked.

"Oh, Jesus," I said. "I'm not sure I want to fly in that."

"Me, either," Rather said. "What time is the next flight?"

"Not for six hours," I said, "and there's no guarantee that the plane then will be any better."

We stood around until they were just about to close the doors, and, crossing our fingers and several other parts of our anatomy, we ran on board. The flight was, fortunately, uneventful.

I had a rented car waiting for us at the Monterey airport, and we drove to Soledad. All the arrangements had been made for Rather to see Sirhan. I assumed we would be whisked right through, from the guardhouse to Sirhan's cell. I was shocked and upset when the guard at the gate put in a call to the superintendent's office. I pointed out to the guard that all the arrangements had been made, that we were expected.

"Of course, Mr. Isaac," the guard said. "But the superintendent did want me to let him know when you arrived. It'll just be a moment, I'm sure."

That's all I need, I thought. Here CBS spends thousands of dollars and flies one of its top newsmen all the way out from New York, and now the whole thing may go down the drain. I can be very nervous about some things. When I find that officials are starting to act officious, I get nervous.

"Would you please follow me to the superintendent's office?"

My stomach flipped. I was concerned that there would be more official red tape. The superintendent is obviously going to give us some excuse about not having the permission of the vice-chairman of the Senate Ethics Committee or something. I could see it happening.

He was smiling.

"Come in, come in," he said. "Mr. Rather. Mr. Isaac. My, what a pleasure! Won't you gentlemen join me in some coffee?

"I wanted to see you before you went to Sirhan's cell. You see, Mr. Rather, you are without question the favorite newscaster in our house. My wife thinks you are just great, and I've been looking forward to meeting you."

As we walked from the office to the building where Sirhan was imprisoned, Rather and I exchanged glances, and smiled at each other.

"It happens all the time," Rather said.

"Dan, when you've got it, you've got it," I said.

It has often been said that lawyers are first cousins to entertainers. Trial lawyers, particularly. There has to be a streak of exhibitionism in our makeup. Most of us love that part of our profession that has us standing up and talking, reaching out to move an audience—whether it be a judge or a jury—and trying to convince them of the justice of our position. I think we may be something like entertainers, but we have to be more. While we are doing our thing, playing our part, we don't have a script. We have to ad lib. And yet our ad libs must be within a rigid framework of legal procedures. They must be helpful to our clients, and they must be convincing.

As Dan Rather and I walked down the corridors of Soledad, many guards and prisoners recognized him. I felt it must have been good for Rather to know that his face was so well known—even inside a prison. As we drew closer to X-Wing, where Sirhan was kept, I resumed my wondering and worrying about how the meeting would go. It was, as it turned out, useless worrying.

Rather and Sirhan met. They talked. Sirhan began with a quiet intelligent discussion of Rather's book. Sirhan said he was particularly interested in the way Rather had portrayed some of Nixon's aides. I smiled. I could see that Rather was amazed, both that Sirhan was familiar with his book and with his intelligent critique of its contents.

The guards brought in coffee and lemonade. The talk went on. Rather quickly moved on to ask Sirhan about the Kennedy assassination. Sirhan gently but firmly stuck to his position—he remembered nothing. Rather asked him some very pointed questions. What about the notation in his diary, found by the police when they investigated his apartment, that he planned to kill Kennedy, and on the day that the assassination actually happened? Sirhan was very hazy about having written the words, "R.F.K. must die." He did explain that he followed the teachings of the Rosicrucians and that he had read in their literature that if you wrote something down it might happen. Rather questioned him incisively, but politely.

The guards came back. This time they had lunch, neatly and tastefully arranged on trays. A tray for me, a tray for Rather, and a tray for Sirhan. I thought that was rather interesting. I was secretly amused at the sight of prison guards serving Sirhan Sirhan his lunch on a tray.

Rather and Sirhan kept on talking. The newsman moved on to later events. The second gun theory. Sirhan was reasonable. He said he knew nothing about that, of course, because he had no recollection of the events of that evening. But he had faith in his attorney—here he nodded in my direction—and told Rather he put great store in what I said. He spoke, throughout the entire interview, in a very moderate fashion. There were no histrionics, merely a calm and reasonable answer to whatever question Rather posed. I would have characterized Sirhan that day as open, friendly, polite, almost eager to have the next question so he could answer it as fully as possible.

Finally, four hours after we arrived, we left. The two men shook hands and smiled.

As we walked out of the prison to our car, Dan Rather turned to me and said, "Godfrey, when you said I would like Sirhan, I didn't believe you."

I knew what was coming.

"But you understated it. I liked him a lot. Sirhan Sirhan is a very interesting man."

The Rather interview reflected that picture—it showed Sirhan as he was. I would have preferred it if there had been a taped interview, because I knew that the actual words would strengthen that image, that my client was no wild-eyed fanatic (at least not any more) but a calm and reasonable and intelligent person. Still, Rather's report was fair and I felt the first round in my battle to change public opinion about Sirhan had been fought. We had taken one step forward.

The next step came out of the clear blue from the County Building in Los Angeles. The assassination buffs had never stopped their maneuvering, their sermonizing. County Supervisor Baxter Ward, a former television newsman, had a well-earned reputation as a tenacious investigator. He had long been interested in the Robert Kennedy case, and had sparked an interest in his colleagues. For some weeks, the supervisors had been discussing the case and going over all the evidence again, particularly the good old second gun theory. They had previously appointed Thomas Kranz to investigate the case with instructions to report back to them directly. They wanted me to come and testify.

Little time was allotted to me, but I utilized it by making an offer I thought Ward and another supervisor, Kenneth Hahn, would find intriguing. I invited them to come up to Soledad Prison to talk to Sirhan. It was, I felt, a golden opportunity to change public opinion a little more. I knew that where the supervisors go, there, too, would go newsmen and television cameras. Thus, there would be another public look at Sirhan. I was confident that my client would comport himself admirably and thereby help to change public opinion a little more by letting the people get to know the Sirhan I knew.

"I promise you," I told the superivisors, "that if you come to Soledad prison, my client, Sirhan Sirhan, will speak to you fully and openly."

And so arrangements were made for those two supervisors, Kenneth Hahn and Baxter Ward, to come with me to Soledad to interview Sirhan. It was on June 2, 1977, we made the trip.

The authorities had stationed a guard in the room with us at first, but I insisted he be removed. There was certainly no need for a guard for security reasons and his presence might inhibit our talk. The supervisors supported me and the guard was removed.

Sirhan had been freshly barbered, cleanly shaved, wore a clean T-shirt and trousers. He was more nervous than I had seen him. I suspect he felt this was important to him. Perhaps he attached more importance to the visit than it actually warranted.

"Just relax, Sirhan," I said. "Take a deep breath and relax. This is all going to be very informal, just a nice chat."

As if to illustrate my point, I took my jacket off. It was a little warm in the room provided us, which fortunately made my gesture reasonable. Hahn and Ward took their jackets off, too.

"That's right," said Hahn. "We'll all relax and have a nice, pleasant talk. And I'm sure you'll tell us the truth, because it's important for the sake of history that you tell us the truth."

"I will, sir," said Sirhan.

"Good, good. Now, then, Sirhan, are you a Christian?"

That was out of left field. Sirhan blinked.

"Yes, sir, I am."

"Good. Put your faith in God and Jesus Christ and every-thing will be all right."

They were there to talk to Sirhan, to ask him questions, but first Hahn launched into an inspiring sermon. He spoke about God, about religion, about the Christ figure. Sirhan listened politely. Hahn's colleague, Baxter Ward, was edgy. He tried to ask some serious questions about the assassination in between Hahn's theological philosophy, but he was having a hard time. And poor Sirhan was thoroughly confused. He tried to pay attention to Hahn but then Ward would suddenly shoot a question about the assassination, and he would be caught in the crossfire.

"You must tell the truth, Sirhan," Ward said. "Now, when

you arrived at the Ambassador Hotel, did you carry a gun?"

"Remember, my boy," Hahn said, "if you put your faith and your trust in Our Lord, then nothing and nobody can harm you."

"Yes, I had a gun in my car, Mr. Ward. Yes, I will put my trust in Our Lord, Mr. Hahn." Sirhan tried to answer them both at once.

Sirhan politely told his story again. The same story. He didn't remember anything. He related how, afterward, everybody told him he had done it so he believed he had done it, but he had—still has—no recollection of any of the events of that dreadful night. He was sorry, but that was just the way it was.

"Is there anything we can do to help you refresh your memory?" Kenneth Hahn asked.

Sirhan told him how, in his original trial, he had suggested that perhaps if he had been taken again to the scene of the crime—the Ambassador Hotel kitchen—it might have helped him to recall some of the incidents.

I could see the reaction of Hahn and Ward. I knew that both of them were anxious for something concrete to come out of their visit. We all looked at each other, and the same exciting idea flashed among us. Hahn was the first to speak.

"Do you think," he said, "that if you went back to the kitchen of the Ambassador Hotel now, it might help you to recall what happened that night?"

"I don't know," said Sirhan. "I just don't know."

"Would you be willing to try, for the sake of history?"

"Yes, for the sake of history I would try."

Then Baxter Ward had another idea. He asked Sirhan if he would be willing to submit to hypnosis. He knew that, sometimes, a memory can be restored in the hypnotic state. Sirhan didn't answer, but looked at me for some hint as to what to say.

"Let's discuss that idea at some other time, Baxter," I said. "Then you'll get an answer to your suggestion."

I was concerned about subjecting Sirhan to yet another hypnosis. Just after the Kennedy assassination, he was hypnotized by methods I have grave doubts about. They had sought to force him to admit to the killing by repeatedly telling him he had done it. Now I was concerned that in hypnosis, many years later, he might recall what he had been told in that earlier hypnosis. This could cloud the issue, rather than clear it up. I concluded that I would try to avoid hypnosis as long as possible, and I suspected that might be forever.

The interview lasted several hours. Sirhan told them how much he respected me, which was nice but unessential, so I cut that off. Finally, we stood to leave. Hahn embraced Sirhan and gave him a final shot of religious courage, a final little sermon about faith and hope.

We left to brave a regiment of newsmen. Later, I was told that there were more reporters—both from the print medium and from radio and television—than had assembled anywhere since the Elizabeth Taylor-Richard Burton wedding. I don't know if that's true or not, but I do know that there seemed to be hundreds of press people at Soledad Prison that day.

Hahn, Ward, and I managed to find a place away from the press and its constant barrage of questions, and we talked. I was delighted to find that both of them had come away with a positive image of Sirhan. They seemed to accept his loss of memory. They accepted his statements that he had searched his soul and had tried and tried to recall what had happened, but that that period in the Ambassador Hotel kitchen was a total, irretrievable blank. We talked as we got back in the car, as we drove back to the Monterey airport. Both the supervisors felt that Sirhan was bright and intelligent. Hahn used the word "humble," which I found particularly interesting.

"I think this has been an historic meeting," Hahn said; and Ward, the old investigative television journalist, nodded his agreement. Good, I thought. They would go back to their colleagues and report on how history had been made. I hoped they would then comment publicly on how Sirhan had been cooperative and likable and, yes, even humble. My own desire at that point was to present one more positive picture of Sirhan.

The rest of that day was very strange. We had spent so much time with Sirhan in the prison that we missed our return flight to Los Angeles. There wasn't another for hours. Ward was on his way to Seattle, so this didn't affect him; but Hahn scurried around the airport, talking to people, trying to find some way back to Los Angeles. I was at the counter, trying to assure myself of a seat on a later flight. And then I heard Hahn calling me—"Godfrey, come quick." He said he had a ride on a Lear jet back to Los Angeles. I looked around and saw him beckoning to me, then running out a back door.

I quickly concluded my business at the counter, then rushed out back to where I had last seen Kenny Hahn. It was an area where many private planes were parked. I looked around for a Lear jet, but there was no jet of any kind. I was sure that they had left without me and was going through one of those what-do-I-do-now periods, when I saw Hahn and several others standing next to a twin-engined Cessna.

"Kenny," I said, "where's the Lear jet?"

"This is it," he said, beaming proudly.

It wasn't a jet at all, Lear or otherwise. It was crowded, with the only available seat for me being the co-pilot's chair. That is where I sat, and I must say it was a fascinating flight. The pilot, a friendly pro, explained things to me, let me take the stick a few times, and Ace Isaac got us safely back to Van Nuys Airport, where we landed. The pilot landed it, of course.

There I was at Van Nuys Airport, but my car was at Los Angeles International Airport. The two airports are miles apart.

I should never have underestimated Hahn and his capacity for getting things done. I had only begun to voice my concern over how I was going to get my car and/or get home when Kenny Hahn grabbed my arm and pulled me along. He hauled me over to a helicopter and pushed me aboard and climbed in after me. No sooner had I sat down and fastened my seat belt than we took off. I hadn't the vaguest idea whose copter it was or where it was going. But I figured that where Hahn was going, there I would go.

It was my first time in a helicopter, and I couldn't help but be aware of the absence of wings. Hahn wasn't an experienced helicopter passenger, either, and he took my hand and said these things made him nervous. We landed, after getting a new and lovely view of the city, on the ABC building. This, it turned out, was the local ABC station's helicopter and, as we landed, we were rushed into the studio for a live newscast with Jerry Dunphy and Christine Lund; we went through all the questions again. It seemed like old hat to me, but Kenny Hahn, always good-natured and ready for action, flashed the good old politician's smile and was as fresh and charming as he had been hours before.

I was still miles away from my car and my home. Hahn once again grabbed me by the arm, hustled me down the elevator and out the door. This time there was a big black limousine waiting. He asked me if I minded if they dropped him at his house first, then the limo would take me to the airport where I could pick up my car. I said no, of course not.

Our next stop brought me some insight into Kenneth Hahn, the man behind the politician. We stopped at his house. I had expected some sort of pretentious mansion. He was, after all, the dean of the Los Angeles County Board of Supervisors. He was, obviously, a very successful politician. I knew enough about politics and politicians to know that they have a knack for getting rich, and here was a man who had been a leading political figure in California for several decades.

We turned down a simple street in what was almost a ghetto, or as close as sunny Southern California has to a ghetto. The big black limousine glided to a soft landing in front of a very modest home. It was neat and clean, painted and polished, in a neighborhood where most of the homes

weren't. Its value was, obviously, minimal by today's standards. Most of the faces that turned in our direction were
friendly and respectful—and also black. You could almost feel
the affection they felt for this powerful man, who stayed close
to his constituents. Other whites had obviously moved, but
not Kenny Hahn. You could sense the veil of protection
around him. I understood why he had stayed. It was his home.

He is a successful politician. And, I think, a very good
politician. He stays close to his people. They love him for it,
and vote for him, year after year, election after election.

The whole episode with the supervisors was another step
forward in providing a new view of Sirhan. In their interviews, when they came back from Soledad and spoke to the
press, both Hahn and Ward showed a better understanding of
Sirhan. To them, my client would no longer be simply a hated
image. Somehow, Sirhan had touched them; their public
statements, referring to him, were not vitriolic now. They had
taken a risk in visiting him, and I appreciated their political
bravery. I wanted to do something to show that the visit had
been a forward step in the search for truth.

I continued to think about Sirhan's statement that at one
time he wanted to return to the Ambassador Hotel kitchen to
see if it would jog his memory. In addition, Sirhan was
anxious to be cooperative and helpful, looking toward the day
when he hoped to be released. Knowing that there would be
much criticism, I nevertheless concluded that it was incum-
bent upon me to petition the court for permission for Sirhan
to return to the Ambassador.

There were positive things that could result if Sirhan
returned to the scene. Primarily, we would be implementing
our stated resolve that we were willing to try anything in the
continuing effort to find the truth. We would be doing the
only thing then available to us to help remove the memory
blackout and were willing to live with the results, whether the
restoration of his memory was good or bad for him. I felt
there was some small chance that the visit to the hotel kitchen

might release whatever it was that was inhibiting his memory.

I was deeply concerned that our court action might be considered a publicity stunt and bring about some unfavorable comment. In the end, after weighing the pros and cons, I made my decision. Whatever the consequences, I decided to move forward and I brought a motion before the Superior Court, formally requesting that prisoner Sirhan Sirhan be taken from Soledad Prison and brought to the kitchen of the Ambassador Hotel in Los Angeles. I requested a restaging of the Kennedy killing, which might help Sirhan regain his memory and shed some new light on the assassination of the Senator.

The first judicial action to my motion was one I had not expected. The Court, on its own motion, set a new date for my hearing and requested that I serve a copy of my motion on the Ambassador Hotel. The hotel promptly contacted me and told me that it was all right with them, provided that the restaging be done at night. They wanted to disturb as few guests as possible. They also asked that the county provide adequate security. It was, I felt, an enlightened position on the part of the Ambassador Hotel. It was not long thereafter that the hearing was held.

We appeared before Judge William Hogoboom, who had succeeded Judge Wenke as presiding judge of the Superior Court. He quickly, and I felt sarcastically, denied the motion. I didn't quarrel with his ruling—after all it would have been a precedent and precedents are always risky—but I did take exception to the tone of that ruling. He compared my argument to an old wives' tale and asked if I had considered astrology. It was a strange reaction for an experienced and respected judge. I could understand his ruling, but I could not understand his compulsion to resort to sarcasm. A simple ruling would have sufficed.

Although my motion and perhaps my last legal step had been unsuccessful, I knew that it had not been a failure. One of my original goals had been to shed some light on the dark unexplored corners of the assassination, and we had done so.

I decided to take no further legal action in the case. There was probably nothing I could do. I came to the conclusion that, from that point on, everything I did should be directed toward one goal—securing a release date for Sirhan and concentrating on those things that would be helpful in getting him out of jail. The public opinion campaign was absolutely essential to that.

Time would be our ally. The more days, weeks, months, and years that went by, the more the public would forget its initial anger. I hoped that, by letting the case become ancient history, the people would no longer hate Sirhan with that first burst of raging passion.

There is a reason for not pursuing any other legal avenues. I think doing so would be harmful to the public. Any further litigation would be expensive—all litigation is expensive—and why should the public have to pay any more for rehashing old facts? I think that, too often, trials and retrials go on and on, long after they accomplish anything, and they cost the people millions and avail them nothing.

Summing up, and looking back, I do not regret my defense of Sirhan at all. It was costly to me in many ways, but I considered it then—and now—as something that had to be done. When I undertook the matter, millions of people had nagging doubts about what the truth was and whether there had been a governmental cover-up. These people were entitled to seek answers to those questions, and I helped provide some answers. When I undertook his defense, Sirhan was tortured by not knowing whether or not he killed Senator Kennedy. He was entitled to a genuine effort to try to get some answers, and I gave him that.

I would have liked to have found all the answers, but it was not to be. I do not know if Sirhan killed Kennedy. There remain many curious aspects, many unexplained details. No one knows the answers now, and I have come to believe no one ever will.

Chapter Three

ONE DAY IN 1969, Ralph Kaplan had a toothache. He went to see his dentist. Of such small things are careers made and broken. If you are a fatalist, this story should give you comfort. Because of Ralph Kaplan's toothache, a brilliant scientist had his career and possibly his life saved, and it opened new career horizons for me. I had my most difficult decision, my most emotional moment, and, all in all, I think my most satisfactory case.

Kaplan's dentist was Dr. Yoshio Yamaguchi, a fine dentist, a decent man, and, as you may suspect from the name, a Japanese-American. At the time of Kaplan's visit to Yamaguchi, another Japanese-American was in serious trouble. Dr. Thomas T. Noguchi was the Chief Medical Examiner-Coroner of Los Angeles County. He had been fired by the county's chief administrative officer on sixty charges, most of which alluded to his emotional instability. In short, they said he was crazy.

Noguchi and Yamaguchi were friends. And Yamaguchi was concerned for his friend's career. He mentioned that concern to Kaplan, who was a distinguished journalist and, at the time, an assistant to Los Angeles Mayor Sam Yorty. Yamaguchi said that he was afraid Noguchi was being poorly represented legally. He wondered if Kaplan knew a lawyer who might help.

Kaplan sat in the dentist's chair, his mouth full of cotton, and thought of me. I was his lawyer and his friend. As soon as the cotton was out of his mouth and he could speak, he said, "Dr. Yamaguchi, I'll speak to my lawyer about Noguchi."

At the time, I was representing Kaplan in a personal injury matter. I wasn't happy with some aspects of the case, and was considering withdrawing. When Kaplan called and said he wanted to talk to me, I jumped to the wrong conclusion. I thought that it was his case he wanted to discuss. And I felt this was a good time to tell him of my reservations. We arranged to have lunch in the Venetian Room at the Beverly Crest Hotel. As soon as we sat down, I got to the point.

"Look, Ralph," I said, "before you start in on the case, I want to tell you that I've been giving the matter a lot of serious thought and I'm afraid . . . "

He waved me off.

"Later, Godfrey. First, I have to ask you—do you know who Tom Noguchi is?"

This was from out of left field. I knew I had heard the name.

"Yes, I think so," I said. "Noguchi? Isn't he the coroner?"

"That's right," Kaplan said. "Do you happen to know him?"

"No."

"Godfrey, he needs you. He's in big trouble. You're the only man I feel can help him. You have the legal knowledge and you have the trial skill."

"Thanks, but what's his problem?"

Kaplan told me as much as he knew about the situation.

Then he asked me if I would meet with Noguchi and the dentist, Yamaguchi, and hear the whole story. They wanted to meet me that same afternoon, and were ready to come to my office. Yamaguchi had even broken all his appointments so he would be available. I agreed to give them a half-hour.

That's how it began, the famous Noguchi case. If you lived in Los Angeles, you know it. Of its kind, the most sensational trial of them all.

At that first meeting, I learned the facts, at least from Noguchi's standpoint. And, after many months and much investigation, the facts from Noguchi's standpoint stood up. He was telling me the truth at that first meeting, and from then on he told me the truth. It appeared that he was the victim of a vicious racial attack.

Noguchi had been a pathologist in the Los Angeles County Medical Examiner-Coroner's office, under the old Chief Medical Examiner-Coroner, Theodore Curphy. When Curphy resigned, the county searched for a replacement. Applicants from all over the world vied for the prestigious position. In the end, it was awarded to Noguchi, who had achieved a reputation for brilliance. Curphy had handed him the toughest cases. It was Tom Noguchi who had performed the autopsy on Marilyn Monroe.

Noguchi was a brilliant scientist, and in some ways a pioneer in his field. He was a native-born Japanese and had lived in Japan until he was twenty-eight. His father had been a surgeon in Japan and had practiced well into his eighties. Young Tom Noguchi, a teenager during World War II, had been so eager to become a doctor that he studied through all the bombings of Tokyo, working in candlelight when the city's lights went out.

For some reason, he grew up with the desire to come to the U.S., a curious dream for a Japanese who lived through World War II. It was just something that happened, and he can't explain it, but it became almost an obsession with him. After the war was over, and after he had completed his medical training, he wrote more than 200 letters to American hospitals, seeking employment. He got one answer, from a hospital in Loma Linda, in Orange County, outside of Los Angeles. He took the first plane and presented himself to the Loma Linda Hospital. This was in 1956; Tom Noguchi was twenty-eight years old.

He worked in emergency wards and he worked in obstetrics wards and he worked in pathology labs and he worked at his English, and he gradually became known as a talented and efficient forensic medicine specialist. Curphy hired him for the County Medical Examiner-Coroner's office and came to rely on him more and more.

Noguchi became the champion and in some ways the developer of a new technique for coroners, the psychological autopsy. In addition to the purely physical aspect of examining a dead body for cause of death, Noguchi felt that in cases where suicide was suspected, something more was indicated. He would assemble a group of behaviorial scientists, when he had such a case, and have them look into the background of the subject, to determine if there was any chance that it might not be suicide. They would prepare a psychological profile which, together with the physical profile from the regular autopsy, often produced startling information.

He was appointed to his post in 1967. In 1969, when I first knew him, he had acquired a national reputation for his ability and his thoroughness. He had done the difficult autopsy on Senator Robert F. Kennedy, which was a model for how an autopsy should be done. He was a fellow of the American Academy of Forensic Sciences and belonged to many other professional groups. In many quarters, he was considered a genius in his field.

But there were some other quarters, it became apparent, where his tremendous skill and ability would not be enough.

The Los Angeles County government was ruled, sternly, by the Board of Supervisors—five old-line, old-time, hard-nosed politicians. They were Ernest Debs, Warren Dorn, Burton Chace, Frank Bonelli, and Kenneth Hahn. The day-to-day administrative duties were the province of the county's Chief Administrative Officer, The C.A.O., an old, crafty, and very tough gentleman named Lin Hollinger. They used to say that when Hollinger said jump, 90,000 Los Angeles County employees went up in the air.

For the first year that Noguchi was coroner, there were no problems. Noguchi did his job, managing to stay out of Hollinger's way, and the Board of Supervisors simply watched from the sidelines.

Los Angeles kept growing. The growth brought more and more crime, more and more dead bodies for the coroner's office to examine. Noguchi's staff hadn't grown, and Noguchi felt there was a well-established need for more personnel, particularly more investigators. He went through channels, requesting, from C.A.O. Lin Hollinger, that the county appoint additional investigators to help with the work load. Hollinger turned the request down.

Noguchi, very naive in the ways of American politics, decided the need was so great that he would go over Hollinger's head. He applied directly to the Board of Supervisors, writing a report in which he told of the shortage of help in his department and requesting that they hire additional investigators. The board, who may have assumed that Noguchi had gotten an OK from Hollinger, approved the request and the extra investigators were added to the staff.

Hollinger heard about it and was furious. He had said no and this upstart—this Japanese upstart—had gone to the Board and gotten the help. Noguchi didn't know it—not yet—but he had made an enemy, an enemy who was powerful and, it turned out, vindictive.

As accomplished as he was in forensic pathology, Noguchi was naive in politics. He had no idea what was in store for him when he was summoned to Hollinger's office.

The C.A.O., a tall, white-haired man with ruddy cheeks and flashing blue eyes, flashed those eyes at the Japanese doctor in great anger.

"Dr. Noguchi," he said, without a greeting or an invitation

to sit down, "you will never embarrass me again."

Noguchi didn't even know what Hollinger was talking about. He looked at the politician with a quizzical look on his face.

Hollinger drew his finger across his throat, in the slitting gesture that seems to be universal. Noguchi knew what that gesture meant. He was being told he was going to be ousted, but he still didn't know what offense he had committed.

Hollinger told him, in strong terms. Noguchi tried to explain that he was unaware he had committed an offense in going to the Board of Supervisors. Hollinger was in no mood to listen to any excuse or explanation. In fact, there are those who feel that Hollinger had merely been waiting for some chance, any chance, to come down on Noguchi. Many have suggested that there was resentment because Noguchi was Japanese. Others feel he was just not a member of the insiders club of Los Angeles County. Noguchi was definitely an outsider and had to go. To Hollinger, an old hand at political in-fighting, this timid, trembling, stammering newcomer looked like easy prey.

Noguchi left that meeting, upset and confused. He had only been doing his job. How had he managed to make such a powerful enemy? He didn't know what to do, so he did nothing.

Some days later, Hollinger summoned Noguchi to his office again. This time, he waved the doctor to a seat and shuffled through a file full of papers before he began to speak.

"Dr. Noguchi, you will have to go. We've had many complaints about you."

"What complaints?"

Hollinger picked up a bulging file, and waved it under Noguchi's nose.

"You have to resign," he said.

Noguchi tried to look at the papers in the file, but Hollinger quickly stuffed it into a drawer, out of sight.

"No, I will not resign," Noguchi said. "I have done nothing to resign for."

Hollinger said he had found him a good job. If Noguchi resigned, he said, he would see that he was appointed chief pathologist at Rancho Los Amigos Hospital. Hollinger said the pay was the same as that he was getting as Chief Medical Examiner-Coroner.

"It's a good job, doing what you like to do, and getting the same money as you get now," Hollinger said.

"I like the job I have," Noguchi said.

"No," said Hollinger, banging his big fist on the desk." You cannot stay in this job. You have to resign."

"Why?" Noguchi persisted.

"I showed you all those complaints. We can't have that. You must leave at once."

Noguchi got up and left the office. For a few days, he was determined he would not quit. But then he began to think that it would be bad to be in a job where he wasn't wanted. It was a very Oriental way of thinking, the idea that he had lost face and that he could not continue under such conditions. He came to the conclusion that if he was not wanted, he would leave. So he wrote a letter of resignation and was about to forward it to Hollinger.

He was advised to consult an attorney. He did, discussing the situation with a lawyer named David Smith. Smith wisely told Noguchi to withdraw his resignation. If he did resign, Smith told Noguchi, he would never have any legal recourse later.

So Noguchi sent a telegram, withdrawing his resignation and, instead, stuck to his guns and his job.

Around that time, the newspapers began to be full of little stories, all alluding to Noguchi's strange behavior. Someone was systematically leaking a series of items to the *Los Angeles Times,* the *Los Angeles Herald-Examiner,* and to suburban papers, which all had the same import. These stories hinted at Noguchi's odd behavior and mental difficulties. Some talked about how he abused the personnel in his department. There were intimations that he was addicted to drugs. Gradually, the Southern California public was acquiring the impression that the Chief Medical Examiner-Coroner, Thomas T. Noguchi, was a crazy man.

The press, at first, seemed to be sympathetic to Noguchi. They reported the stories that had been leaked, but tried to get him to comment, gave him the chance to rebut the stories. Noguchi's lawyer, David Smith, was handling his relations with the press and, while the newspapermen seemed to like Noguchi, they had for some reason developed an antipathy to Smith.

It was at this point that Noguchi's friends, including the dentist, Dr. Yoshio Yamaguchi, became concerned for his welfare. That was when Yamaguchi spoke to Kaplan, his patient, and Kaplan spoke to me, and I met with Kaplan, Yamaguchi, and Noguchi.

That first day we met, Noguchi was glum and depressed.

"Counselor," he said, sunk low in his chair, "I appreciate your taking the time to talk to me. But I have to tell you—I think this is mission impossible. They're out to get me."

He had, by that time, become convinced that the whole thing was a calculated and deliberate attempt to get rid of him. He wasn't sure why. Only later would I decide, to my own satisfaction, that the motive was basically racial discrimination.

I told him that day the same thing I tell all my clients. There is no such thing as a guarantee in the law business. I said his case might not be winnable, it might indeed be mission impossible as he had said, but I told him that in my opinion he had to fight, or else the world would believe the charges.

"Even if we lose," I said, "when we're done you'll be in a better condition than you are today. Better, because you will have denied the charges in front of the entire public. Even if we lose, we will make the public doubt those charges."

He had been suspended before our meeting, and the C.A.O. had filed formal charges against him with the County's Civil Service Commission. The charges at that time consisted of those sixty-one accusations of strange, odd, and irrational behavior. Later, a sixty-second charge would be added under spectacular circumstances.

"If you agree to it," I said to Tom Noguchi, "I promise you a fight you won't believe and will never forget."

This is just what he got. Later, after it was all over, Noguchi told me he hadn't believed me when I'd said that, but came to realize I was telling the absolute truth.

He nodded. OK, we would fight. It turned out to be a fight that was an all-out war. It was the hardest fight of my career, the most difficult, and the most tiring. For months, we all worked seven days a week, often twenty hours a day. The county was determined to get him and I was equally determined that they wouldn't. The battle lines were drawn.

As I got into the case, examined the evidence, such as it was, investigated and probed and asked questions and weighed the answers, a strange thought entered my brain. The more I considered it, the less strange and more sinister it became.

I am ordinarily not one to see conspiracies behind every event, to suspect prejudice, to imagine intolerances. I am not naive and yet I tend to think people are generally pretty good. Once I become convinced that someone is evil, I can be forceful in fighting him, but generally I think well of people. And so, at first, in the Noguchi case, I believed that Hollinger was acting out of some principle—a twisted principle, perhaps, but still something he felt was justifiable.

But as I learned more about the case, I came to believe there was no principle involved at all. Hollinger's motives were suspect. Although he said he had much evidence to support his position, all the indications were that he was motivated by his dislike of Noguchi's cultural background.

This was brought home to me when I examined the sixty-one charges against my client minutely. Among them:

He was too emotionally upset to continue.
He was addicted to amphetamines.

He was addicted to barbiturates.

He had thrown a shoe at a black chauffeur.

He had said he wanted 707 jets to crash so he could perform the autopsies on the victims and become famous.

He had smiled at disasters.

He had wanted Mayor Sam Yorty to die in a helicopter crash.

There were more, but the tenor of them all was the same. It occurred to me that, considering all the charges together, many of them suggested the behavior pattern of kamikaze pilots.

The Hollywood film version of a Japanese World War II kamikaze pilot was a man who smiled at disaster, who was somewhat unbalanced, who pepped himself up before battle with drugs. I doubt if there was a conscious attempt to paint Noguchi as being of the kamikaze mentality, yet it was a curious, fascinating similarity. Perhaps it was subconscious, but the result was the same. Noguchi was being portrayed as crazy, drug-addicted, imperious, caring nothing about death. In fact, inviting death. A man who smiles as he approaches death. A kamikaze.

It seemed clear to me that Noguchi was the target, because of plain, old-fashioned prejudice. They were out to get him because he was a Jap, that's all there was to it. As a Jew, as a representative of a race who has heard about prejudice, I was incensed. As a lawyer, who values justice, I was angry. As a human being, who had fought for human dignity, I was mad as hell.

Perhaps I went into the case with more emotion than is recommended for a lawyer. We are supposed to be objective, cool and detached, but I was hardly cool or detached in the Noguchi case. I am upset by prejudice and intolerance. And, after I came to know Noguchi and found him to be an outstanding person, I got madder and madder and more and more determined to help him.

I notified the Board of Supervisors, the Chief Administrative

Officer, whom I had not yet met, and the county counsel that I was representing Dr. Thomas T. Noguchi.

At that point, Noguchi had been suspended and replaced, temporarily, by one of his assistants. I made an official request upon the board that they were not to fire Noguchi until a hearing was held to determine the truth or falsity of the charges against him.

I arranged a meeting with Hollinger, County Counsel John Maharg, Assistant County Counsel John Larson, and Deputy County Counsel Martin Weekes, the man who later would be my adversary in the hearing. I made them a proposition—if they would reinstate Noguchi as Chief Medical Examiner-Coroner and make a public statement to the effect that all sixty-one charges against Noguchi were untrue, then Noguchi would resign. I said that my client did not want to make a fight out of this, but he would certainly not resign under this sort of cloud.

"No," said Hollinger, and stalked out of the room. He would tolerate no discussion, nor consider any settlement. He was intractable.

The next step was that the Board of Supervisors put the firing of Noguchi on its agenda. In a nice, neat, parliamentary way, a motion was made and seconded that Chief Medical Examiner-Coroner Dr. Thomas T. Noguchi be fired forthwith.

"Gentlemen," I said. I walked down to the front of the Board's meeting room and addressed the supervisors. "My name is Godfrey Isaac and I am the attorney representing Dr. Thomas T. Noguchi. Before a vote is taken on Dr. Noguchi's termination, I would like to be heard."

The Chairman of the Board, Eugene Debs, acted as though I were not even there.

"All those in favor of the motion," he said, "please signify by raising their hands."

All five of the board members raised their hands. Debs said, "The motion is carried. Dr. Noguchi is fired," and he and the others got up from their chairs and walked out. I was left standing there, hardly appearing like an all-conquering advocate.

Debs had not only refused to listen to me, he had totally ignored me. He would have paid more attention to a fly buzzing around his head. I stood there, my hands on the railing, consumed with fury, but managing to keep a smile on my lips. I told myself, at that moment, that I would put Dr. Noguchi back in his job.

The board meeting had been covered by live television; and there I stood, looking ineffectual, with the whole city observing my moment of extreme discomfort.

"Mr. Isaac," said a TV reporter, "how does it feel to be speaking to empty chairs?"

I couldn't resist.

"When the supervisors got up and left the empty chairs," I said, "that was the first time I saw an intelligent look in this room."

The entire Southern California basin, from Santa Barbara to a little north of San Diego, chuckled over that remark; it was carried in the newspapers the next morning, and they chuckled again. I don't think the Board of Supervisors was doing much chuckling, however. My little wisecrack did nothing to improve the climate between us.

There was something else in the morning newspaper. One of the reporters had gone to each of the five supervisors and asked them all, point-blank, what they thought of Noguchi. And one after another, they said, in effect, that he was crazy. Some used the word "upset" and some said "disturbed" and some said "emotionally unstable," but it all boiled down to the same thing—they all thought, or at least they all said they thought, that my client was crazy.

And one of the supervisors, Warren Dorn, turned his fire on me, too. He was quoted as saying that the only reason I was in the case was for publicity, because it was a case that could not be won.

I must say that barb nettled, which I suppose is what barbs are intended to do. In any event, for the rest of the time that I handled the case, I often thought about Dorn's remark in times of stress. And it helped inspire me to increased efforts.

I began assembling a team to prepare for the hearing that I was demanding. First, I contacted Clyde Nicholas Duber, my indefatigable private eye, to do a little digging here and there.

Roena, my wife, loved the investigative aspects of law cases, and she was very good at coordinating it all. When something had to be found out, she could find it out or find someone who could find it out or, at the very least, know whom to ask to find out whom to ask.

She was brilliant, she was tenacious, and she was even a little ruthless. I had a taste of that, as she kept after me day and night until I agreed to let her head up the investigation. I had Duber and Jim Briscoe, another ace investigator, and others, but they all had to report to Roena.

There was a lot of investigation to be done. Each of the charges against Noguchi, or many of them, involved factual things. Did he take pills? If so, what kind? How many? When? Where? Did he throw things at people? Get witnesses and their names. Did he say terrible things to people? Find more witnesses. And, of course, find witnesses for our side, witnesses who could testify to his sanity, his common sense, his coolness and capability under fire, his emotional stability.

Meanwhile, I insisted that Noguchi submit to a barrage of psychological and psychiatric testing. I knew that a large part of this hearing would swing on the testimony of experts in this area. It might turn out to be a battle of their experts against our experts. And I wanted to have the best and the most competent. My ace in this area was Dr. Frederick Hacker, who had his own clinic, The Hacker Clinic, the largest private psychiatric clinic west of Menninger's. Hacker and his staff did a complete workup on Noguchi, giving him a battery of tests and hours of interviews with their array of outstanding psychologists and psychiatrists. I felt that with those results in my arsenal, and with Hacker, an outstanding witness, on my side, I would win in the battle of mental experts.

After Noguchi's firing, I had requested a hearing before the

Los Angeles County Civil Service Commission (Chairman, O. Richard Capen, and members, Harry Albert and Thelma T. Mahoney) and it seemed to me to be a classic case of conflict of interest. The same men—the Board of Supervisors—who had fired Noguchi had appointed the Civil Service Commission. Now the commission was being asked to determine whether the men who had appointed them were in error on the Noguchi matter. I wondered whether they could rise above political reality and judge this case on its merits. Somehow I doubted it, but I believed I would show them such a powerful case they would have no choice.

I went over the charges time and time again, and got angrier each time. So many were simply untrue. Yet I was concerned because, in some of them, there were elements of literal truth, but distorted and twisted.

There was, for example, the one about Noguchi handing out his business cards at the scene of a disaster and other inappropriate times. Sounds strange, doesn't it? But you have to realize that Noguchi was only a few years removed from Japan, and handing out business cards is a way of life there. Meet anybody, anywhere, any time, and you exchange business cards. They hand them out the way we shake hands. And so, to Tom Noguchi, the idea of handing out business cards is second nature. He never even gave it a second thought. Wherever he went, he would reach into his pocket, pull out a business card, and hand it to whoever he met, with a bow (polite) and a smile (friendly). So, sure, the charge was true, but meaningless. I was certain I could make that clear in the hearing. And the same with many other charges.

We spent hours, days, weeks going over those charges to make sure there wasn't a rattlesnake hiding somewhere in that innocent woodpile. I didn't want to find myself caught by surprise. I hammered at Noguchi to tell me everything he could think of about each of the charges.

I began talking to others, people on Noguchi's staff I knew would be witnesses, maybe for them, maybe for us. One of the key witnesses would be Charles Maxwell, who was chief of the

mortuary division of the coroner's office. My first meeting with
Charlie Maxwell was one I'll never forget.

We met in his office. The coroner's office, you understand.
Maxwell was busy; he said he had to go into the operating
room and we could talk there. He asked me if that was OK, if
I thought I could take it.

"No problem," I said. He led the way and I sauntered in
after him, as nonchalant as though I was going to watch an
afternoon on the croquet lawn.

It turned out to be anything but croquet. I looked around,
and all about me were gurneys with dead bodies stretched out
on top of them. I forced myself to look at them—old, young,
male, female, white, black—and while it was unpleasant, it
was bearable. I was sure I would be OK. As Maxwell went
about his job, I talked to him about my job, about Noguchi.
As we talked, they wheeled another gurney in, just next to me.
There was the body of a young woman who had been rather
attractive. I felt embarrassed for her, stretched out there for
everyone to see. I wrenched my eyes away, back to Maxwell.

We talked for a few moments more; then I couldn't resist
turning back to look at the girl. There had been a change.
They had opened her up, using a cut I think they call
"canoeing," and she had been opened up from top to bottom,
literally. I felt myself turning green. All my resolve, all my
bravery—and almost all my lunch—began to vanish. I think
Maxwell noticed that I had begun to change shade, and was
now fast approaching apple greenness.

"Are you OK, counselor?" he asked.

I nodded, gave him a small wave, and walked away. Out.
With dignity, but with all possible speed.

That was only a minor setback in my work, however. I
managed to see Maxwell many times, as well as many others
on Noguchi's staff in the coroner's office. We assembled
mountains of material, and I became more and more convinced that I had a fighting chance to win the case. It
wouldn't be easy—it rarely is—but there was a chance.

My conviction that we stood a fair chance of winning was

not shared by my chief adversary, Martin Weekes. The deputy county counsel and I met frequently, in the normal processes of legal work; he kept taunting me about the ease with which he would win the case.

"You are doing your client a disservice," Weekes said to me one day.

"How so?"

"Giving him hope, that's how so. There is no hope, Godfrey."

"Oh, come on, Martin," I said. "You know as well as I do that there are no certainties in law."

He laughed.

"This is the closest thing to a certainty there is, Godfrey. Your man is crazy. There is no way I can lose this one."

I have seen positive lawyers in my time, but I had never seen one as positive as Martin Weekes. His supreme confidence made me a little apprehensive, I must confess. How could he be so sure? Did he know something I didn't know? Was my increasing fondness for Tom Noguchi blinding me to the realities of the case? Was I becoming too involved to see the truth?

I took some time to reassess it all, as objectively as I could. And the more I did, the more I was certain—we did have a fighting chance. It would be tough, but it wasn't impossible.

One thing I knew for sure. In this case, public opinion was vital. In a jury trial, the people who decide the case are often sequestered and have no access to newspapers, radio, or television, so the press does not affect their deliberations. But this was not that type of trial. We were preparing for a hearing, and the decision would be made by the three Civil Service Commissioners, who would not be sequestered and who would, therefore, be free to read the newspapers, listen to the radio, and watch television. Hence, they might react to public opinion, as reported by the various media, since they were, after all, creatures of the political process.

The big thing, then, was that the press and television be allowed into the hearing room, so they could cover the entire proceedings and make a full report to the people. It was my hope that the readers, viewers, and listeners would then sympathize with Noguchi and even become incensed at the unfair treatment to which he was subjected. I wanted the commissioners to react, consciously or subconsciously, to the public viewpoint I hoped to create. I have tremendous faith in the public, provided they have access to all the facts. In the Noguchi case, I was convinced that, if the public heard the whole story, it would be indignant and demand justice. It was a damaging blow when the Civil Service Commission announced that the hearing would be closed. The press had requested an open hearing, but they had been turned down.

They were not about to give up—nor was I. One of the local radio men, Art Kevin, who was president of a Los Angeles newscasters' association, asked me to address his directors. I did. I told them how I felt, how it seemed to me that my client would only get a fair hearing if the press would be allowed to cover it. They passed a resolution stating their determination to open it up. That was nice to hear, but it was just a resolution and, unfortunately, meant nothing unless implemented. The association, together with other members of the press, turned on the pressure. There were editorial cartoons, graphically illustrating the press position that this was a gag situation. Radio and TV commentators hammered away on the same theme. The Board of Supervisors finally instructed the Civil Service Commission to open up the hearing.

They stated, later, that they had done it because they felt that Noguchi was crazy and if they opened the hearings up, the public would know he was crazy and they would therefore avoid any possible criticism in upholding his firing.

I didn't care why they did it. I was simply jubilant that they had done it. I had been afraid of a hearing in the dark, with nobody outside the hearing room becoming aware of what was going on. I knew that, with an open hearing, our chances to win had increased a hundredfold, maybe even a thousand-fold. I had that much confidence in the rightness of our cause, and in the ability of the public to detect that rightness.

Chapter Four

THE HEARING BEGAN on May 12, 1969, a typical California spring day—gray and overcast in the morning, becoming sunny and hot by noon.

Casual observers around the Hall of Administration in downtown Los Angeles might have wondered who were those people carrying signs and walking into the Hall of Administration. It was Tom Noguchi and his wife Hisako. It was his adopted daughter Masako and five or six of her friends carrying signs that we would use during my opening statement and which we had spent weeks preparing. Roena and I walked with the others and we all must have looked like a small army on the march. Some of the news commentators stated that for the first time they thought Tom Noguchi had a chance when they saw us entering the building with our posters and tripods.

The first session of the hearing was in the Board of Supervisor's hearing room, which holds about 700 people. The room was mobbed and the excitement was high.

Martin Weekes and I made our opening statements. His was choked with emotion to everyone's surprise. He said that across the city that morning there was another group assembling; with trembling voice he went on to describe the funeral of the black man at whom Tom Noguchi was accused of throwing a shoe. He almost sobbed as he told how the man had died of cancer. At the time I was wondering whether the county was now going to hold Dr. Noguchi responsible for cancer. The Weekes opening statement was a turnoff to the media, who were skeptical of both the emotionality and the content.

My opening statement was much more on the factual side. I tried to lead the commission step by step and point by point to what I considered an inescapable conclusion, namely that Dr. Thomas Noguchi should be reinstated as county coroner. I displayed poster after poster illustrating my remarks, and I was beginning to feel a great surge of confidence in our case.

The president of the Civil Service Commission told Martin Weekes to call his first witness and, as I had anticipated, he wasted no time in attacking Noguchi. The first witness was Herbert McRoy, Noguchi's deputy. Almost at once Weekes got McRoy to testify to a series of facts that he felt showed Noguchi's peculiarities.

Q: Would you describe the manner of speech of Dr. Noguchi during . . . conferences?

A: Well, during some of the conferences, being a layman I would have to interpret it in this manner: that Dr. Noguchi appeared to be intoxicated and that he slurred his voice quite often and that he was not able to continue a trend of thought more than three or four minutes, then he was off to something else.

Then a few moments later:

Q: Now did you observe Dr. Noguchi take anything (at lunch)?

A: Yes, I did.

Q: How often?

A: I cannot recall a luncheon that I had with Dr. Noguchi after he became coroner that he did not take some type of medication.

Q: Did you ever see the medication in question?

A: Yes, I did.

Q: What color was it?

A: I saw on several occasions Dr. Noguchi taking a green beaded substance in a capsule that was—I would say was green and clear and at the same time a coup—this was a capsule—and at the same time a couple of pills, one pill being larger than the other.

Then some minutes after that:

Q: Did Dr. Noguchi ever make any statements to you with reference to air crashes?

A: Yes, he did.

Q: And what—first, when did he make the statement?

A: I recall statements that were made shortly after the first helicopter crash.

Q: That would be approximately May of 1968?

A: Right.

Q: And what statements did he—first, where did he make it?

A: He made the statements in the office.

Q: Who was present?

A: The secretaries were present on some occasions. I believe Mr. Maxwell was present on other occasions. I'm sure on some occasions I was with him alone.

Q: All right. What statement did he make with reference to these air crashes?

A: Well, shortly—when—shortly after the first helicopter crash he wished for 707s to go down.

When he sat down, Martin Weekes gave me a smug little smile, as though repeating his boast that this was a case he couldn't lose; his attitude was that McRoy's testimony was just a sample of the invincibility of his case.

In fifteen or twenty minutes McRoy had testified that Noguchi's behavior was that of an intoxicated man, that he had been an inveterate pill-taker, that he expressed a desire for airplanes to crash. I knew that I had to neutralize his testimony and fast.

After a few preliminary questions in my cross-examination there came this exchange:

Mr. Isaac: May I have permission, Mr. President? I left some of my paraphernalia on the other side of the table. May I go over and get it?

Commission President Capen: Yes.

Q: Mr. McRoy, can you observe what's in my hand?

A: Yes.

Q: I'll now place them back in this vial and will ask you some questions about them shortly.

Then I moved onto other matters while McRoy's eyes followed that mysterious vial. What I had held in my hand were some green capsules, something I hoped like the ones he had testified that he had seen Noguchi take every day at lunch. But I wasn't going to let him examine them closely for a while. I wanted him to think about them and stew about them and worry about them.

Finally I got back to the pills and to the matter of the lunches McRoy had had with Noguchi:

Q: How many times out of—did you have lunch with him approximately 65 times in 1976?

A: I had lunch with Dr. Noguchi more than 65 times.

Q: How many more?

A: I would estimate that I had lunch with Dr. Noguchi between 150 and 200 times.

Q: And in not one time out of those 150 or 200 lunches did

you ever see him when he didn't take a pill, is that correct?

A: That is my testimony.

Q: You don't ever recall going to lunch with this man when he did not take a pill?

A: That is my testimony.

Q: How many times out of the 150 or 200 lunches that you had with him did you see the pill that he took—or a capsule?

A: I would say three or four times.

Q: So you don't know what color they were, do you?

A: On the two or three occasions that I saw them, I do.

Q: Have you ever seen Librium? Are you familiar with it?

A: No, I'm not.

Mr. Weekes: If you're going to show him something, may I see it?

Mr. Isaac: All right.

Q: I show to you a small green and white capsule, half of it is green and half of it is white.

I represent to the commission, it's a Roche; that it's to the best of my knowledge and belief—I haven't done a laboratory analysis—but that it's Librium.

Mr. Weekes: I object to that. That's certainly improper. If he wants to establish what's in the tablet I think we ought to have somebody that's competent to testify in that regard.

Mr. Isaac: Exactly. And I would suggest that when Mr. Weekes puts the witness on the stand to testify against the man who's fighting for his job, we have somebody competent to testify what the medication is.

The hearing room burst into applause. It showed me that when the evidence was presented forcefully, Tom Noguchi could be switched from villain to hero. My belief that public opinion would be vital in this case was strengthened. The commission president had to rap sternly with his gavel and scold the audience: "Let me say this to the people that are present at this hearing: This isn't a theater where we are applauding various performances and I think we can dispense with all applause regardless of who is testifying and who is questioning, whether it be Mr. Weekes or Mr. Isaac."

I then went into a lengthy bit of legal sleight of hand involving capsules, showing McRoy some, then showing him an assortment and asking him to pick out the ones I had shown him before, and there was no question I had him thoroughly confused. That, of course, was my point. I had green capsules and yellow capsules and green-and-white capsules and other kinds. Finally I got him to admit that it was "difficult to identify" the capsules that he had seen only a few moments before. The whole capsule testimony had fallen. If he could not identify capsules he had just seen how could he identify capsules he had seen months before?

Our triumph with the capsules was covered on radio and television, and it was clear that we had won the first round. There was no time for overconfidence, however, because I knew that one after another the charges and wild accusations were coming up. I had to prepare for and handle them one by one, without exception.

Weekes and the people on his side of the fence felt that McRoy was their biggest gun. They had great confidence, I believe, that his testimony would wrap it up for them right at the beginning. He had been close to Noguchi. He was the one who insinuated Noguchi was a drug addict with that capsule-taking routine. He was the one who cast aspersions on Noguchi's sanity with the testimony about Noguchi's talking in an intoxicated fashion.

My cross-examination had disposed of McRoy as an effective witness, and his accusations were no longer believable.

Another of the opposition's major witnesses was Ethel Field who had been Noguchi's secretary. Some of the charges that McRoy had not mentioned, Ethel Field did.

Q: Now were there any incidents of swearing in your presence?

A: Yes, sir.

Q: What words did he use, ma'am?

A: Well, frequently he said "Goddam it" and then other times he said "Son-of-a-bitch." And once I heard him say "Go to hell." He told that to me. And then once when he received a letter from a certain doctor he was very upset about it, and he kept saying "Goddam son-of-a-bitch pissing peters."

Q: Did you find his language offensive?

A: Well, I was rather shocked.

And they had her repeat the now famous charge that Noguchi wanted planes to crash. The press began calling this "Noguchi's prayer for disaster."

Q: Did Dr. Noguchi ever make any statements to you with reference to air crashes?

A: Yes, he did.

Q: What statements did he make to you in this regard?

A: Relative to the helicopter crashes, he said that this would make him well known and that he had hoped others, you know, helicopters would crash and that this would be in his jurisdiction. And that he would—the press would be there and that he would become well known internationally and nationally.

Q: Then with reference to the other aircraft crashes what statement did he make?

A: He also said that he hoped some other large jets would crash so that he could handle the case.

Another of the charges relates to the Robert F. Kennedy autopsy and the accusation that he felt this would also help him achieve fame. Ethel Field's testimony was the key to their establishing that.

Q: Were you present in the office before Senator Kennedy died but after he was shot?

A: Yes, sir.

Q: Did you observe Dr. Noguchi at that time?

A: Yes, I did.

Q: Did he say anything to you with reference to Senator Kennedy?

A: Yes, he did.

Q: And what did he say?

A: Dr. Noguchi said that he knew President Kennedy . . . Senator Kennedy was going to die; that it was only a matter of time and that he was waiting for him to die so that he could perform the autopsy, and that this would make him well known.

It was all powerful testimony against Dr. Noguchi, and the commissioners seemed to be accepting it at face value. I knew that, once again, damaging testimony had to be neutralized. Fortunately, both Roena and Clyde had interviewed Ethel Fields and I had the results of their interviews. I began cross-examining her cautiously, spending a great deal of time on relatively unimportant matters. Finally, I was ready to move in.

Q: When after you talked to Mr. Duber and after you talked to Mrs. Isaac and after you talked in the presence of Martin Weekes did you get the full story?

A: I think after the discharge had come through—the suspension—after March 4th.

Q: From whom did you get what you call the full story?

A: Well, partly from the papers.

Q: So that a good part of your testimony . . . that you have given here is based upon what you have read in newspapers?

A: Yes, and what I have obtained from Mr. Weekes and Mr. McRoy—what they have told me.

Q: So that your testimony after April 15th is based on the newspapers, on what you have obtained from Martin Weekes, a deputy county counsel, and Herbert McRoy, is that correct?

A: Yes, sir. I had no other information on this situation.

Q: Are the things that you said before you talked to Mr.

Weekes, before you talked to Mr. McRoy, and before you read the newspaper true?

A: About what?

Q: Did you read about the so-called prayer for disaster in the Los Angeles metropolitan dailies?

A: I don't take the *Los Angeles Times.* All I take is the *South Bay Daily Breeze.*

Q: Did you read in the newspaper about Dr. Noguchi's behavior about Kennedy?

A: Yes, sir.

Q: And did you read in the newspaper about Dr. Noguchi's statement about air disasters?

A: Yes, sir.

In a sense it was incredible. As prepared as I had been for the hearing, I had no prior knowledge that Ethel Fields would testify as to acts of Noguchi that she had only read about in the newspaper and heard about from others. Her testimony was based on what she had read in the *South Bay Daily Breeze.* I looked over at Weekes who had the decency to look embarrassed. Somehow, I knew then that the County's case was crumbling. There was a long way to go, but Ethel Field's testimony was totally discredited.

I turned the knife a little more. Upon my further cross-examination she admitted that she had typed a petition on Noguchi's behalf, a petition that said, "He has administered his office with honesty, integrity and leadership, not only for we, the County, we, the employees, but also for all the citizens of Los Angeles County. We honestly believe that the resignation of Dr. Thomas T. Noguchi would be a loss to the County and all involved." In essence, I had gone full circle with her. Not only had she testified to things she did not know about, but now was confirming that she typed a petition lauding his honesty, integrity, and leadership. Weekes in his redirect examination tried valiantly to rehabilitate her, but the damage had been done.

I have to admit that I began to feel elated, but I was well

aware that there was a long way to go, and I knew that it was still a perilous road. You could almost feel in the air that the momentum was switching to our side, but even as in a sports event, momentum has a way of going one way and then the other. It was about this time, after my hard cross-examination of those two key witnesses, that many at the hearing coined a name for me—"The Meatgrinder." I was determined to keep on grinding, to take one witness at a time and, if possible, not to leave one of them whole.

The hearing dragged on for over a month, and as witness followed witness I seemed to gain more energy and Martin Weekes seemed to be fading. In a trial of this type, it is important that you hear every word, consider every possible objection, and think ahead to your own testimony which may be coming. There is never a moment when you can relax. On the other hand, there is nothing that I have experienced that is as stimulating. Trying such a case is like being on a continual high.

Despite the success with the lay witnesses, I was also aware that psychiatric testimony would be very important. As I anticipated, we were not too far into the hearing when our respective witnesses on Dr. Noguchi's mental status were called. I had chosen Dr. Frederick Hacker because I knew him to be not only one of the outstanding men in his field, but also an incredible witness. Some doctors are extraordinary at their craft, but turn out to be terrible witnesses. They say too much or too little, mumble or shout, lose their temper, or are irritating. Somehow Fred Hacker has that combination of traits that makes him believable, admirable, and persuasive. He testifies with dignity, purpose, and an admirable degree of certainty.

In this case he was highly motivated to appear. It was Hacker's belief that this case could lead to a very dangerous precedent if Noguchi's dismissal was upheld. He felt that all public officials would have to do, in that event, would be to say that Mr. X is crazy and they could summarily fire him and nobody could challenge their action. He told me that many persons felt there was virtually no defense against such actions. However, he hoped the successful defense of Dr. Noguchi would show that a defense is possible and that our victory would help others.

I agreed with Dr. Hacker's evaluation, but Tom Noguchi's welfare was my main concern. After talking to Hacker, however, I felt additional inspiration in the realization that if I could succeed in this one case I would be helping others for years to come who might be fired from their positions without cause and upon the unsubstantiated pretext that they were crazy.

Hacker and I had very interesting conversations during this period concerning people who are accused of being insane. We agreed that once a person is accused of being crazy, anything and everything he does from that point forward could be viewed as proof of his mental condition. Whether a person being observed scratches his cheek, wears a yellow cap, or constantly clears his throat, if he has been accused of being crazy, even such simple acts as that make you believe the charge is true. Recognizing that eccentricities may be catapulted into craziness by the observer, Hacker and I concluded that we would have to prove affirmatively that Thomas Noguchi was emotionally stable and had no mental disorder. We examined and analyzed the psychological tests that the Hacker Clinic had given Tom, and Dr. Hacker spent many hours in a clinical evaluation of Noguchi.

As we had expected, the question of Noguchi's normalcy became a major issue. Martin Weekes hoped to carry the day with one question of Dr. Hacker.

Q: [By Mr. Weekes]: Would you say, assuming all the pressures under which Dr. Noguchi had to function, that he was normal?

A: No, not normal. Super-normal. It's certainly not normal for a man to do all the things he has managed to do.

Hacker went on to say later: "Do not confuse unusual with abnormal. Dr. Noguchi may be unusual in some areas, in his drive, in his ability, in his accomplishments, and yes, in some of his customs and habits. But that is not abnormal."

Then he ad-libbed, something which I consider to be one of the most appropriate statements I ever heard from a witness: "Remember," Dr. Hacker said, "that the house of normalcy has many rooms."

In the war over Noguchi's mental condition, there was no question that we had once again destroyed one of the county's major premises. Our witnesses were bright, perceptive, and articulate, and theirs did not stand up to cross-examination.

About thirty days after the first charges were leveled at Dr. Noguchi and some time before the hearing had begun, Martin Weekes suddenly added one more charge against Noguchi. In many ways it was the most serious of all. The final charge had little to do with those accusations pointing toward craziness. It went to the heart of Noguchi's professional ability, and in this charge the county accused Noguchi of bungling the Robert F. Kennedy autopsy. It claimed that he had disassociated, was unable to complete the autopsy, and had mishandled it. It went on to assert that others had to complete the autopsy because Noguchi could not.

In preparation for the hearing I had assembled witnesses to testify to Noguchi's skill during that critical Kennedy autopsy. As an example, one of the witnesses I called was Dr. Victor Rosen, a brilliant young pathologist from Sinai Hospital in Los Angeles. He had reviewed the entire autopsy protocol and was prepared to give his evaluation. I called him to the stand and questioned him.

Q: Did you have an opinion as to the manner in which the autopsy and autopsy report were prepared?

This was followed by some legal wrangling. Weekes objected and I defended the question and finally Commissioner Capen overruled the objection and Rosen answered.

A: My opinion is that this was an autopsy that had been performed in a manner which would serve as the prototype for autopsies of great—great medical legal significance. This was more than just an autopsy and I think this is—the performance of this autopsy exemplifies what I consider Dr. Noguchi's approach to forsenic pathology, that is, that it was a medical-legal investigation complete from beginning to end. More than an autopsy.

Later:

Q: In what way, doctor, was this different from other autopsies you have seen?
A: This autopsy tied together in greater depth clinical findings and a summation of the anatomic evidence into a unit. This autopsy was what I would call a complete autopsy, as complete as a pathologist can make one. It was highly organized.

There was more. Rosen, too, was a good witness. I had other witnesses who all testified, or were prepared to testify, as to Noguchi's skill and organizational abilities during the time of the Kennedy autopsy. Suddenly, Weekes leaped to his feet to object and asked if we might approach the bench. Weekes and I came up and conferred privately with the three commissioners.

Weekes was agitated and adamant and demanded that the commission not listen to testimony about the Kennedy autopsy. His point was that he did not want any material about the Kennedy autopsy aired in public. He maintained that the autopsy had been bungled; if that testimony were brought out it might lead to an international incident since Noguchi's autopsy report was placed in evidence in the trial of Sirhan Sirhan and led to Sirhan's conviction. It was an astounding declaration from the man who had filed the charge and made it public. I wasn't buying.

I became as adamant and as agitated as Weekes. I expressed

my incredulity to the commissioners and pointed out, as forcefully as I could, that Weekes had made a public charge against Noguchi concerning the autopsy and it had been carried in every newspaper in town. Now, suddenly, the very man who had made the charge was claiming it would start an international incident. It was one of the few times I have resorted to profanity in opposing a motion. I told the commissioner that Weekes did not know what the hell he was doing. I said that it was a better example of insanity than any I had heard in this hearing.

"I am not going to make an international incident of this," I said, practically thundering, "but I intend to present irrefutable evidence that Noguchi performed a near perfect autopsy." Weekes and I were unyielding, and we pushed for our respective positions. Sensing that he was about to lose the point, Weekes suddenly asked for an hour recess so that he could go back and consult with his boss, County Counsel Maharg.

The hour stretched into an even longer period as we all, including the commissioners, waited impatiently. Finally, Weekes returned. He stated that the county was prepared to withdraw the charge that Noguchi bungled the Kennedy autopsy in order that there be no testimony concerning it. Commission President Capen turned to me and asked me if I would stipulate to the withdrawal of the charge. He probably heard the loudest no of his entire career. I insisted that they could not make a charge publicly, disseminate it in the media, have half the world believing it, and then simply withdraw it. However, I added, I will so stipulate provided the County of Los Angeles states on the record that the autopsy of Robert F. Kennedy was perfect.

Weekes said he could not do it, would not do it, and in any event did not have the authority to do it. I made it clear I would settle for nothing less.

After all, that charge had been aired and it reflected seriously on Noguchi's ability in the area where he made his livelihood, the area where he had established his reputation. To settle for anything other than a total withdrawal of the charge and an admission that it was and always had been erroneous would be doing my client a disservice.

When Weekes said no, they would not stipulate that the autopsy had been perfect, I insisted that we would have to continue with the hearing on that question. At least, if that happened, I knew that I could produce a parade of witnesses, to attest to the fact that the autopsy was a good one, and in that way Noguchi and his efforts would be vindicated.

We were literally at a stalemate, haggling for hours. Finally, the commission invited us to its office to discuss the matter. Both Weekes and I remained firm and unbending in our position. Each of us waited for the other to weaken. It must have seemed at times as if we would be there forever. Finally, Weekes again talked to his superior. He returned and, in a voice that you could barely hear, whispered, "The county agrees that the autopsy was competent."

Despite the fact that I had been adamant about the use of the word perfect, I happily settled for the evaluation of competent. I knew then, as now, that nothing is perfect. This brought the first real emotion from Tom Noguchi that I had seen since the hearing began. He was ecstatic. The thing he treasured the most, his reputation as an incredibly talented pathologist, was secure. We had literally forced the county to back down on the most damaging charge of all.

I was happy too. There were a lot of people who flocked around me, congratulating me; many of them said they felt that this was a turning point in the case.

It is hard to pinpoint one time or another that turned the whole case around. This particular reversal, however, inspired headlines, news comment, community reaction, and really buoyed our spirits. One thing is for sure. It was a significant victory, and we were certainly on our way to our goal.

In the public mind, perhaps the charge that was hardest for them to swallow was the "prayer for disaster." The idea that a human being, and especially a county official, could actually have been heard to say that he hoped airliners would crash was, to everyone, unthinkable. I knew that I would have to turn that around if I were to have public opinion solidly behind my client.

When Noguchi and I had first talked, I asked him if he said that. He didn't remember it specifically but admitted that he could have said something like it in jest.

Almost all of the coroners across the nation have told me that people in their business make jokes all the time. It is a sort of nervous release and does not relate to any actual intentions on their part. It is almost like a valve to allow tensions to escape harmlessly.

It was, in effect, gallows humor. Black humor. Morgue humor. Call it what you will. I had my investigators dig up examples from other walks of life in which death is a constant companion.

Doctors, among themselves, often joke about death and dying. Policemen and firemen do it to relieve the tension. Others do the same. It turned out that it was not unusual for men and women who work in coroners' offices to do it, and I brought this out in court.

Weekes called other witnesses to testify to hearing Noguchi make that statement about hoping airplanes would crash. Some added that he looked very serious when he said it. That was quite possible; Noguchi is a great dead-pan comic. He sometimes loves to shock people with outrageous statements told with his inscrutable Oriental face showing not a sign of humor.

Maxwell, the chief of the mortuary division, had testified to having heard Noguchi make that unfortunate remark. When I cross-examined him, I got him to soften it through this exchange:

Q: When Dr. Noguchi talked to you about the caseload when you had the discussion about an accident, you recognized that he was being facetious, didn't you?

A: About what accident?

Q: When you were talking about how many people there were going to be and he said, "We need an aircraft accident," you didn't take him seriously did you?

A: No, of course not. I didn't expect this would cause an accident, no.

Similarly, I was able to have most of those who testified to having heard that remark, or something similar, to admit that it could have been in jest or that such remarks were often made by people in the office.

When I presented my own witnesses, I made a point of getting some to talk about the frequency of morgue humor among employees in this and other coroners' offices. Dr. Victor Rosen, the pathologist who had testified so strongly about Noguchi's skill in the Kennedy autopsy, said this in his testimony:

Q: Did you observe whether Dr. Noguchi had a sense of humor?

A: Yes, I did.

Q: And how would you describe it?

A: I think Dr. Noguchi has a marvelous sense of humor. We pathologists have senses of humor that might not be understood by nonpathologists. In the line of work that we are engaged in, dealing with death and disease so much, a sense of humor is more or less a survival kit for us. If we are constantly effectively immersed in morbidity as we are, being able to make light of these events can ease—make it easier for us to practice. This is sort of a gallows humor as you may hear the term or graveyard humor, as other individuals have termed it.

Q: This is common practice among pathologists?

A: Yes, it is. I'm afraid sometime that if the remarks we made—if the general public were to hear them may be misunderstood. I know things I have said in a hospital setting or in an autopsy I would never say in a social setting.

Another of my witnesses for Noguchi, one of the most famous of European coroners, Dr. Bernard Knight of Cardiff, Wales, testified that on slow days the joke around the Cardiff coroner's office was that they ought to go out and hit a pedestrian.

Between effectively cross-examining the opposition's witnesses and bringing on men like Rosen and Knight myself, I think that I totally demolished the "prayer for disaster" charge. I showed it to be what it was—a joke. Maybe a bad joke or a tasteless joke, but just a joke. I think I convinced the public that was all it ever was. Nobody, certainly not Noguchi, had any real wish to see airliners crash.

At the time the charges against Noguchi were first circulated, some Japanese Americans had gotten together to help in his defense and to combat anti-Japanese prejudice. Early on there was very little enthusiasm, and many even reflected a concern that Dr. Noguchi might embarrass the Japanese American community. I think it is fair to state that it was a slow-moving group. Many of them had listened to the charges and suspected Noguchi of being a little crazy.

After the hearing commenced and as my cross-examination began to attract more attention in the media, the attitude of the Japanese community began to solidify in favor of Thomas Noguchi. Some bright, effective Japanese professional people formed a group and called themselves Japanese United in Search of Truth, which boiled down to JUST. They were galvanized into action by the county's withdrawal of the Kennedy autopsy charge. At that moment, they began to have total confidence in Thomas Noguchi. They realized that the county was not only not infallible but had admitted to a basic mistake. They made plans for a big dinner to raise money and support the Noguchi defense. They optimistically booked the Roger Young auditorium and guaranteed the caterers that they would sell 200 dinners. When I heard that, I was deeply concerned about getting 200 people to come to the dinner. I remembered how only weeks before they called a meeting and the total attendance was, I believe, five. Before, many Japanese had been embarrassed. Now, however, enthusiasm was growing, but I was still concerned that they had guaranteed too many dinners.

The extent of that change was dramatically illustrated the night of the dinner itself. They had guaranteed 200 dinners—and they had to turn away an estimated 500 people. The place was packed to capacity. The Japanese Americans were now thoroughly aroused and angry. No longer was Tom Noguchi an embarrassment, now he was a hero. Now he was their public official who, just because of the color of his skin, was being discriminated against and persecuted. They were in a mood to do something about it.

I was the guest of honor and was to be the principal speaker. As I looked out at the crowd and the people rushing to get in, I allowed myself a small self-congratulatory pat for having stuck to my position with reference to the Kennedy autopsy charge. It had been the catalyst that sparked this enthusiasm. I had merely been doing my job, but it was exciting and gratifying to hear the words of praise that were being heaped upon me. Some lauded me as a friend of the downtrodden, a champion of the oppressed. When I rose to speak there was a rousing reception; as the entire audience stood, I looked out and thought to myself, "Oh my God, what if I lose?" Meanwhile, however, I was optimistic in the words I spoke—yet cautioned the audience that there was much to be done. Whatever it was I said that night seemed to work, and the JUST Committee enthusiastically went out and raised funds to assist Dr. Noguchi.

The next day, as the hearing resumed, Gordon Nesvig, the County's Chief of Personnel, buttonholed me in the corridor outside the hearing room.

"Godfrey," he said, shaking his head in a combination of annoyance and awe. "What have you done? I fired a crazy man and you are turning him into a folk hero."

I would like to think that is precisely what I had done.

Now, after the Kennedy charge withdrawal and after I had successfully explained away the "prayer for disaster" statements, the public had swung solidly behind Noguchi. I sensed in the hearing room that the three commissioners had joined that swing. You can feel those things, and I felt now that they were showing a concern they had not evidenced before. I could see, in the eyes of Weekes and the others at the opposition table, that they realized they were now in a fight, a fight they very possibly might lose. No longer was this, as Weekes had said, a case he could not lose.

The county had a few guns left, chiefly the testimony of Lin Hollinger, the County Chief Administrative Officer, the man who had precipitated the whole incident. Hollinger took the stand with an attitude like a god from Olympus. He always had, I thought, an exaggerated vision of himself. For years he had run the county with an iron fist, an administrator who brooked no opposition.

Hollinger testified and I could tell he felt it was his mission to nail Noguchi to the cross. He testified that his people had investigated each and every one of the charges—the Kennedy autopsy had not been any of his doing—and they had authenticated each and every one of those charges. They were all true; and even one of them would be sufficient to warrant firing the man, he said. According to Hollinger, the firing was absolutely justified and he would do it again.

He was definite, positive, totally in command, totally sure. He spoke in an authoritative voice, shaking the hall with the power of his accusations. I couldn't wait to get a crack at him in cross-examination. I hoped to continue the success I had had with previous cross-examinations.

The television cameras were allowed in the hearing room and covered the case most of the time. At first they had covered it all, but gradually their coverage slackened. Roena often tipped them off as to when something exciting was about to happen, and they would put in a quick call to their stations and go on the air. Now, she said, as I got up to cross-examine

Hollinger, now you'd better have the cameras on and rolling. They were.

I pinned him to the wall.

"Mr. Hollinger, isn't it true that you recommended the discharge of Dr. Thomas T. Noguchi because you believed he was too emotionally disturbed to perform autopsies?"

"Yes, that's true."

"Mr. Hollinger," I went on, "isn't it true that when you asked Dr. Thomas T. Noguchi to resign, you offered him a post at Rancho Los Amigos Hospital as a pathologist?"

"Yes, I did."

"Mr. Hollinger, would you tell this commission why you were ready to assign a man that was too ill to operate on dead bodies to a place where he'd be performing services for people who are still alive?"

He didn't know what to say. He turned pale. He sputtered. He coughed. He actually could not think of an answer.

The Hollinger answer or, perhaps it is more accurate to say, lack of answer, was carried on television. Later, many reporters were to tell me that my cross-examination of Lin Hollinger was the straw that broke the camel's back. Many felt after Hollinger's testimony that we had indeed won the hearing. But the decision was still many weeks off.

As I think back over the entire case, I feel that the cross-examination of Hollinger was the testimony that most affected the commissioners. It seemed to me that they would have been thought to be ridiculous if they had upheld the firing of a doctor charged with being too mentally ill to perform an autopsy and yet offered a pathologist's position at Rancho Los Amigos. It never made any sense to me and I do not believe it made sense to them. Suddenly, it was clear that Thomas Noguchi was obviously capable and his behavior was obviously within the bounds of normalcy. For the first time the Civil Service Commission must have been forced to ask itself, "Why was this man fired?"

The hearing went on and the trend continued. One witness

after another for the county was unable to defend his own statements. I would like to take full credit but I cannot. Our position was just and the facts were carrying it out. I believe that is why our witnesses held up well. They testified to simple truths: Noguchi's ability, his character, and his professional competence. Under cross-examination by Weekes, they stood firm.

Finally, on a Friday afternoon just before we were to adjourn for a weekend, I made the electric announcement: "Members of the County Civil Service Commission, ladies and gentlemen, on Monday I will put Dr. Thomas T. Noguchi on the stand." It was the moment people had been waiting for. Needless to say everyone was curious about what Noguchi would say in his own defense. The hearing had gone on for six weeks at that time, and here was the man himself about to tell his side of the whole story.

Roena and I had just moved into a new house. I invited Tom Noguchi to come home with us. I wanted him there so we could go over his testimony, step by step. He was, as usual, a delightful guest. He took off his jacket, rolled up his sleeves, began helping me out in the myriad little carpentry chores one has with a new house. He hammered nails and screwed in fixtures and helped out as we talked.

Mrs. Noguchi insisted he come home that Friday, Saturday, and Sunday night, no matter how late it was when we finished. He went home about three or four in the morning because it took us that long to do what we were doing. I was determined that Noguchi's testimony would be clear, accurate, to the point. This was his rebuttal and it had to be right.

There is an old saying among lawyers: If the person accused of wrongdoing does not get up in court and deny that wrongdoing, then the trier of fact will generally find that he is guilty as charged.

In other words, an accused had better stand up in court and say loud and clear, "I didn't do it," or else he'll probably lose.

That was why I wanted Noguchi to testify. I wanted him to

stand up in the hearing room and, with the eyes of the world on him, deny any wrongdoing.

I questioned him for hours on end over that critical weekend. I am a pacer by nature, and I paced as I hurled question after question at him. He was more of a sitter so he sat, following me as I walked, and he answered as best he could. The problem began to emerge in those words—"as best he could." He just wasn't very good as a witness for himself. His answers seemed wishy-washy. Some people make good witnesses for themselves, some do not. It has nothing to do with guilt or innocence; it's just in their nature. Noguchi, no matter how innocent he was, tended to sound guilty. He had trouble with the language, which meant he hesitated as he groped for the right word. Hesitation is bad. It smacks of evasion. Often, even after the hesitation, Noguchi picked the wrong word. Rather than give a straightforward, simple answer, he tended to ramble and equivocate. He'd stick in a word that sounded bad. He'd use the right word but have an inflection that made it sound wrong. I knew him to be innocent, but I was concerned about his ability to be convincing in his own defense.

I was deeply concerned. I felt I had to continue working with him until I could shape him into the witness I wanted, the witness I had to have. For me, and I suppose for Noguchi, it was an emotionally fatiguing weekend. I may have driven him too hard and past the point of optimum return.

Finally, late Sunday night, I decided that I would not call him. Tom and Roena were incensed. Tom had lived for this chance to get up in the hearing room and tell the world his side of it. For months he had been silent. I had not allowed him to talk to the press, so he could tell everything at the hearing. And now I was going to tell him he would not be called? He and Roena both insisted that it was unthinkable. Roe said it would look bad if now he didn't testify, it would look very bad. Everybody was waiting to hear what Noguchi would say. He had to testify. And, in part, she was right. I had told everyone Noguchi would testify, and if he didn't it would seem strange indeed. So I agreed to keep trying. They both threw their arms around me. We began working again— question, answer, question, answer.

Nothing changed my mind. I would review an answer with Noguchi time after time, and somehow the answer never sounded right. For some reason this brilliant, accomplished man who had given great testimony in hundreds of cases in his professional capacity blocked when the questions involved himself. I was reminded of that old saying that lawyers are never good witnesses.

It was 3:30 on Monday morning—six hours before the hearing was to reconvene. I wanted no more questions.

"I've made my decision," I said. "And we are going to have to live or die by it. I won't put you on the stand, Tom. I'm sorry, but you just would not be a help to yourself. This is the hardest decision I've made in almost twenty years of practicing law. It just had to be made, that's all."

Tom and Roena were stunned. I knew I was right. If Tom's answers to my questions were not satisfactory to me, imagine how it would be when he was cross-examined. Weekes would go after him like a shark after a bloody tuna. I knew that my adversary had to be working as hard that weekend as we were, readying himself for that encounter. I knew that Weekes would ask him if he'd committed each of the offenses, one after another, an endless parade. I knew that just the question would make headlines. I felt that Weekes would baffle him with fancy questions, confuse him with idiomatic English— Tom's knowledge of English was good, but our slang often baffled him—and Tom would have to resort to that always weak-sounding reply, "I do not understand the question." The more I thought about it, the more I knew I was right. Noguchi should not testify. I stood by my guns even though he and Roena tried to get me to change my mind again.

Finally, Tom went home. I am not sure whether he agreed with me, but his confidence in me was such that he would abide by my decision.

After Tom left, I stayed up drafting a statement informing the commission and the public that Noguchi would not testify. I had the statement typed. I slept a few hours, although not very soundly.

We went to the hearing the next morning. There was more excitement than ever. More reporters. More television cameras. More people trying to crowd into the pitifully few seats. And all because Noguchi was expected to tell his side of the story.

I stood up and read the statement. The gist of it was that Dr. Noguchi's primary concern was the welfare of the county and the preservation and maintenance of the finest coroner's office in the nation. Because of that, Dr. Noguchi had decided not to testify against members of the coroner's office who had testified against him. He did not want to add to the dissension that already existed. He wanted to preside over the preservation, not the destruction, of the office of the County Medical Examiner-Coroner.

Pandemonium broke out. The hearing room exploded. People jumped up shouting. Some were angry. Some were disappointed. Some were hostile. The three commissioners were visibly upset. Weekes was red in the face, furious, and yelling at me. He finally got the attention of the commissioners as Capen gaveled the place into something like order. Weekes said he had prepared all weekend for the chance to question Noguchi and it wasn't fair. Those were the words he used, it wasn't fair, that now he wouldn't be able to cross-examine Noguchi. Later he told the press that he had found Noguchi's Achilles' heel but he was being denied the opportunity to exploit it.

When I talked to the press, I reiterated the position I had taken in the statement. Noguchi was a man of integrity. He had concluded that he couldn't in all conscience testify, because if he did he would have to say certain things about some members of his staff who had testified against him, and by saying those things he would necessarily be doing harm to the morale of the office.

Aside from the fact that I felt Tom Noguchi could not

testify, the statements that I made reflected his true feeling about the office he loved. It was gratifying to see how many reporters understood the statement and complimented Noguchi for his self-sacrifice.

My main reason, of course, was legal strategy. We started out this affair way behind. We had not only caught up but, it seemed safe to say, passed the opposition. We were now ahead. Putting Noguchi on the stand could conceivably reverse that favorable position. I thought we had everything to lose and very little to gain. At this point in the proceedings, I would do everything to keep us ahead; keeping Noguchi off the stand was just one of those things. I simply wasn't going to risk all we'd gained with Noguchi on the stand.

I was sure I was right, although I received a lot of criticism. It all began the second I read the statement in the hearing room, when Weekes labeled me "unfair." That was only the beginning.

At the first break, Kenneth Hahn, one of the Board of Supervisors, cornered me in the hallway. He was breathing fire.

"Isaac," he said, "you've just made the biggest mistake I've ever seen in a legal matter."

That seemed to be the opinion of many that hectic day. People would look at me and sadly shake their heads or draw that imaginery circle around their ear to indicate I had done a crazy thing. Even my friends told me they thought I had committed a grave legal boner, and a few urged me to reconsider. But the decision was made and I stuck to it.

We wound it all up a few days later. I argued the points I had made, including Noguchi's ability and his normalcy, as proved by my witnesses and my experts. The opposition argued the points they had made about his inability and his abnormality, as testified to by their witnesses and their experts.

Then it was over. And the waiting began. There was no jury, no judge, just the three commissioners. They had as long as they wanted to render their decision. Nobody had any idea how long it would take, as there had never been a case like this one.

So we waited. Weeks went by. I moved on to other cases, of course, but kept my eyes and ears open. Every day there were rumors about the Noguchi case. One day somebody who knew somebody who knew somebody would learn, positively, that Noguchi was through. The next day, from an equally unreliable source would come definitive word that he was sure to be reinstated.

By coincidence I was involved in another Civil Service hearing when one day Capen, the President of the Commission, came over to me and said, "Godfrey, we are prepared to announce our decision in the Noguchi matter. Is July 31st OK with you?"

"Sure."

He walked away. I tried to interpret his question and his attitude and the expression on his face and even the way he walked. Did it all add up to a firing or a reinstatement? It seemed to me just from what he said and the way he said it, that we had won. No guarantees, but would he have said it that way if we had lost? I was pretty sure I was right, but I was still concerned. In fact, I was so concerned I hedged my bets. I wrote two statements for Noguchi to read to the press. A victory statement, gracious in victory; a defeat statement, aggressive in defeat. I gave them to Tom to study so he'd be ready no matter what happened. I didn't tell him that I thought we had won, because in case we lost he would be twice as unhappy.

The hearing room was full on July 31, 1969. About 700 people had jammed in and, of course, the area for the press was crowded to capacity. We were all nervous, tense, anticipatory. Then Capen rose and the place quieted down.

"We, the Civil Service Commission of Los Angeles County," he said, "after hearing over one million words in over six weeks of testimony, find that not one charge against Dr. Thomas T. Noguchi has been proven. He is reinstated forthwith as Los Angeles County Chief Medical Examiner-Coroner and awarded full back pay."

The room burst into cheers. Roena was sobbing on my shoulder. Tom was shaking with emotion, alternating between laughter and tears. Roe was between us; I reached around, putting one arm on Tom's shoulder and my other hand on Roe's arm. The camera caught that moment and that was the picture that spread out on the front page of the *Los Angeles Times* under the screaming banner headline—NOGUCHI CLEARED. A few veteran news photographers told me the photo was a classic because of its spontaneity, because of the composition, because of the presence of the accused, his lawyer, and his lawyer's wife.

Something beautiful happened after that, and it happened with no planning and no preparation. Tom walked out of the hearing room and started walking toward his old office, the coroner's office. It was only a few blocks away. I walked at his side, and many people walked behind us. As we walked more and more people fell into the trailing group, and soon we were a small parade. As we strolled slowly and sedately, Tom whispered to me he was making "a ceremonial walk back to my office."

There were people lining the street. They had heard the news, and they applauded and cheered; Tom graciously nodded or waved or, when he recognized a familiar face, he called out and smiled broadly.

We reached the office, and Tom's associates were there; they too applauded and opened the doors wide so we could go in. The reporters and photographers, who had been part of the parade, crowded in behind us as Tom entered his office for the first time since he had been suspended.

"Dr. Noguchi," called one reporter, his voice slicing through the general din. "How does it feel to be back?"

"My chair looks the same." Noguchi said.

We all laughed. And then it hit me that it was all over, that we had won. I think it hit Tom at that moment, too, for his eyes sought out mine; we looked deep into each other's souls and there was a rapport. That was, I think, one of the greatest moments of my career.

I have had cases that brought me greater financial return by far. I have had cases that brought me greater acclaim. I have had cases that were perhaps won despite greater difficulties. But somehow that moment after winning the Noguchi case remains one of my supreme joys. Tom and I have often relived it, sipping a martini or some Japanese tea, and the memory never fails to raise my spirits.

When it began the case seemed to be a losing proposition. You will remember even Noguchi had said it was "mission impossible." When it was announced that I was going to represent Noguchi, people were so anti-Noguchi that they were abusive. Once Roena was in Ménage à Trois, one of the celebrated Beverly Hills beauty salons, having her hair done, when a woman came over and began screaming at her abusively because her husband was representing "that crazy man." A few lawyers told me that taking on such an unpopular case could do me irreparable harm—"You won't be able to practice in Los Angeles County after this one," one told me. It turned out he was wrong. I turned it around. I made the cause a popular one, and much of the popularity of the cause rubbed off on me. The Noguchi victory brought me a great deal of success, a tremendous amount of new and profitable business.

The next time I met Martin Weekes, he was still bitter. He congratulated me, but then he said, "Godfrey, you know you have done a terrible thing. I am so convinced that Noguchi should not be coroner that I am sure when he returns to that office, a tragedy is inevitable. Some day, somehow, he's going to do something awful."

He hasn't. As this is written, it has been about ten years since Noguchi resumed his post. He has become generally recognized as one of America's outstanding coroners. There has been no tragedy. He's matured into a master administrator of an ever-enlarging department. He has matured as a person, too. He no longer drives himself as hard as he once did. He no longer has anything to prove because I helped him prove it, out there in public. He now works shorter hours than he formerly did, and he is now able to delegate authority and let some of his subordinates do some of the key work. He has grown in self-confidence, too, and has become a skillful and popular speaker. He still has an accent, but that no longer troubles him. He spices his talks with humor and the audiences love him. I've often been in the audience when he speaks, and I think that now, perhaps, I might put him on the stand.

Shortly after Noguchi was reinstated and began serving the county as Chief Medical Examiner-Coroner again, there was the brutal Tate-LaBianca murders. It was a weekend. I was working in my office when suddenly Noguchi burst in. He was visibly upset and excited. He had to use a phone, he said, because he had been called to a case in Beverly Hills; he had to make a call and this was the only phone he could think of.

He managed to tell me something about it. It was the brutal slaying of Sharon Tate and her friends. He shook his head. He had seen some terrible things in his career, he told me, but this was by far the worst.

Later some irrational people even blamed the rash of murders on the reinstatement of Noguchi. How foolish people can be.

I learned a few lessons from the entire Noguchi matter. One concerned the fickleness of politicians.

Debs, the supervisor who totally ignored me at the hearing, and Hahn, the supervisor who told me what a stupid thing I had done in not letting Noguchi take the stand, had within a matter of weeks apparently forgotten those incidents.

Debs called me up because he was facing a stiff reelection campaign. Without so much as an apology or even an embarrassed mumble, he asked me if he could come to my office one day and if Roena could be there. He wanted to take a picture with us. We did on the theory that bygones are bygones. He had the picture taken with his arms around the two of us, a big buddy-buddy smile on his face. We were now political assets to him.

And Hahn, who is really a nice man, is now a big fan of Noguchi. And of mine. He often tells people how great we both are. The Noguchi case cost the county a fortune. It hurt some people. It could have been avoided if the Board of Supervisors had simply let us respond to the charges before firing Tom. It could have been settled in a few quiet, inexpensive, and painless days. But apparently that isn't the American way.

Chapter Five

SIRHAN. NOGUCHI. A legal career is made up of many cases, most of which involve people whose names none of us have ever heard. It is true that handling a front page case is fun and stimulating, but that is not the heart of any lawyer's practice. Most of us who are practicing law spend our professional careers representing clients who are ordinary people, but who have problems that are important and significant to them.

I was attracted to law because it always seemed to me a profession that was interesting and held great opportunity for service, accomplishment, and recompense. In my youth I often fantasized about being a lawyer. I consider myself one of the fortunate people of the world, because I have had the opportunity to live out my fantasies.

It seems to me as far back as I can remember, I wanted to be a lawyer. When I was in grade school and high school, when anybody asked me what I was going to be when I grew up, I universally replied I was going to be a lawyer.

I was born in Chicago, but was brought up in Kansas City, Missouri, which is the place I consider my hometown. My father was a salesman who sometimes made a living and sometimes did not. When I was very young we lived in an assortment of apartments and moved often because my father was unable to pay the rent. It may be that a good part of my personality was formed in those early years. My family had no money and I used to walk downtown with my father because he could not afford to take a streetcar. Money was a source of difficulty. There was never enough. There never was quite enough to eat, to wear, and certainly there was not a spare nickel, ever, for luxuries.

I suppose a case could be made for the proposition that my drive to succeed was nourished in the soil of that childhood poverty. It is certainly not a conscious motivation, but I am aware that our early backgrounds have a great deal to do with our later behavior. I began working at an early age, and most parents today would not allow a child to do so. I always had a regular job from the time I was in junior high school. My first regular job was as a copyboy at the old *Kansas City Journal-Post*. I worked fourteen hours a day, and my mother would cry when I came home exhausted. My fatigue was transitory, however, because my paycheck always revived me. I had various jobs all the way through high school, often working seven days a week as well as going to school.

After I graduated from high school, I went into the service and served for nearly three years in the Army. I went to Camp Abbot, Oregon, for my basic training. Because of my aptitude test scores, the Army sent me into the Army Specialized Training Program at Sacramento Junior College for assignment to an engineering school. While in Sacramento, I walked along streets lined with orange trees and vowed that after the war I would return to California.

From Sacramento I was transferred to the University of Utah, where I studied engineering. From there I was assigned to Camp Bowie, Texas, where my outfit was loaded with boys from Texas A&M. For some reason, in those days, most of them had a very vocal variety of anti-Semitism; nothing personal, they just dubbed me "Jew-bastard." As never before, I vowed not to put labels on people.

Probably that experience helped me crystallize my desire to become someone. It also inspired me to fight the Nazis, and I volunteered for overseas duty with the infantry. A bunch of my buddies and I decided to volunteer, but as it turned out, I was the only one who did. Shortly thereafter I was on a troop ship heading across the Atlantic Ocean. I fought with the 16th Armored Infantry Battalion of the 13th Armored Division. My outfit rushed through Germany with Patton's Third Army and on into Austria, where we captured Berchtesgarden where Hitler had his retreat.

In Germany, I observed some of our good, clean, American GIs become nearly as brutal and cruel as the Nazis. It left me wondering about human nature; I was amazed at how we react within our environment. The whole rotten business left its mark on me. I came out of the service with a better understanding about people, life, and senseless death. That understanding has contributed to my becoming a better lawyer. It preceded my career-long opposition to capital punishment. It made me aware.

I was discharged when I was twenty years old. Although I wanted to be a lawyer, I was in a hurry. As an alternative to law, I decided that I would become a teacher, a noble profession, and I entered the University of Southern California and was on my way. Despite the change in the course of my education, I had a constant inner fight, and in the end I could not turn my back on my first love, practicing law. My dream to be a lawyer was stronger than any reality.

Shortly before my first wife, Norma, and I were to be married, I made the decision that I was born to be a lawyer. I told Norma in almost an ecstatic manner that the decision was made and irreversible. As I stood waiting for her approval and understanding, she turned pale. It was as if I had slapped her.

I had shattered her dream of being married to a teacher. Her fantasy bubble was burst. We probably should not have gotten married after that, but we were in love and we continued our wedding plans. I thought she accepted my goals.

My choice of careers was never again the subject of any conversation between Norma and me. Sixteen years of marriage, two children, and we never once spoke about that subject that was so important to both of us. It must have been festering inside Norma though, for each of those sixteen years, but she never said a word.

Then, in 1964, we stood in the hallway outside the Santa Monica courtroom where we were getting our divorce. And suddenly that festering wound broke, and all the accumulated hatred and passion erupted. Norma turned to me and spat, "I fell in love with a teacher," she said, "and all I got was a trial lawyer."

She had helped me get through law school as she had promised she would. For the three years I attended Loyola Law School, she worked and never begrudged a cent of her earnings. I worked, too, of course, but certainly her efforts were essential. And then I went out, and the first years were struggling years and she stood at my side. Gradually success came and I started making money, a little at first and then more and more. Each step ahead was, as it turned out, like a knife at her throat. Why? I don't know the answer. When I had lawsuits that brought fat retainers, she became upset and cried. When I suggested that we could now afford to buy a Cadillac, she said if I bought a Cadillac she would divorce me. She often said that she didn't believe in people making as much money as I made, that it was obscene and indecent.

Despite her protstations on the subject of money, when it came time to talk dollars and cents at our divorce, she had no hesitation about asking for $2,000 a month for alimony, which was, at that time, almost as much as I made on a regular basis.

But in 1948 when I entered law school all of that was ahead

of me. I should have known from Norma's initial reaction to my decision to go to law school that I should have run from her, but I stayed. I followed my heart in both matters, the matter of love and the matter of career.

I applied and was accepted at Loyola University School of Law. I decided on Loyola at that time because it was a smaller school and I felt it would be more conducive to the educational process. It was a decision I have never regretted. I feel I received a good legal education there and good preparation for the years to come.

In my first year at Loyola I made the highest average that had ever been made until then by any first-year law student. I was tremendously elated and I continued to work and study. By my senior year I was elected president of the Loyola Law School's most prestigious organization, Loyola Board of Bar Governors. It was looked upon as a curiosity that a Jewish student would become president of the Student Bar Association at Loyola, which was a Catholic institution. But that was all—just a curiosity. There was never a problem or a difficulty over religion there.

As I look back to my law school days, it is of interest to me that I made my highest grades in criminal law, family law matters, and torts. I did not do as well in corporations and taxes. Law is a huge field, and as it gets bigger and more complex, no one is an expert in every phase. From law school on, it has been criminal law, family law, and trial law that have held my interest and that have brought me to this point. I never hesitate to consult an expert when I am faced with a tax problem or a corporate matter. Sometimes I feel that I was born to be a trial lawyer.

My first real break in entering the trial law field came about on one of the days that I was taking my bar examination. It was October 1951. During the lunch break I was sitting on a bench in the park, near the old Elks Temple in downtown Los Angeles where they gave the test. I ate the sandwich and Coke I brought with me. Then I soaked up the sun and flexed my tired hand, tired from all that writing I'd done all morning. One of my Loyola classmates came over to the bench and sagged onto it wearily.

"Hey, Godfrey," he said. "I heard about a job that sounds like it's right up your alley."

"Tell me."

"There's this lawyer, I got his name and address written down here somewhere, and I hear he's looking for a young guy to help him. He needs a trial lawyer and that's your thing, right?"

It sure was my thing. I took the name and address, and the next day I went to see him. His name was Paul Gordon, and he had an office on Hill Street.

He hired me immediately, so I had a job in the legal profession, even before I knew if I'd passed the bar exam. Gordon paid me $250 a month, which was then, to me, a princely sum.

I got my basic legal training from Paul Gordon. He was a brilliant teacher. Not that he taught, he just performed and I observed. Gordon was a bright, feisty, tough, hard-working pro. As I write these words, I know that Gordon is still practicing and whatever he does, he does well. I became his protégé, and it was the best possible start for me.

I did many things for him, and he let me do more and more. I went with him everywhere, watched as he talked to clients and witnesses, sat with him in court, went with him as he talked to judges in their chambers. I was his shadow. In December, the bar exam results were published and I had passed. Gordon congratulated me and raised my salary to $350 a month; it felt like I was on easy street. Norma and I really celebrated that night with a fancy dinner and the finest wines we could get.

On January 9, 1952, I was formally admitted to practice law in the State of California. Paul Gordon told me he was grooming me to try all his law suits. Many things Gordon did are things I still do today.

One of Gordon's habits I invariably follow even now. When he got a new client, he had an inflexible policy. After the first meeting with the new client, he writes him a long letter in which he tells him exactly what he proposes to do. He includes a key paragraph stating that there can be no guarantees as to results. He will do his best and he will try to do such and such, but he can make no guarantees, no promises of success. I write such a letter to all my new clients today. Right at the outset, I tell them there can be no certainty of success—and Paul Gordon was the man who taught me that.

Gordon taught me a great deal. Law school is one thing, but there is nothing like the reality of day-to-day legal practice to teach you the hard cold facts. I was with Gordon a little less than a year, but I have always felt that I received five years' worth of education in that period.

I remember the first trial I ever had. It was scheduled on the afternoon of the morning that I was admitted to practice law. I had only been a lawyer for about three hours when I appeared in court. When I stood before the judge for the first time to plead for my client, my legs were so shaky that I braced myself against the table. And an interesting thing occurred that first day. As I continued my opening statement, it began to become easier. By the time the afternoon was over, the shaking was history. The next time it was even easier. Gradually, I became very relaxed in court. In recent years many have commented that I am so at ease in a courtroom I look like I own the place.

As the months passed, Paul and I became very close. I had a tremendous amount of respect for him and the respect became affection. From the way he acted I was sure that he returned both the affection and a growing respect for my ability. At one point, he took me out and generously bought me a new suit. He said it was time I began to look like a successful lawyer. I took it home and modeled it for Norma. She turned her back on me and my new suit.

In September of 1952 when I had been with Gordon for

about ten months, he said he had a case to try in the San Francisco area and wanted me to come along. He also invited Norma, saying that this would be a good opportunity to get to know her better. It would be something of a pleasure trip as well as business, and we would all enjoy it.

En route he talked and asked questions. He told Norma how much he had done for me. He must have mentioned the suit he bought me several times. It was a strange conversation, it did not sound like the Paul Gordon I had known in the office. I believe he was trying to impress Norma with how generous he was to me and how my future lay with his firm.

We attended to the case in San Francisco, and Gordon said he was going to fly home. Norma and I drove back. The morning after our return, I came into the office as usual. He was waiting for me.

"Godfrey," he said, "I have to talk to you. I got some very disturbing vibrations from Norma in the car the other day."

"What do you mean?"

"Well, I will make it crystal clear. I got the feeling from her that you are planning to leave me. Are you planning to leave me?"

I had never thought of leaving. I liked working with Paul Gordon and felt I was set for the foreseeable future.

"No, Paul. I haven't even thought about leaving."

"Well," he said, leaning forward and looking me square in the eye. "I tell you what I want from you. I want you to look me in the eyes as we sit here and I want you to tell me that you will never leave this office."

"Paul, how can I tell you that? I can assure you that I have no plans whatsover to leave you and, in fact, the thought of leaving has never crossed my mind. But I cannot promise I'll never leave, because who knows what could happen in the future?"

"Is that your final word on the subject?"

I couldn't believe this conversation. I shook my head in disbelief. What had happened?

"Yes, I guess it is. I don't have plans to leave and I don't want to leave and I hope I don't leave. But I just can't promise you that I'll never leave, and I don't see how you can expect me to make such a promise."

He gave me a long and searching look.

"All right," he said. "If that's the way you feel, maybe you should leave right now."

"Right now?"

"Exactly. Today. This minute."

I walked out of his office in a daze. How had this strange and frightening conversation begun? It was insanity. But the bottom line was that I was fired. Twenty minutes later, Gordon came in to tell me he had decided to give me two weeks, so at least I had a chance to consider my next move.

After that strange experience, when a man I thought liked me and respected me let me go without any reason that I could fathom, I decided that I would never again work for anyone else. I would be my own boss where I wouldn't have to be subject to the peculiar whims of anyone else. Never again would somebody try to force a promise out of me that I would never leave, then ask me to leave when I couldn't make that promise. From now on, I would do the hiring and, if necessary, the firing.

I spent those two weeks looking around, and I finally found a modest office in a downtown Los Angeles building for $80 a month. It wasn't much, but it looked good to me. Of course, I couldn't afford a secretary or anything like that. I opened my own office in those humble surroundings with only a desk and a couple of chairs.

I didn't sit there waiting for cases to come to me. I knew enough about lawyers and how they operate to know that for some attorneys court cases are a nuisance. Lawyers who specialize in business matters look on court appearances as an unnecessary drain on their time and their energy. They'd rather be doing other things than going to court. But since going to court was what I loved, I figured that maybe I could take over some court appearances for some of the business lawyers. I set out to do just that.

I began going door to door in buildings that I knew had a high number of lawyers as tenants. I would barge in, introduce myself, and say that I would like to handle their court cases, any court cases no matter how small or inconsequential. Sometimes I couldn't even get past the receptionist. Sometimes the lawyers would see me, but I often had the feeling that they would like me to get lost. Most were polite but they had nothing. A few had minor cases which they let me handle— cases involving fees of $10 or $20. I took them all. The experience was good, and the $10 or $20 was always welcome. But it was a discouraging period for me which fortunately only lasted a few months.

Which brings us to the second turning point in the early years of my career.

My door to door wanderings brought me one day to the office of a lawyer named Walter Egerman. I was about to tell him that I was available to try any lawsuit for him when I recognized him. I had been at a cocktail party at a relative of my father's a few weeks before and we had been introduced. This time I had a little bit of a wedge.

Fortunately, he recognized me at once also. He seemed very friendly. We chatted for a few moments about the party where we had met. I had a gut reaction that this was going to be a profitable experience. Over the years I have learned that my gut reactions are often accurate.

I told him that I was beginning my own practice and that I was looking for cases. I offered to take some of his suits off his hands to free him for other things. He immediately looked interested.

"I've got a bunch of junk here," Egerman said, gesturing to a haphazard pile of files behind him. "I'll give them all to you, if you want them."

"As far as I'm concerned," I said, "there is no such thing as a junk suit. I'll take whatever you've got."

He swiveled around in his chair, picked up the files, and dumped them in my lap. I think there were eighteen or twenty of them. They made such a hefty pile that I staggered out of the office with them, little realizing that they were launching my career.

Egerman said I could keep whatever I made from those "junk" cases, but if I did well with them he'd like to be recompensed for his time. I said I'd pay him for his time whether I did well with them or not.

Back in my office I went through the files and set to work. There weren't big cases, obviously. I went to work on them as though they were. To me, each of those cases was as big as the Lindbergh or the Loeb-Leopold trial. As the cases began going to court, and I showed up totally prepared and giving my all, the results were gratifying. None was a big winner, although the sums began to add up. Regularly, I made out a check for Egerman for what I felt was his portion of the proceeds. I made it a point to deliver each of my checks to Egerman in person, to reinforce his impression of me as a hard-working, honest, ambitious young man.

He kept saying each time I showed up with some money for him how amazed and delighted he was. Eventually he told me that he had thought those cases were all hopeless, and he had just handed them to me as a way of getting rid of them. Now here I was turning them into money for both of us. He smiled and clapped me on the back.

One day he did something more important. He telephoned me and said, "Godfrey, join me for lunch today. One o'clock at the Beverly Hills Hotel. That OK with you?"

It sure was. I assumed that it was a special occasion, and you can bet I arrived at the Beverly Hills Hotel on time. We had a good lunch. Then he sprang his surprise.

"The office next to mine has become vacant," he said. "I would like you to take it. I've been watching what you've done with those junk cases and I have a feeling that you and I can make some big money together."

It sounded great but I did not want to sound too enthusiastic.

"Don't rush into this. Think it over. I sense we could be good for each other, but I don't want to rush you or force you into making a step you're reluctant to make."

Think it over he said. I thought it over—maybe two seconds. This was the break I had been waiting for. I quickly agreed; then he told me his other news. There was a divorce case. He had a retainer of $2,500, and he wanted us to work on it together, on a fifty-fifty basis. There was a check in my hand for $1,250; that was very important money in those days.

I moved to Beverly Hills next to Walter Egerman. I became a Beverly Hills lawyer, and I'm still a Beverly Hills lawyer. Over the years from time to time I've had my office outside the city limits of Beverly Hills, but somehow I have always been thought of as a Beverly Hills lawyer. I still am in Beverly Hills and consider it one of the most beautiful cities in the country.

Egerman handed me a personal injury case that was coming to trial. He felt it could not be won. The opposing attorney was one of the most famous insurance defense attorneys of his day, Ray Stanbury. Walter felt that not only the facts were difficult, but that I could never win against Ray Stanbury. It was my first jury trial, and one of the greatest thrills of my early days was getting on the telephone to tell Egerman that I had received a jury verdict for $10,000. That was a substantial sum then and Stanbury was furious. The trial judge was also furious; he felt the defense should have won, and he set the verdict aside. Egerman asked if I would like to drop it. By now I guess I was getting a little bit cocky and I replied, "Never."

My feeling was that if I could win it once I could win it twice. The insurance company was upset about my verdict and sent in a different high-priced and renowned defense lawyer. I was determined to repeat my victory. I drove to Redondo Beach where the accident occurred, and I literally went door to door for blocks around the site of the accident, scouting up new witnesses to the old accident. The famous old pro who opposed me was confident, ready, and prepared to destroy the witnesses I had used in the first trial. When I presented totally new witnesses, he was angry. The results, however, were the same, I won again. This time the judgment was for $6,000. Egerman was impressed. I was thrilled.

Within a few months I received my largest fee to that date in a divorce case, thus celebrating the end of my second year as a lawyer with a $4,000 fee. That equaled one year's pay with Paul Gordon. I was on my way.

Chapter Six

In the summer of 1954, my real legal life was beginning. Events began to happen with increasing swiftness. It was as though I had started something that was beginning to snowball.

Egerman and I had a nice working arrangement, which was helpful to us both. Paul Gordon had begun my practical law education; Egerman and his associate, Leo Gold, polished it. Soon, another man would enter my life and contribute to my street education—also important to trial lawyers.

It wasn't long after I moved into the office next to Egerman that I needed and could afford to hire a secretary, my first. I was lucky. I hired a girl named Babette Levine. She was dedicated, wise, and attentive. She was also, of course, very qualified and an experienced legal secretary.

She had been with me a few weeks when a new client was referred to me, Harvey Karman. He was an intelligent, educated young man and he was in jail. He was charged with murder arising from the death of a woman he had allegedly aborted.

I was very excited about my first murder case. Divorces and accidents are interesting and sometimes challenging, but when a young lawyer realizes that he is going to defend a man accused of murder, there is something inside him that suddenly grows up. Many laymen feel that murder cases are where the thrills are. The simple truth is that they inspire the lawyer to deep dedication to his craft, and they bring about nagging doubts as to one's own ability. I threw myself into the preparation of this trial, because I was determined to be equal to the task.

This case would need expert investigation. Until now I had personally gathered the information I would need during a trial, and I interviewed witnesses myself. Now I was entering a more sophisticated world, and I decided to seek out my first private investigator. I discussed this with my secretary, Babette, just as I often discussed other important questions with her. Babette reacted with her usual enthusiasm and immediately suggested a private detective that her former employer had considered the best in the business. I relied upon her advice, and I placed a telephone call to Clyde Nicholas Duber.

Duber came bounding into my office and my life the next day. He was, and still is, a medium-sized man, full of vitality and enthusiasm and tremendously experienced at his job. We immediately hit it off; it turned out to be the beginning of a friendship that has lasted a quarter of a century. Through Duber, I moved into other circles. I moved into the area of Hollywood and Hollywood stars. Duber knew them all. He introduced me to many of them, and I came to represent many of them through the years.

I was now meeting people who lived in a different world than I had known. I had been brought up in a rather old-fashioned, moral family, and those characteristics are hard to shake off. The Hollywood crowd that was now becoming part of my social life held to a newer and less structured set of mores.

As Clyde (some people called him Nick, but he's always been Clyde to me) and I became more friendly, I became more and more aware of the world in which he lived. I knew that I would have to understand this new world if I were to mature into an effective attorney able to deal with all aspects of it. I knew that the Mike Hammers and the Sam Spades were creatures of fiction created for movie audiences, but I also sensed that they were based on truth. Clyde Duber understood what was going on in a part of the world that I had only read about. I would have to know about the streets of the city in order to adequately handle clients charged with crimes.

I was becoming busier, and Duber worked for me more and more. Often evenings were the only time we could meet and discuss the pending cases. Restaurant Row, as a certain stretch along La Cienega Boulevard in Los Angeles was then known, was Duber's turf. Every maître d' on Restaurant Row knew Clyde Duber, and they came to know me too.

Often our restaurant conferences would be interrupted as Clyde greeted one famous person or another and introduced them to me. There was one night in particular. We would often have cocktails with our dinner. I have always been a moderate drinker, but I recall this one occasion when I overdid it. I was seated at a table at a Sunset Boulevard restaurant when John Wayne sat at the adjoining table. He and I began to talk politics; we were worlds apart. Somehow, each of us punctuated a point being made by belting down the cocktail at hand. Despite the difference in our political philosophy, he was soft-spoken, said what he thought, and kept right on drinking—and so did I. Finally, I headed for home. On the way I kept bumping into the curb. Although I drove slowly, the curb kept coming up and assaulting my tires. I vowed that night never again to drink so much that I could not drive straight, and for all these years I have kept that vow. As I nursed a hangover the next morning, though, I could not help but smile at my misery. I remembered those earlier days in Kansas City when I went to a movie every Saturday afternoon and never dreamt that one day I would engage in a drinking bout with the Duke.

Duber was always telling people how good I was. I would suggest to him that he moderate his statements, as it sometimes became embarrassing. He was irrepressible, however. He had really become a fan of mine. He was continuously telling me to charge more.

I think the case that inspired him to all of these complimentary comments was the Meyer case. There was a very fine psychiatrist whom I had met on several occasions. He was conservative, brilliant, and totally reputable. He called me one day, sounding agitated and upset and telling me that he needed help. He did. His brother had been arrested and was accused of oral copulation with another man at a drive-in restaurant in West Los Angeles. He wanted me to handle the case.

I wasted no time in getting Jimmy Meyer out of jail. I had him brought immediately to my office and proceeded to interview him. His appearance gave me pause for thought as I sat and studied him. He had on extremely tight pants and even looked as if he had on a touch of lipstick. I was concerned that any observer would conclude that he was a homosexual and thus, in the observer's mind, likely to be guilty of the charge. I felt that his appearance might have caused a zealous officer to believe him guilty of an act that he may not have committed. He swore that he was innocent. He was intelligent, sensitive, and persuasive. I agreed to defend him.

I read the police report. In it the officers stated that they had been in the vicinity of a drive-in restaurant and saw Jimmy Meyer enter the rest room. The officers then drove to the side of the rest room and parked their car in front of the only window. One of the officers stood on the left front fender of their Ford automobile and looked through the window. He stated that he had a clear view of the booths in the men's room. He concluded that while he was observing the two booths, he observed Jimmy Meyer and another man perform the illegal act for which Meyer had been arrested.

Robert Hill, my legal assistant, and I drove to the drive-in. It has always been my practice to take a look at the scene where the crime is supposed to have occurred. This case cemented that practice for all time. I parked my car where the cops said they had parked, under the only window in the men's room. First Bob and I checked to make sure there were no occupants. Then, one after another we stood on the fender of my car. Neither he nor I could believe what we saw. More accurately, neither of us could believe what we could not see. He and I looked from every square inch of the window into the room and to our amazement discovered that it was impossible to see into the booths where the action was said to have occurred. There was no question, the police had just plain lied. The problem I was faced with was proving it in a courtroom.

I called Clyde Duber to continue the investigation. I told him what Hill and I had discovered. Clyde was incensed but dubious about the chances of proving that the police lied. He reminded me that jurors generally believe the police. He did not believe that a court would allow the jury to come out to the drive-in and stare into the window of a men's room. He could not understand why I was grinning as he talked.

"What's with you?" he inquired.

"I'm going to take the men's room into court," I said.

And that's exactly what I did.

I found a carpenter who agreed to go to the drive-in, take measurements and build an exact replica with actual dimensions of the entire men's room. It was meticulously built with every corner and every aspect identical to the real men's room. It was complete to simulated toilets, partitions, and booths. I had it originally assembled in a warehouse. The carpenter built it such a way that it could be disassembled and reassembled inside the courtroom. He also built a wooden car fender the exact size and at the exact height from the ground as the Ford car fender which the policeman stated he had stood on. I had it assembled in a warehouse and I could not wait to hear the police testify. I knew that they had a surprise in store.

The matter came to trial before Judge Stanley Mosk, now a Justice of the Supreme Court of the State of California and then a Superior Court Judge in Santa Monica, California. He was a bright and perceptive jurist, and I was pleased to have him as the judge. The jury was impaneled and the case began. The police testified that they had driven to the restaurant, parked near the men's room, stood on the fender of their car, and peeked in the window. Then they testified in lurid detail every act they claimed to have seen. It became my turn for cross-examination. I asked the court for a recess and had the carpenter come in, rearrange the entire front of the courtroom, and erect the model that he had so painstakingly constructed.

As I began my cross-examination the policeman on the stand kept looking at the model. If he was nervous it did not show. I advised the court that the exhibit was an exact replica and offered to put the carpenter on the stand to testify. The district attorney conferred with the police and then stipulated that the model was accurate. I then asked the policeman to stand on the fender we had constructed, and to show us where he looked in the window to see the acts he had described.

The officer went from point to point and tried in every way to see inside the booths. He became agitated and upset. He finally stood on that fender, looked back at the jury, and said, "You cannot see inside the booths from this window." I put on no further testimony. Oddly enough there was a hung jury. The few jurors who voted conviction admitted privately that they thought Meyer was a homosexual. It was incredible to me that they had completely ignored the uncontroverted facts. I immediately reset the case in front of Judge Mosk, waived a jury, and stipulated that he could reach his decision based on the evidence introduced at the first trial. This experienced jurist looked up and without hesitation stated, "I find the defendant, Jimmy Meyer, not guilty."

Clyde Duber has not outgrown the sheer enjoyment he got watching that policeman in court, dancing from position to position, trying to see through that glass. He laughs about it today and still says he has never seen anything to equal the time I brought a men's room into court. It was that case that made Clyde Duber a fan of mine.

As one case followed another, I began to assemble my own arsenal of what I considered to be very important legal truths. At the same time I learned that some of the axioms that I had learned from the day I commenced law school simply were not true. As an example, for years lawyers have been saying that cases are won or lost on the facts. This is almost universally held as being gospel. However, facts do not occur in the courtroom. A trial comes on for hearing many months or even years after the fact. Cases are won or lost on what the facts appear to be. It is the appearance of facts that we lawyers present to judges and juries. I have kept this in mind and time after time the recognition of this truth has been of service to my clients.

When you are as active an investigator as Clyde Duber was twenty years ago, I suppose it is only a question of time until some of your enemies try to set you up. This happened to Clyde, and it was an upsetting and nerve-racking experience for him. I was accustomed to having him call me to report on cases he was investigating, but the call I received one day was different than any that had preceded it. His first comment was, "They are after me, Godfrey, and I want you to help me."

He was excited, indignant, and his voice a bit throaty.

"What are you talking about, Clyde?" I asked.

He replied, "They're out to get me. I have been arrested on a bribery charge and it's a frame-up."

I calmed him down and invited him to the office. After he told me the whole story I was convinced that he was absolutely innocent but that powerful pressure was being brought to set him up. He had handled the investigation on a particular case and was now officially accused of paying a witness a large sum of money when the witness agreed to stay away from court, even though he had been subpoenaed. The attorney employing Duber on that particular case was Walter Anderson, a fine lawyer and a part-time city attorney for Manhattan Beach. Anderson was generally respected.

The charge against Duber was totally illogical. He was supposed to have paid the witness $1,000 not to testify, but it made no sense. The money had not come from Anderson, nor was there any claim that it came from the client of Anderson. The only person left was Clyde Duber, and I knew that he would never have paid someone $1,000 of his own money because it made absolutely no difference to him whether the man testified or not. Careful investigation and an objective analysis of the facts led to but one conclusion. Clyde was innocent, but someone was out to get him. He had stepped on a lot of official toes in his day as he pursued various investigations, and apparently one of those toes was out to kick back.

This was perhaps the worst period in Duber's entire career. He felt that the police department and the district attorney's office wanted to nail him. He kept urging me to more and more effort. No matter what I did in those days, he wanted me to do more. He kept insisting that I was the only man he would trust, so I began working almost night and day.

This was one of the few times I saw Clyde lose his objectivity. No matter what statement I would elicit from any witness, he would want more. He kibitzed and he cajoled. He was a great detective but a terrible client.

At one point he was calling me so often that I felt I would just have to have a discussion with him. One evening we were at his home in Culver City sitting around his kitchen table, which in that house was the social center. Clyde and Virginia, some of his operatives, and I went over the case time and time again. Finally, I led him by the hand out of the kitchen and into one of the other rooms.

"Clyde," I told him, "I will try this case for you and I will break my ass doing it, but you have to stay the hell out of it. You have got to let me handle it my way."

In all the years I have known him, that was the closest we ever came to an argument, and those words were probably the harshest I had ever directed at him. Then I laid it on the line. I told him that I would have to try the case my way and he would have to let me alone or else I could not do it at all. The message got through to him. He understood what I was saying, and he promised from that point on to let me represent him without interference from him.

Clyde's matter was set for trial in the old Hall of Justice in Los Angeles. One of my most vivid memories of that old building is Clyde Duber pacing up and down the hallway at every court recess. He was a nervous wreck by the time the case was called. A jury was chosen, opening statements were made, and the prosecution put on their case. It was not a strong case, but standing alone and unchallenged, it would have sustained a conviction.

The police had prepared their witnesses well, and although I felt that my cross-examination was adequate, I knew that the case would be won or lost on the testimony of Walter Anderson and Clyde Duber. I had always heard that lawyers were notoriously poor witnesses. I guess this is because they find it hard to set lawyering aside and just answer the questions being asked. I was more than a little concerned about Anderson but I need not have been.

He certainly made a great impression physically. He looked like every lawyer wishes he looked. He was tall, handsome, a young face with a shock of white hair giving him that perfect balance between experience and youthful eagerness. He testified that he had, in fact, wanted the witness in question to testify and that what the witness had to say was beneficial to his client. He would have had no reason to want him silenced, and he had not instructed Duber to offer him money to keep silent. He had not given Duber any money for such mission, nor had he authorized or requested it.

He was cross-examined by James Kolts, at that time a deputy district attorney and now a Superior Court Judge. Kolts was a fine hand with cross-examination. Anderson held together and his testimony could not be shaken. He said just enough but not too much, and did not try to be smarter than Kolts.

One exchange remains vividly in my mind. Kolts had become frustrated at the cool and intelligent manner in which Anderson was fielding his toughest questions. Finally, he snapped at Walter.

"You're considered an expert at law, aren't you, Mr. Anderson?"

Walter looked up, all innocence, and softly replied, "Thank you, counsel."

As concerned as I had been about Clyde's nervous state, he too delivered. He was an excellent witness. He denied the charge simply and believably. He answered the questions that were asked of him without embroidering on them. I do not know what Kolts was anticipating, but he never shook Clyde up by a single question or on a single point. In the clutch Duber was the smooth performer he had always been.

It was time for closing arguments. In a criminal case the prosecution has both the first and the last argument. They open and close. The reason for this is that the people must carry the burden of proof. Thus, I knew Kolts would have the first word and the last word with the jury. I have always considered summation to be one of the pivotal stages of any trial and one of my strong points. I had thought about this closing argument morning, noon, and night for days. I delivered the argument with confidence and hoped that I was persuasive. When I finished, Duber was all smiles.

"Godfrey," he said to me. "You've done it again. They'll acquit me without even leaving the jury box."

Kolts gave his closing argument, and suddenly it was in the hands of the jury.

The jury filed out of the box. Clyde's smile began to fade. We went back into the hallway and both he and I began pacing up and down. In some ways this time is the hardest in every jury trial. We had done everything that was going to be done and now there was no opportunity to do more. Clyde kept talking about the things we could have done, should have done, might have done. As the hours went by without a verdict, it took all my efforts to try to calm Clyde down.

The jury deliberated for five or six hours; then they finally buzzed, indicating they had reached a verdict and were ready to announce it. We went back to our seats in court. I closed my eyes and folded my hands while I waited—the tensest moments of my life are those jittery seconds before a jury announces its finding.

"We, the jury, find the defendant, Clyde Nicholas Duber, not guilty."

I began to breathe again. I turned to Clyde and the change in him was absolutely miraculous. Five seconds before he had been a craven shell—haunted eyes, sunken cheeks, cold and clammy complexion. But as soon as he heard that cheerful verdict, he immediately reverted to the old Clyde Duber. His color was back, the old sparkle was in his eyes, the old jauntiness to his posture.

"What else could they have done?" he asked with a shrug.

I just laughed. What was there to say? You'd have thought it was just another day to Duber, rather than the trying experience it had been. I smiled at him and he smiled back. He understood. I got up to do my customary pleasant chore of thanking each of the jurors and Clyde turned and embraced me.

"Godfrey," he said, "I'll never forget this."

I've had a lot of clients over the years who have said the same thing in the first flush of appreciation after a favorable verdict. Most of them have quickly forgotten. Clyde Duber never forgot. That was over twenty years ago and ever since he has been telling everybody within earshot that I'm the best lawyer there is. I know he is prejudiced in my favor, but it is always nice to hear.

I was long past being naive by the time of Duber's arrest;

nevertheless, it was an eye-opener for me. I knew that it was possible to harass a citizen for political reasons, but this was my first close experience with such a thing. It is a shocking concept and, in those days, few believed that type of thing could happen. It was not until twenty years later when the Watergate scandal was on the front pages that the entire country came to realize that prosecutions could sometimes be born of political aggression.

I believe the great majority of people in government are honorable. However, I am also acutely aware that there are some who are not. The difficulty lies when the few find ways to influence the many. I believe the prosecutors in the Duber case were sincere men of integrity, but they had been spoon-fed erroneous information by certain members of the police department. Prosecutors, after all, are advocates too.

There was a victory party the night of the verdict in the Bantam Cock, Clyde's favorite Restaurant Row hangout. For me, that was a joyous moment. As I walked into the restaurant a bit late, the whole table of Clyde's friends and associates stood up and applauded.

The case had a secondary effect on my life. Virginia Duber had been very upset by the whole affair. She felt humiliated by the publicity and felt that her neighbors looked at her askance. She insisted that they move, so Clyde and she sold their home and bought a house in the upper reaches of Mandeville Canyon. Naturally, I often went there to visit for dinners and parties and just simple social evenings. Both Norma and I loved the rustic beauty of the canyon, so when I began to make more money and we felt we could afford nicer living quarters, we bought a house in Mandeville Canyon, too. I always thought our home there looked like a picture postcard. I really loved that house and would have been content to stay there forever. But two years after we bought it and moved in, Norma and I were divorced and we had to sell the house.

It was in the Dubers' Mandeville Canyon house that I met

even more Hollywood celebrities. Duber had often done work as a private detective for the stars. Before I knew him, he had been retained by Jerry Geisler, one of the most noted of Hollywood attorneys, on a famous case. When Lana Turner's daughter was accused of stabbing gangster Johnny Stompinato, Lana's first call was to Geisler. Geisler's first call was to Duber. Together, Geisler and Duber made the decisions and did the investigating that led to a resolution of that case.

Norma and I were at the Dubers' Mandeville Canyon home for a party one evening. Virginia was a very skillful hostess and her parties were always exciting and fun. The weather was pleasant, and this one was outside. We were enjoying ourselves, talking and laughing and eating, when suddenly the little band Clyde hired broke into "Over the Rainbow." We looked over and there was Judy Garland. She was still with her husband, Sid Luft, who was an old and good friend of Clyde. Later in the evening, Clyde signaled me to follow him into the kitchen; there were Judy and Sid, and the four of us sat around the kitchen table. It was only a minor encounter but it would eventually lead to something more major.

In recent years, Clyde's favorite watering hole has been the Luau Restuarant on Rodeo Drive in Beverly Hills. He holds court there most evenings and enjoys seeing many of his old friends. Occasionally, I would drop in to say hello and perhaps to have a drink. One evening, in the summer of 1978, I stopped by on my way to an appointment and found Clyde talking with Stephen Crane, the owner of the Luau, famous restaurateur and ex-husband of Lana Turner. Steve looked at me and said, "Godfrey, I'm glad you came by. I need you." He then retained me to represent him in his latest divorce action. Once again, I met another celebrity through Clyde Duber.

I have generally enjoyed people associated with the entertainment industry. Sometimes the legal problems of actors and actresses are exaggerated because of their prominence. It is true that highly volatile performers are often bombastic in their demands and certainly are subjected to far more publicity about their personal lives. Many incidents that might go unnoticed become publicized when the participants are famous.

Mrs. Marlon Brando requested an appointment with me one day. She said it was imperative that she see me as soon as possible. She told me that Saturday morning was the only time available to her. It has been my preference to keep my weekends free from work to get away from the grindstone, but I have made too many exceptions to recount. When a meeting was requested by Anna Kashfi, the former wife of Marlon Brando and a noted beauty, I made another of my many exceptions.

On weekends there is a guard stationed in the lobby of my building, and visitors must sign in and out. When I got there precisely at 11:00 A.M., which was the time for our appointment, I signed in and noted that Mrs. Brando had preceded me by fifteen minutes.

I hurried up to my office; I never liked to keep anyone waiting, especially a famous beauty. On the way up I tried to remember her background. I had read that she had been born in India and that she was reputed to have a rather tempestuous personality. Representing her might be a challenging experience.

I floated off the elevator and entered our reception room with a smile on my face, prepared to welcome her. She wasn't there. I went back to the elevator area, looked around, but she wasn't there, either. Perhaps she had gone to the ladies' room. I unlocked my office door, sat behind my desk, and waited for Anna Kashfi Brando to appear. Minutes went by. Fifteen minutes. A half-hour. When I realized I had been sitting there doing nothing but waiting for an hour, I became annoyed. I assumed she must have changed her mind. Just as I was leaving my office, she raced into the reception room with her eyes blazing; and when Kashfi blazes her eyes, they are burning. She was madder than hell and talking so fast I almost couldn't understand her. I gestured for her to follow me into my office, sat her down, and finally calmed her sufficiently so she could tell me what had happened. It was an unusual story, and I probably would have thought it amusing if I had not been waiting for an hour.

She had signed in with the guard at the desk in the lobby at 10:45. There was a nice looking, middle-aged, white-haired man behind her.

"Mrs. Brando," he said. He either recognized her picture or had good enough eyesight to see the name she had written in the guard's book.

"Yes?"

"It's very nice to meet you," the man said. And Anna Kashfi Brando jumped to the conclusion that the man was Godfrey Isaac, the lawyer she had come to meet.

The man held out his hand, gave her a warm smile. She took his hand, and smiled in return.

"It's nice to meet you, too," she said.

"How about going down the street and having a bite of breakfast?" the man suggested. She agreed, and off they went.

They sat down in the Old World Restaurant and had breakfast. She poured out her story. He was sympathetic. He commented intelligently, gave her good advice, made sensible suggestions, and discussed legal ramifications knowledgeably. She was very pleased with him and felt she had made a good choice of lawyers. They sat there dallying over their coffee, and finally she said, "I want to thank you so much, Mr. Isaac, and I think I am in good hands."

The man looked at her in great surprise.

"Oh my dear woman," he said. "My name isn't Isaac. My name is Schnabel."

It turned out to be a lawyer named Daniel Schnabel who also had his office in that building. He had quite innocently recognized Mrs. Marlon Brando that morning and greeted her out of politeness, inviting her to breakfast merely because he enjoyed being in the company of beautiful women. He had

been having a very delightful morning, entertaining a charming and attractive lady, and out of the goodness of his heart,
gave her legal advice free. He felt it was all a fortuitous
meeting—but she was furious. In fact, it occurred to her that
it was a plot.

"Do you think Marlon set it up?" she asked me. "Do you
think that man Schnabel is working for Marlon?"

I said I didn't think so, but she wasn't convinced. She was
so bitter at Brando that she saw his hand in everything that
happened to her.

"Believe me, Mrs. Brando," I said, "this time Marlon had
nothing to do with it. It was simply Daniel Schnabel exercising his normal and healthy appreciation of a good-looking
woman."

Finally I got her off the subject of Schnabel and onto the
subject of her legal problems. I liked her, and we became
friends. Eventually she met Roena, my wife at the time; Anna
and Roena became very close.

In due time I brought a proceeding on Anna's behalf,
taking Brando to court and seeking additional child support
money. The case appeared finally in Los Angeles Superior
Court, and the presiding judge was Edward Brand. Brand was
very familiar with movie people. His brother, Harry, was
publicity director for 20th Century-Fox for many years, and
Harry's wife, Sybil, was very important in Hollywood society.
The Sybil Brand Institute where Los Angeles houses its female
criminals is named for her.

Judge Brand took a particular interest in this case. He often
called Anna Kashfi Brando at home to discuss certain aspects
of the proceedings or to give fatherly advice.

When Anna first told me about this, it was difficult for me
to believe her. However, I called the judge to ask him whether
he had been telephoning Anna. He immediately stated that he
had and explained that his sole interest was in resolving the
case quickly without any more of the fireworks that had
previously occurred. I accepted his explanation, but I strongly

recommended to the judge that he not place any more telephone calls to her, and that he limit his participation in the case to the courtroom.

When the hearing itself began, Brando took the stand; I questioned him at length, which was an experience. He is a brilliant actor, and I felt that his testimony was yet another magnificent performance. He had even taken great care with his appearance. He was a gray man—his hair was gray, his clothes were gray, and somehow he had managed to even make his skin seem gray. He obviously wanted to give that impression, the impression of grayness, of lackluster, of bland nothingness. It was a strange color to assume, but it was good showmanship.

I thought that the actor was sincere in his protestations of love and affection for his child. I also knew that Anna loved the boy deeply. But Marlon and Anna had no love for each other. In fact, I believe that Anna would have cheerfully ripped Marlon apart, had she been able to do so. I felt great sorrow and sympathy for the boy. That feeling was heightened during the trial. His parents did not even call him by the same name.

If Marlon was on the stand, the boy was called Christian; if Anna was on the stand, the boy was called Devi. You can imagine how confused the boy must have been— compounding the usual mother-father dichotomy of a divorce, there was the question of his name. One boy with two names.

The curious thing is that all of us involved in that trial— lawyers and judge—followed the parents' example and called the boy by two names. Whenever the remarks pertained to the boy and his father, he was Christian; but if we were referring to him and his mother, he was Devi. The stubbornness of the parents had infected us all.

As the case proceeded, Judge Brand, an articulate and witty man, said to me in court one day, "Mr. Isaac, do you realize that you are Mrs. Brando's seventeenth attorney?"

"Who's counting, Judge?" I said.

"Furthermore," he went on, ignoring my attempt at humor, "Do you realize that there will soon be an eighteenth?"

The judge really knew his litigants. It wasn't long before I suggested to Anna Kashfi Brando that she might be happier with another attorney.

I still liked Anna very much, but by this time we had come to disagree on the best method of resolving the case. While I was still representing Anna, the judge decided that Christian/ Devi should be sent to a private school and not live with either party. It was not that either, at that time, was not a good parent, but rather to avoid further battles. Judge Brand suggested they consider a particular school. Then the trouble started. Marlon felt he should inspect the school. Anna countered by saying that before Marlon inspected the school, she should see it. It was important to her that she see it before Marlon did. It developed that it was equally important to Marlon that he inspect the school before Anna did. They could not agree on which one should go first.

Brando's lawyer, attempting to be a Solomon, proposed that we hire two limousines, put Marlon in one and Anna in the other, and that they drive to the school at the same time.

I thought that was a reasonable solution, but Anna didn't. She was entitled to her position, and I respected that. However, at that point, I felt that she would be happier with another lawyer. Later I heard that there was a parade of lawyers after me, and the battle raged on.

Chapter Seven

ONE OF DUBER'S OPERATIVES was a man named Phil Irwin. Irwin had been hired by another private investigator to tail Marilyn Monroe. Apparently, Joe DiMaggio wanted to know where his ex-wife was going the many afternoons and evenings she would suddenly disappear.

One night, Irwin was off-duty and happened to spot Marilyn Monroe's car outside an apartment building. Irwin knew that one of the tenants of that apartment house was a woman who was reputed to be a lesbian.

Irwin felt that he should immediately report this information to his boss. He put in a call to Barney Ruditsky, the private eye who had him working on the case. It was not long before Ruditsky showed up on the street outside the apartment building with one of Joe DiMaggio's good friends, Frank Sinatra. DiMaggio also arrived. Marilyn's car was still there. The more the men conferred, the more excited they got; it was finally decided that they were going to bust in and confront Marilyn. Sinatra thought it a splendid idea.

Irwin and Ruditsky looked at each other. They knew they had no legal right to bust in anywhere. They were also concerned that if they did bust in on an apartment and found Marilyn in a compromising situation, there was no telling what DiMaggio might do. They were worried.

Irwin and Ruditsky now realized they were in a spot that could easily cause them serious problems. DiMaggio and Sinatra were determined to break in. Ruditsky and Irwin knew that such an action could only lead to disaster. Ruditsky simply pointed out the wrong apartment. He knew there would be trouble, but felt it would be less serious than if he pointed out the right apartment. I guess he thought that God would be kind to them, and there would be nobody home in the apartment he indicated.

God wasn't that kind. Ruditsky kicked in the door, and a little old lady screamed in fright and protest. All of the men fled. The screams brought the police. They called it attempted burglary. In the confusion, Marilyn Monroe also slipped away, and nobody ever knew in whose apartment she had been, or for what purpose. At that time no one knew what had happened.

Eventually, someone reported the true facts to the police. After that a State Senate Committee was formed to investigate private detectives. The incident became known as the "Marilyn Monroe Wrong Door Raid," and it was to become the most publicized inquiry of the Senate Committee. Phil Irwin was subpoenaed to testify about what he knew concerning the whole crazy event.

Somehow Irwin got the idea in his head that because of his testimony Sinatra was going to have him killed. He became paranoid on the subject and began carrying a gun with him wherever he went.

One afternoon, I walked into Duber's office. As I opened the door, I was staring directly into the barrel of a gun pointed at my head. It seemed cold, black, and very serious.

It was Phil Irwin. He had been in the office, and when the

door opened, he assumed it was the imagined Sinatra-paid assassins coming to fulfill their contract to eliminate him. So Irwin pulled his 38-caliber revolver and leveled it at the door. One false move and he seemed quite prepared to pull the trigger.

I never before—or since—looked into the muzzle of a gun. You can be sure that I not only made no false moves, I made no moves whatsoever. I froze.

"Hello, Phil," I said.

"Hi, Godfrey" Irwin replied, slowly lowering the gun.

"Why don't you put that thing away?"

"I'll just keep it handy. They're out to get me, you know."

"Not me, Phil. Not me."

When Hollywood producer Sid Luft was divorcing Judy Garland, he asked me to help out. From time to time, we talked about his divorce from Judy and other legal problems of his. We became friends. Years later, in 1966, Sid told me that he wanted me to represent Judy in a divorce action that was pending between her and Mark Herron, whom she had married after her divorce from Sid. Sid still had a great deal of affection for Judy and, of course, they had two children in common, Lorna and Joey. He was incensed that Herron was demanding alimony in the divorce action. He had come to the conclusion that Judy should have me for her attorney.

I told him that I would be happy to represent Judy and would fight like hell to keep Herron from getting alimony, but Judy herself would have to retain me. I would not agree to being retained by Sid as her surrogate. He obviously spoke to Judy, because it was not long before I received a call from Judy Garland asking me to meet with her at her home in Brentwood. As is my custom, I arrived at her door on the dot. Her chauffeur, Lionel, admitted me and directed me to the living room where I sat and waited and waited and waited.

As it turned out I waited nearly two hours for Judy that afternoon. I am afraid that I am impatient. I did not think that I would wait two hours for anyone. Yet, I waited for Judy Garland. By this time I thought I was immune to the glamour of entertainment figures. Somehow it was different with Judy. I knew her to be one of the superstars, and I did feel excitement at the prospect of representing her. As I waited in her living room on Rockingham Drive, listening to the Judy Garland records that were being played for me, part of me regressed to those high school days in Kansas City when I sat and watched her on the movie screen. She had been one of my favorites, and somehow in this instance there was a refrain that I could not stamp out.

Finally she showed up only slightly apologetic. I almost became angry at her seeming callous disregard of my convenience, but it was overshadowed by the interest I took in what she was saying. We sat opposite each other in the living room. It seemed to be difficult for her to speak with me about her problems; conversation was halting and did not flow easily. As we progressed in our talk, however, she seemed to become more at ease. Suddenly, she stood up and told me she liked me and wanted me to help her. I told her I would. It was as simple as that. I was representing Judy Garland.

She had changed unbelievably over the years since I first met her at Clyde Duber's. That night years before, she had been fat and looked bloated. Now, she was so thin it was almost painful. Her weight did not affect her personality, however. She became animated, her eyes were bright, and she was constantly alert. I left her standing at the door watching my departure.

Once I became her attorney two things occurred. First, she showered affection upon me and sometimes seemed to genuinely need my presence. Secondly, she became demanding of my time and felt free to call me at any minute of the day or night. She had a suitor but as time went on, she called me more and more often. When my telephone rang between 2:00 A.M. and 5:00 A.M., I always assumed it was Judy. Often she would rouse me out of a sound sleep and her famous voice would say, "Darling, come right over, I need to talk to you."

I continuously refused to answer her summons at impossible hours, mainly because I was concerned that it would become a habit. In relatively reasonable hours, when I would race to her house because she claimed to be in some desperate straits, it was generally a minor question that could have easily been asked on the telephone.

With it all, she was charming and funny and I liked her very much.

One time, she invited me over for dinner at 8:00 P.M. She said she was making Shepherd's Pie; she wanted me to share it with her. I thought since she herself was doing the cooking there probably would not be a delay. I got there at eight and Lionel let me in. He said she was in the other room but would be with me shortly. She appeared at about 2:00 A.M., and that was when we ate the Shepherd's Pie, somewhat overcooked.

Judy began to ask me to escort her places. I was divorced then, and when I was available I began to squire her to various events. I enjoyed her company, and it was a stimulating experience to be with her on special occasions.

Because of my divorce I was living separate and apart from my children, David and Julie, who were then about twelve and eight respectively. I spent every other weekend with the children and looked forward to my time with them. One Saturday night, when the children were with me, Judy called. She wanted to know what I was doing.

"I have David and Julie with me," I said.

She then demanded to know what our plans were.

"They just got here," I said. "We haven't decided yet what we're going to do."

"Stay there," Judy said. "We're on our way."

In fifteen minutes or so, Judy's car drove up to my apartment on Linden Drive in Beverly Hills with Lionel at the wheel. She said that Lionel would take David and Julie over to her place to play with her two youngest—Joey, around twelve, and Lorna, who was, I think, fourteen or so.

"You and I have to get to know each other better," she said, "and with our kids having fun together we can have the evening to ourselves."

My children were very pleased with the prospect of going off to play with Joey and Lorna. They happily said good-bye and left with Lionel.

When they had gone, I fixed us a drink. Then I said, "Okay, Judy, what do you feel like doing?"

She didn't say a word. She simply stood up, took my hand, led me into the bedroom, and removed her clothes. Not a word, not a sound, not even much of a change in her expression.

At that moment I felt a great tenderness toward her, and I reached out for her. We made love and I responded to her need. While we were together she was warm, funny, and loving. It was a moment that I will always remember. At that time, Judy Garland was a warm, giving person, and the mantle of stardom was far from either of our minds.

That evening in my apartment lasted until almost 5:00 A.M. Just as I was prepared to get some much-needed sleep, Judy asked me to drive her home, which I did. I checked on my children who were sleeping peacefully in the guestroom, having been attended to by Lionel. I then went back to rejoin Judy in her bedroom. On every mirror she had scrawled in lipstick the words, "I love Godfrey." I felt deeply touched by that.

One day she told me she had been invited by the president of Brazil to be queen of the first music festival of its kind in Rio de Janeiro.

"I won't go unless you agree to go with me," she said.

I was a little hesitant because of the pressure of cases, so she had the Brazilian consul in Los Angeles call me.

"Mr. Isaac," he said, "have you any idea what it's like to be the personal guest of the president of a country?"

"No, I haven't."

He proceeded to explain to me all the wonderful things that were in store for me in Rio as Judy's escort and the personal guest of the Brazilian president. He described luxury upon luxury, magnificence piled on magnificence.

"I think I'll go," I said.

Judy was delighted. We made plans. Then, a few days before we were to leave, she called and said she had decided to bring another man with her. This was the young man she had been going with when I met her. She told me the Brazilians had agreed to let her bring two guests. I debated that development for a while; then I decided to go. I had never been to Rio and all the plans had been made.

The night before we were scheduled to fly to Rio, Judy called and said she had made a change in plans. Instead of flying we were going to travel by boat.

"Judy, that's impossible," I said. "We have to be there the day after tomorrow for the opening of the festival."

"Either we go by boat," she said, and her voice could get hard when she wanted it to, "or I don't go."

We did not go. I was annoyed at Judy. However, I understood her mercurial temperament and her swiftly changing moods. I accepted her as the person she was. If I had not known it before, I was now aware that superstars often have fragile egos and perhaps greater difficulty in personal discipline than the rest of us. I made up my mind that, although I would continue as Judy's attorney, I would back away from any further personal involvement. We remained friends.

Her business affairs were, at the time, in a mess. I know that the previous year she had grossed about three and one-half million dollars with CBS but had nothing left. I became increasingly concerned for her well-being, as she seemed to be deteriorating both physically and mentally.

Early in 1967 her divorce trial had been set. She was genuinely terrified. By this time I knew her very well. Even having experienced some of her difficulties with strangers and the almost painful shyness she would exhibit, I was still not prepared for the terror she displayed as we approached the Superior Court hearing room on the day of her divorce.

I held her trembling hand tightly as we rode up in the elevator to keep our court date. When the elevator doors slid open, it was like stepping into another world. There were photographers' lights everywhere, and the heat and light were intense and uncomfortable. I could feel Judy sag, her legs weak and unable to hold her up. I gripped her tighter so she wouldn't fall. I practically had to carry her to her seat in the courtroom. As the court convened, the presiding officer, Commissioner Edward Nichols, said, "Mr. Isaac, will you please approach the bench?"

When I got there with the other attorney, Nichols waved the other man away. He wanted to talk to me in private. What he had to say was that Judy Garland was his favorite singer and his wife's favorite entertainer.

"When the case is over," he said, "would you be good enough to bring your client into chambers so you might introduce her to me?"

"Certainly, Your Honor," I said.

I went back to my seat, and I found Judy still shaking with fear. I patted her hand and said she had nothing to worry about. The judge was a big fan and I was totally confident. She was only moderately calmed.

The proceedings went smoothly as I expected; then I said that she should come with me to the commissioner's chambers to meet him. She said she didn't want to do that. I insisted, saying that I had promised him, and the least she could do was meet the man and shake his hand. Finally, she agreed, went back and was her charming self. The commissioner was ecstatic.

I had another client who was a celebrated star. That was the beautiful and talented actress, Dorothy Malone. She was involved in an odd legal battle with her ex-husband, Jacques Bergerac. The issue, strange as it seems, was over what language their daughter, Mimi, was to take in school. It may seem odd to the rest of us, that these two would waste time and money over such an issue, but it was deadly serious to them.

Jacques was, of course, French. Because his daughter was half French, he felt that she should learn French. Dorothy had been raised in Texas. She said that many people spoke Spanish in Texas, and she wanted Mimi to study Spanish. Jacques said French was the only language his parents spoke, and he felt it was only right that the girl study French so she could communicate with her grandparents. Dorothy said that when she visited old friends in Texas, it would be handy for the girl to speak Spanish. Besides, in California most of the servants are from Mexico and it would be helpful for Mimi to learn Spanish so she could communicate with the servants.

The battle had been going on before I got involved and it would continue after I left the case. The two principals would eventually spend thousands and thousands of dollars in legal fees and court costs on the issue of what language Mimi would take in school.

When we got to court, the judge, an old-timer named A.A. Scott, took the bench. He peered down over his glasses at the two litigants and he said in his soft, but definite, voice, "In this Bergerac matter, I have just read all the papers. I want you to know that I took French when I was in school and it didn't hurt me. Now what is the problem here?"

It was clear to me from the tone of Judge Scott's pronouncement that we were in trouble. The judge seemed to take personally the fact that Dorothy preferred Spanish when he, the judge, had studied French. Nevertheless, I put up a vigorous fight for Spanish. During the hearing at one point, I asked Dorothy to have her mother remain outside the courtroom. Her mother deeply cared for Dorothy and felt so militantly about the child taking Spanish that I was concerned there might be an outburst in court. Her mother resented my action. After the judge ruled that French was an appropriate language, Dorothy retained an appellate lawyer to handle the appeal and I was done.

Dorothy was a likable, friendly, and intelligent woman. Her beauty was far more than skin deep. I thought the issue that we were trying was not exactly earth-shaking, but I found Dorothy to be an exceptional woman. One evening I invited Dorothy out to dinner. It turned out we lived only four or five blocks apart. Dorothy was an interesting contrast to Judy. When the evening arrived for our dinner date, we fixed the time, I arrived on the dot, and Dorothy was ready. I was almost shocked at her promptness after my experiences with Judy.

As we entered my car in front of Dorothy's home on Linden Drive, she told me that in order to avoid publicity and because of the court proceedings, she would like to go to an out-of-the-way restaurant where she would not be recognized by anybody. I knew of a little place in Santa Monica, considerably off the beaten path, where I was certain nobody would bother us. That's where I took her. As we walked in and were shown to a back booth, the piano player looked over, saw us, and said, "I'd like to dedicate this next number to that beautiful actress, Dorothy Malone," and he pointed over to where we had just sat down; the whole restaurant burst into applause. The next day there was a comment in the columns that Dorothy and I had dinner together. I learned then that for a star there is no such thing as a restaurant that is off the beaten path. For stars, the beaten path is everywhere.

I have also had clients from other branches of show business. There was, for example, the noted rock-and-roll composer and record producer, Phil Spector. Spector was the young genius of rock music, a man who made millions with his songs and records. He is a pal of the Beatles, individually and collectively, and had produced some of the albums John, Ringo, Paul, and George made by themselves. In fact, John Lennon and Spector were very thick and have been involved in several projects together.

Jay Cooper called me and asked me to meet with him and Spector. Cooper is a top entertainment lawyer in Los Angeles, a man of many parts who was a musician first, then a lawyer. He knows the entertainment world from both sides. He called me and said he represented Phillip Spector. I said, "Who?" and he patiently gave me all of Spector's impressive credits and told me they felt they needed my assistance.

Cooper explained that one of Spector's fortes had been to create rock groups. The Righteous Brothers were his creation. So were the Ronettes. He told me that the Ronettes were named after their lead singer, a girl named Veronica— Ronnie—Bennett. She was, Cooper said, an extremely beautiful girl, somewhat unusual, and she was also Mrs. Phillip Spector.

Ronnie and Phil Spector had, Cooper continued, adopted three small sons. This marriage was supercharged with emotion and tempestuous episodes. The grand finale had just occurred. Spector had literally thrown his wife out of their house. Naturally, divorce was on her mind, and Cooper wanted me to meet with Spector and consider representing him in the divorce action.

Phillip Spector swaggered into my life. He was, I suppose, in his early thirties then. He was hugely successful, obscenely rich, and terribly sure of himself.

Roena saw him first. She had just come to the office and had gone through the reception room en route to my office, and she said, "Who is that man out there?" I asked what man, and she explained that there was a small, sensitive man out there, who radiated power and charm; she was consumed with curiosity about him. That was Spector, the kind of person everybody notices. Somehow he is electric, and he knows how to project that electricity.

He came in, and I could understand Roena's curiosity. He was dressed in a black suit, a white shirt, a black tie. My first thought was that this was Little Lord Fauntleroy, surely a very prim and very quiet little fellow, obviously a gentleman.

Shows you how first impressions can be totally wrong. Spector may be many things, but a Little Ford Fauntleroy he certainly is not.

We met. We talked. There was a rapport. I agreed to handle his divorce. It was a messy business, that divorce. It involved a custody fight over the three kids, and that's always messy. Both Phillip and Ronnie were asking for custody, and I knew they were going to engage in a mud-tossing contest. Money was an issue, too. Phillip did not feel that Ronnie was entitled to anything. She, in turn, said that he made $50,000 a month, and she wanted her share. He was furious at her demands. First, he said he didn't make a dime because he wasn't working. Then, he added that when he did work, $50,000 a month was peanuts. He claimed that if he wanted to he could make $50,000 a day.

I knew my work was cut out for me. It was going to be an all-out battle. All those details spilled out of him during our first session. He obviously liked me because, before the meeting was finished, Spector insisted that my wife and I be his guests a few nights later. He said there was going to be a closed circuit showing in a theater of a Muhammad Ali fight. He said that Ali was his best friend and later, I found out he had pictures of Ali all over his house.

The night of the fight was an event. Going places with a man like Phil Spector is always a happening. He doesn't operate like the rest of us. The rock-and-roll world lives by different standards and Spector was a pacesetter in that milieu.

There was quite a group going to the Ali fight that night. Jay Cooper and his wife, Spector and a girlfriend, Roena and me, Vic Morrow, the actor, and two other men. One of the men was karate champion Mike Stone. The other was a former United States Marshal named George Brand, who was conspicuously armed. The two men were Spector's body-guards, and before the evening was over, I understood why he needed them.

Spector is the kind of person who likes to pick fights, but

doesn't fight. Virtually everyone he came in contact with at the theater he rubbed the wrong way, or vice versa, and almost automatically words were exchanged. Spector snarled and growled and insulted and yelled. That was fine with Stone and Brand who watched peaceably while "the boss" as they called him did his thing. If anybody said anything back to Spector or gave him a hard look or exhibited any belligerence, the two bodyguards immediately moved in. It was like one of those Hollywood movies of the thirties with the bodyguards protecting Mr. Big and shoving the little people aside.

Spector was dynamic. Roena was just as dynamic in her own way. They were like two fighting cocks circling and waiting for a chance to strike, or two cats on the prowl, snarling and hissing, but not yet ready to commit to unsheathing their claws. They were both very alike, each determined to manipulate the other. Spector made some remarks that Roena interpreted as being anti-female, and she was angry with me because I hadn't taken up the cudgels and backed her up. She went to bed angry.

As it turned out, that would be Roena's last night out in Los Angeles, her last hurrah. It was rather tragic that it was not more enjoyable for her. The day following, we left for a holiday trip north to the Carmel-Monterey area, and she never returned to Los Angeles. She died a week later in Monterey.

After Roena's death, I returned home but did not go back to the office that first week. My time was occupied at home consoling Roena's parents, family, and children. About three days after Roena's death, the telephone rang. I assumed it was one of our many friends offering condolences. It was Phillip Spector and, at first, it seemed to be just another condolence call. He said he had cried for hours when he heard the news, because in that one night, the night of the Ali fight, he had come to have a great deal of respect for Roena. He admired her beauty and respected her brain. He talked on and on.

Suddenly I realized he had switched subjects in mid-telephone call. He had gone through the condolences and was now launched into something else. "I think we've got Ronnie right where we want her," he was saying.

My first thought was to tell him that I did not want to discuss business just then. Before I could say anything though, I could feel my interest being piqued. It was then I realized that although Roena was gone, I was still here and my clients would want their matters handled and without delay. It was like accepting a universal truth. Life goes on.

"What's up?" I asked him.

He told me he had received a tip that Ronnie had overdosed at the Beverly Crest Hotel and started a fire in her room. He sounded excited and pleased. He obviously felt that if this information could be verified, we were well on our way to victory in his fight for the custody of the children. I felt he might be right.

The trial lawyer was obviously taking over from the bereaved husband and I asked for more details. He wanted someone to get over to the Beverly Crest Hotel right away to get statements. I told him that at 10:00 P.M. at night it would be hard to get someone over there. Philip paused only briefly. He said, "In your grief I can't ask you to go over there yourself but, on the other hand, it would not take too long and it would help my case." By this point I felt no outrage and no indignation. I knew that the information could win his action, so I headed for the door. I was excited. As I drove my car toward the Beverly Crest Hotel, I could feel the change in myself. I knew that I was ready for action again, and I knew that if Roena had been able to talk to me at that moment, she would have said, "Godfrey, go ahead and get your work done."

I arrived at the hotel with pad and pen in hand. I talked to the desk clerk and to the bartender and some others. I got all the facts I needed, facts which, when coupled with other information, proved important in the resolution of the Spector divorce. Later, Phillip was to win custody and that particular information which I gathered that night was of great help.

At one point in the Spector affair, he was ordered to pay Ronnie's attorneys $2,500 on account. Spector was in London on business. He called me and said the fee had aggravated the hell out of him. He just did not want to pay money for Ronnie's attorneys. I insisted that he comply with the court order. He said he was going to send it to the two lawyers, Jay Stein and Daniel Jaffe, all in pennies.

"Goddamn it, Phillip," I said. "That's childish. I have enough problems; just pay them their money."

"You serious?"

"Damn right. That's dumb."

"Okay, counselor. No pennies."

I thought that was that. But I underestimated Spector's devious, intricate brain. About a week later, my receptionist buzzed me and told me there were two Brinks guards in the reception room. They wanted to see me.

I went out and there they were all right. Two Brinks guards in their uniforms. They were carrying rifles and they were guarding a wheelbarrow—full of nickels. As soon as I saw all those nickels, I realized that Phillip Spector had promised me no pennies, but he hadn't said a word about nickels.

The guards told me I was required to sign a form saying that I had seen the money, and then they were going to take it down to the Stein-Jaffe office, which was in the same building. I shook my head and signed, figuring that it made no difference at that point and just wanting to finish the matter.

The first thing that happened was that Danny Jaffe, a good lawyer and an easygoing guy, called me up. He was laughing. He thought it was pretty funny.

Apparently, he was the only one besides Phillip who did think it was funny. The judge sure didn't. It was my old courtroom friend, Judge Edward Brand, and he heard about it somehow and hit the ceiling. He had been the person to assess the fee in the first place, and the idea that his order had been obeyed in such an absurd fashion infuriated him. He was quick to note that my signature was on that paper, indicating to him, at least, my tacit participation in the scheme.

He called a hearing. I was in New York on another matter and sent an associate. The judge berated him. My associate, Barry Gold, reported the judge's words back to me.

"I want you to get Godfrey Isaac into this courtroom," he said in full voice. "He is an experienced attorney. He should know better than to countenance such a cavalier attitude toward an order of this court."

He set a date at which I was to be present, and I was to bring Phillip Spector with me. When I told Spector about it, he blew up. He said that if he wanted to pay a fine in nickels he could, or dimes, or any damn thing he wanted.

"It's legal tender, isn't it?" he said.

"Yes, but that's not the point. It's an insult to the court—at least that's the way he feels, and I am inclined to agree."

"I don't give a damn how the judge feels. Wait until I get in court with him. I'm really going to tell him what I think of him. If he fines me for contempt, I'm going to pay it off in nickels again if I feel like it."

I made the decision not to take Spector with me the morning of the hearing. On the one hand, I felt that I could better defend Spector if he were not present and probably soften the blow. On the other hand, I was concerned about what Phillip would tell the court. Phillip insisted that the judge looked like Spencer Tracy, that he was going to tell the judge that Phillip Spector did not take orders from Spencer Tracy. Ridiculous as it all sounds, I felt that Phillip was determined to attack the judge. It seemed much better to leave him home. I did take the precaution of telling him to sit by the telephone in case I needed him.

In court that morning, Stein really poured it on. It was apparent that he felt this was a good opening wedge in the divorce matter, which was still pending. He obviously believed if he could use the nickel caper to demonstrate to Judge Brand that Spector was contemptuous, the judge might rule in their favor on some key issues in the divorce hearing. They must have reasoned that the judge would be angry and, I must confess, it seemed logical to me. Judge Brand was incensed that Spector wasn't there.

"Mr. Isaac, where is that Spector person?"

"He is in the city, Your Honor," I said. "I have him on call and if you want him to be here, he'll be here this afternoon."

"I WANT HIM HERE!"

There was no mistaking that tone.

"I want him here so he can explain why he made a mockery of an order of this court. Is that clear, Mr. Isaac?"

"Perfectly clear, Your Honor. He will be here."

During the lunch recess, I arranged for Spector and his bodyguard, George, to come to my office. I insisted that Phillip dress in a conservative suit with a tie, and not in jeans and a far-out shirt. He arrived at my office, hostile and aggressive. His opening lines were, "I'm not going to take any shit from Spencer Tracy." He was adamant and boisterous and like a time bomb ready to go off. No reasoning affected him. I was beginning to feel that he was totally self-destructive. My evaluation of our case was that we would win, and I felt his behavior could snatch defeat from the jaws of victory.

In the midst of all this confusion, I suddenly started to laugh. That was the first thing I did which caused Phillip to stop talking.

"What's so funny?" he asked.

I replied that I had just had a brainstorm and I knew how he could land on his feet. I proceeded to tell him how I proposed he carry the day. His mood began to change and I could see his enthusiasm mounting. He kept looking at George Brand, his bodyguard, saying, "You know I can carry it off, George, you know it."

We took off for the courtroom with George driving Phillip's Rolls Royce. The three of us were smiling the entire way. When we arrived, we went directly to the courtroom.

Judge Brand took the bench, turned toward Phillip, and bellowed: "Mr. Spector."

Phillip sat at counsel table in his conservative clothes, his hands clasped on top of the table, his head bowed, and his face wearing a contrite and humble expression.

The judge shouted. "How dare you degrade this court and insult these attorneys by paying them in nickels."

Phillip rose slowly and in a quiet, shy voice said; "Your Honor, I want to apologize and beg the court's pardon for what was certainly a foolish and impulsive act."

Phillip looked humble and he continued. "I owe you an explanation and I want to tell you what happened."

He told the court that while he was in England, his wife, Veronica, had called him and told him that her attorneys had been mistreating her. He said that she had asked him to protect her from her attorneys. She had told him that they wanted her to do things that she did not want to do. He went on to tell the court that he was very upset and wanted to help her, but did not know how to do it—while he was in England and the attorneys in California. He said that he wanted to do some act that would teach the attorneys that they should act honorably toward their own client. He said that he knew what he had done was a childish and impetuous gesture, that he should not have done it and would not do it again, but at that moment of anger and wanting to protect Veronica, he felt that it was a protest.

You could feel the judge's attention being drawn away from Phillip and focusing on the attorneys, as the judge seemed to be considering what they might have done.

Stein, feeling the effect on the judge, sat there with a stunned look on his face. He couldn't figure out how the advantage was being turned against him. The judge swiveled around in his chair and turned his most severe look in Stein's direction. Then, without saying a word, he turned back to Phil Spector and began chatting with him. He asked him about his work and his theories on music. He was surprisingly very knowledgeable about rock music and rock stars. He wound up comparing Spector to Chopin, which surprised even Spector and would have stunned Chopin. Stein shook his head in bewilderment. He had expected this business to bring them a sure winner. Instead, now the judge and Spector were chatting like buddies.

We stood up to leave and Spector, playing his part to the hilt, walked over to Jay Stein, thrust out his hand, and said softly and politely, "Mr. Stein, no matter what you've done, I'd like to shake your hand."

Stein turned away.

"Mr. Stein," the judge roared. "The least you can do is shake Mr. Spector's hand."

"Your Honor," Stein said. "This is the same man who, the last time we were in court, accosted me in the parking lot and had his bodyguards threaten me."

"Nevertheless," Judge Brand said, "I think it behooves you to shake his hand now."

With painful reluctance, Stein slowly turned and gingerly shook Spector's hand. You could tell that it was, for him, like sticking his hand into a patch of poison ivy.

Spector gave a last respectful nod in the direction of the bench, and he and I walked out into the hall. Stein was already in the corridor. Spector saw him and let out a yell— "Yahoo!!"—and danced around Stein like an Indian. In a twinkling, the contrite Phil Spector had vanished and the old arrogant and cocky Phil Spector was back.

We walked to Spector's Rolls Royce. George Brand was at the wheel.

"How did the boss do?" Brand asked me.

"George," I said, "that was the first time in my life that I was actually present at an Academy Award performance."

The man deserved an Oscar. Maybe the American Bar Asociation should start giving awards for Outstanding Performance by a Witness in a Dramatic Role. It was certainly an outstanding performance and it bore fruit.

When the matter was resolved, Phil got custody of his three children. Ronnie got a settlement that was, it is fair to say, quite acceptable from Phillip's point of view.

Representing Phil Spector was not my only brush with the rock-and-roll scene. I suppose purists may quibble if I say that the Beachboys were a rock group. In any event, they were a very popular singing group. Their sound was softer, less raucous, and even before my confrontations with Mike Love, I had an appreciation of the Beachboys' talent.

Roena and I had become very friendly with Marge and Gower Champion, a fine dance team and a loving couple. Later, they were separated and got a divorce, and they both moved on to outstanding successes. One weekend, the four of us drove to Solvang, the Danish community north of Los Angeles, to investigate a private school we were thinking about entering our children in. Sometime during that trip, Marge Champion mentioned that her niece, Suzanne, was having problems and needed legal help; she asked me to talk to her. I agreed, of course. A date was set and Suzanne came to see me. She was Mrs. Mike Love, the wife of the lead singer of the Beachboys. Love had lived up to his name and had had a procession of wives, of whom Suzanne was the latest, but hardly the last. Suzanne told me that they were getting a divorce and that Love was being represented by Sidney Traxler, who had the reputation of being one of the toughest of all divorce lawyers. She felt the need to acquire a lawyer who would give Traxler a battle.

It was another one of those messy ones, including a custody fight. At the time I got into it, Michael had been awarded temporary custody of the children, pending trial. He had claimed that Suzanne's lifestyle was such that the children were better off with him. As in all custody fights, each was making accusations against the other and each was insisting that he or she should have the children. I found Suzanne Love to be a very sweet girl with many admirable traits, but at that time she did not have a stable lifestyle. By the same token, Mike Love was often on the road and, even when he was not performing, most of his energy was directed toward participation in an Eastern religion; he would even go visit his own guru in India. Both of them could be described as unusual and neither fit the usual pattern of the traditional parent. I did believe, however, that both loved and wanted their children, but the court had to make a choice. My belief was that the children were best off living with Suzanne's mother and father, a warm and caring couple who also adored the children.

It was a long and sometimes bitter fight. I was not surprised that in the end Mike Love was awarded custody. I felt we had made up some of the ground that had been lost prior to my entry in the case but apparently not enough. Suzanne was entitled to visit the children often, so both had the opportunity to contribute to their upbringing.

The case was closed. It entered my files. And I moved on to other matters.

One day, my secretary said that Mrs. Sue Love had called while I was out. I was surprised, but pleased. I suppose like most lawyers I always have a nagging curiosity in the back of my mind about all my former clients, wondering what has happened to them since our days together. The lawyer-client relationship is a close and personal one. I was pleased to hear that Mrs. Sue Love was calling; I gladly took up the telephone and called her back.

"Mrs. Love?"

"Yes."

"Suzanne, it's Godfrey. I'm really pleased to hear from you. How are you?"

"I'm not Suzanne, I'm Sue."

She went on to explain that she was Suzanne Love's successor, the new Mrs. Mike Love. But, like all the others, her marriage was now on the rocks. She and Mike were separated, and it was time to talk divorce.

"All during our marriage, Mr. Isaac," she went on, "Mike told me that the only attorney who had ever given him a hard time, the only attorney of all the attorneys he'd faced in all his divorces whom he feared, was you. He spoke so much about you that even while we were married, I made a note of your name. I figured that in case we ever split up, I'd want you to represent me because he felt you were the best he'd faced. Well, the time has come."

I told her that I was very flattered by all she had said, but I'd have to think about the propriety of representing another wife against the same husband. I thought about it for a few days, finally concluding that there was no ethical reason why I should not take the case.

So Sue Love—Linda Sue was her real name, but she was universally known as Sue—came in and we got down to cases. She was a bright, spunky, attractive woman. She and Suzanne were entirely different, but they had two things in common; they had both married Mike Love and both had retained me to handle their divorces. At the time, Mike Love was represented by a large firm in Washington, D.C., and the negotiations with the attorneys were carried out mostly over the phone. When it came time for the final arrangements to be ironed out, I said that I would come to their office in Washington. As it happened, I was going to be there anyhow as I had been invited to Washington to attend Jimmy Carter's inauguration and a couple of the inaugural balls.

I attended the inauguration and then I moved on to my legal business. I was staying at the Sheraton-Carlton Hotel on 16th and K Streets and decided to walk to the law offices of Love's attorneys the morning of the meeting. I was told it was cold out, but not until I got outside did I realize just how cold it was. Later, I found out it was a near-record coldness that I braved that morning.

They let me thaw out in a private office for a while, my hands holding a cup of coffee and my backside up against a radiator. Then they showed me into the conference room where the critical meeting would take place. I sat on one side, opened my brief case, and took out my notes. My adversaries sat on the other side.

The door opened, and Mike Love came in. He knew that I

would be there, of course, and he looked at me, grinned, and walked over, his hand outstretched. I stood and shook his hand.

"Godfrey," said Mike Love, "it's nice to see you but I'll tell you one thing—my next wife will never hear your name from me."

I think he's kept that promise. At least I have never represented another Mrs. Mike Love.

Another of my actress clients was Joanna Moore, and her case is memorable to me because, in a curious way, it really had a greater effect on my career than any other. The case itself was not complicated, as far as I was concerned. Miss Moore, a beautiful and lovely lady, asked me to conclude her divorce action with her husband, Ryan O'Neal. O'Neal was already living with another lady, actress Leigh Taylor-Young, and so there was no question about it. The central issue was the custody of their two children. During a divorce, an attorney rarely meets the children of the involved parties, even though their welfare may be entrusted to him. Usually, I prefer to let behavioral scientists talk to the children. I feel this is more appropriate than their being questioned by advocates. In Joanna Moore's divorce, I later was very sorry that I had never met her daughter. That child later appeared with Ryan in a motion picture, and in her first movie, Tatum O'Neal won an Oscar.

It was not long after my representation of Joanna Moore that Ryan O'Neal made *Love Story* with Ali MacGraw. I went and, during the scene when the girl was dying and the boy was sitting beside her crying, I looked around the theater. Many in the movie were crying, too. The scene was powerful and moving.

As I left the theater, I laughed at myself. It occurred to me that I had just finished dealing with O'Neal and found him to be a brash and cocky young man. I knew that he was hardly suffering, hardly unhappy. Of course, Ali MacGraw hadn't been really dying, she had only been acting. I thought of those things as I walked from the theater to my car, and by the time I got into the car, I realized this supported a belief I had long held.

We all react not to facts, but what facts appear to be. Ali wasn't dying and Ryan wasn't bereft—the facts were that both were well and thriving. When people sobbed in the theater, it wasn't because of facts at all, it was because of what these facts appeared to be.

The same thing holds true in court. Judges don't rule on facts and juries don't decide on facts. The facts have occurred outside the courtroom, not in the presence of the judge or jury. The attorneys present their views of those facts, and the decisions are rendered entirely on what those facts appear to be.

I knew that the lawyers who win the most cases are those who can best present their cases, who can give the best light to the appearance of facts. That night at the theater intensified my belief that to be a successful trial lawyer, I should prepare a case for the judge or jury with the same care, thought, and attention to detail that a movie director would use in filming a picture. I later often felt that the courtroom was not unlike a screen and the jury an audience.

Chapter Eight

As my practice was flourishing, my marriage to Norma was deteriorating. We were two people who should never have married. She yearned for the simple life, for an almost pastoral existence. I wanted excitement, achievement, and accomplishment. It is unfortunate that it takes so long for people to discover such basic differences. Our marriage was really over as the year 1963 came to a close, but for some time both of us stubbornly refused to recognize it. Finally, in 1964, we separated, and both of us moved off in opposite directions.

I was never adamant on the subject, but I doubted that I would ever remarry. I had two children and found a comfortable west side apartment. My social life began to flourish, and I settled comfortably into a single existance.

In 1965, the legislature reapportioned the state assembly and senatorial districts in California. I was, of course, aware of this, and more and more my thoughts turned to politics. I had just turned forty years of age and was becoming increasingly aware of the public need for more enlightened legislation, more effective and broad-based legislators, and a realistic approach to the problems of the sixties. I was very highly motivated to make a meaningful contribution to society and to the state that I had grown to love.

It is no surprise that so many lawyers turn their eyes at some point in their careers toward politics. From our first day in law school, the law and legislation become almost obsessions. Every day of our lives, we deal with the law, and there are very few among us who do not believe that if given the opportunity, we could be constructive in making better laws.

For me, the bell had rung and I was determined to find a spot in the political system where I could convert my experience in law into enlightened legislation.

By mid-1965, I made my decision. I declared my intention to run for the state senate. Thus began an exciting, maturing, and sobering experience that I am grateful to have had but doubt that I will ever repeat.

Campaigns in California are indecently expensive, and mine swallowed my entire savings. That is not so bad, but what hurts more when you lose an election, as I later did in the primary, is the deep feeling that so many others have given their money and all in vain. More than a decade later, I still feel a deep appreciation for all the contributors to my campaign, for the many workers who labored in my three campaign headquarters, and for everyone whose hopes were dashed by my defeat. After six months of nightly speeches, constant meetings, innumerable coffee klatches, it came to an end. I have always thought of myself as a winner, but I was to taste defeat at the polls. That public loss helped to season my professional attitude, and although I did not know it then, it gave me a depth of understanding that was to become useful in the years ahead in many of the more visible cases that I have tried—and particularly in 1973, when I was to become involved in Watergate affairs.

There was one unexpected by-product of my political

experience. During the campaign, I spent a large amount of time in a local market that was considered somewhat of a political barometer. Norm's Market just outside of Beverly Hills was a mecca for candidates. Many of us would take time to parade the aisles of that particular market and speak with a cross-section of family shoppers. Although I have no recollection of the incident, I was later told by a woman that she had spoken briefly with me one afternoon at Norm's Market and had returned the literature I gave her, telling me that she knew it was expensive and that she did not want me to waste it because she had not registered to vote. She later insisted it was at that moment that she decided she would become Mrs. Godfrey Isaac.

Her name was Roena Reimer. Whatever her determination may or may not have been, it was four months before we were to meet officially. In October of that year, I was walking down the corridor of the Los Angeles Courthouse and was hailed by Jack Warner, a fellow Beverly Hills lawyer who had intermittently helped in my campaign. He told me that he was teaching a class in business law for the adult education program at Beverly Hills High School. He wanted me to be a guest speaker the next evening on the subject of contracts. I told him that I would be delighted to speak at another time, but that contracts was not a subject I generally spoke about. Jack insisted, but I refused. Later that day, he called at my office and told me that he absolutely had to have a guest speaker and he reminded me that he had helped me when I was running for office. Although I was reluctant, he hit a responsive chord, and I agreed to speak to his class. As we were having dinner, however, all Jack could talk about was the incredible woman he was dating and what a treat it was going to be for me to meet such a spectacular beauty. I listened politely and was mildly interested, but it really meant little to me. I had no premonition of what was soon to come.

We went to the high school, and I found myself at the podium, talking away on the subject of contracts. In the midst of my speech, a latecomer arrived; I watched her every movement as she crossed the back of the classroom, heading for an inconspicuous seat. She was beautiful, meticulously and fashionably dressed, and she moved with an authority that I had rarely seen. Every person in the room turned to look at her, but I had no inkling that for years to come, I would be a part of that same phenomenon. There was no doubt in my mind that she was Jack Warner's girlfriend, because she definitely fit the lavish description he had given me.

After my speech was concluded and the class dismissed, she was the first to arrive at the podium. There was something about her that was compelling. She had a magnificent manner about her, and she dominated the space that she occupied. Her first words to me were an invitation to join her and Jack for a drink after the class. Out of curiosity and politeness, I accepted. We met at a local restaurant and the three of us talked. She was fascinating. Her beauty I had recognized at once, but she was intelligent, bright, and incisive. I knew at once that had she not been Jack Warner's girlfriend, I would have asked her for a date. Since she was, however, it would not have occurred to me in those days to even ask for her telephone number.

I left the two of them and went about my business, and thought very little more about it.

About two weeks later, my secretary informed me that a Mrs. Reimer was on the telephone. I picked up my telephone and she said, "I'm returning your call."

The fact of the matter was that I had not placed a telephone call to her and I told her that. She said she had been out of the country for a few weeks and upon her return, she saw that a Mr. Isaac had called. She just assumed it was me. I did not quite know what to make of it but did suggest she leave her telephone number in the event I should want to call. She gave it to me. Nevertheless, I did not use it. I had no intention of calling her.

A few days later, she called me again. Although I was

unaware of it at the time, when she went to that high school class, she remembered our meeting at Norm's Market and she made a vow to herself that she would become Mrs. Godfrey Isaac and nothing or nobody would stop her. She was tenacious when her mind was made up. In this second telephone call, she said she was across the street at the Nibblers, a local coffee shop, and asked if I would join her for coffee. I told her I would see her there in fifteen minutes. What I did not know was that she was not even in the coffee shop, but when I said I would meet her, she got there as fast as she could. We met at Nibblers and I was fascinated by her. She made it instantly clear that she was interested in me. It was a subtle, not a blatant, communication. It was during this meeting that I first began to feel her power, drive, and fascination. She was truly an unusual woman.

We parted early that evening, because I had to attend an affair at the Beverly Hills Hotel. It was judges' night and after the program, I invited one of the judges to join me for a drink at the bar. As we chatted, I excused myself to get a couple of cigars. As I headed for the cigar counter, I found myself face to face with Roena. She had apparently followed me. There she was, ostensibly casually crossing my path in the lobby. She looked up at me with her big eyes and asked, "Godfrey, what are you doing here?"

It was at that moment that I really knew there was a Roena in my future. Many times during our marriage, men would come up to me and ask how I captured such a gorgeous creature. Usually, I just laughed and said, "How could I avoid her?"

From the start and for the three months until we were married, Roena exerted all of her efforts, every feminine wile and incredible determination in reaching a goal she had set, that we would be husband and wife. From that night forward until her death, I was almost constantly with Roena. Roena was one of the world's most incredible expediters. Shortly after we met, a three-day holiday weekend was coming up. I somewhat timidly hinted that perhaps we could go away together. Roena's reply was one that I have never forgotten. "I will go with you anytime, anywhere. You name it."

That first weekend we went to Palm Springs, and I had a preview of Roena, the organizer. When I suggested Palm Springs, she had merely replied. "Fine. Leave everything to me."

I had no idea where we would be staying or under what circumstances. As we drove in my car from Los Angeles to Palm Springs, we chatted, but she made no reference to our exact destination. When we entered the small desert resort, she gave me the name of a hotel and told me how to drive there. We arrived at a place called the Colony. I parked and was heading for the office, intending to register. Roena stopped me before I had gone two steps. "That's not necessary," she said, "just follow me."

She walked to a particular door and opened it. Inside, a wood-burning fire was crackling in the fireplace. There was a bottle of champagne in the cooler. Fresh flowers were on the table. The bed was turned down. Roena turned to me, smiled, and said, "We're here."

For the next six years, I was to witness Roena's efficiency and attention to detail many times. It would not be until after her death that I would ever have to pick up a telephone to make a reservation, buy a ticket, or plan anything.

That first night in Palm Springs was the first night we shared a bed. By morning I knew that this woman would become my wife, and the thought brought a satisfied smile to my face.

As the weeks passed, we saw each other constantly. Each day I learned something new about her. She talked a great deal about herself, about her past, about her business experiences, about her modeling, about everything. I knew how innovative she was, but in those early days and months, and even years, I did not know how imaginative. Roena had a mind with almost total recall. Her mental powers were awe-inspiring. I felt that she was the brightest person I had ever met in my life. What I had no way of knowing then was that much of what she told me was not true. Her imagination was so vivid, I eventually discovered, that she sometimes created her own world by the sheer inventiveness of her own mind.

Shortly after 1967 began, we were married at a private ceremony at Wilshire Temple in Los Angeles. The only persons there who were not family were Virginia and Clyde Duber. Afterwards, Roena arranged for and hostessed our wedding dinner at Au Petit Jean in Beverly Hills. Little did I realize that years later I would represent the owner of that restaurant, Stephen Crane.

The following morning I had arranged for a wedding breakfast at a restaurant called The Four Trees, then located on Sunset Boulevard, with a good friend, the maître d', Alberto, supervising every detail. Two hundred of our friends joined us; Roena was radiant. The two of us were starting a new adventure together and both of us were optimistic that we would accomplish a great deal.

Then Roena and I were off for Acapulco. While we were there, in our first few days of marriage, there began an erosion of the romance in our relationship and an awareness on my part of Roena's compulsions. Within the first few days some seeds of doubt were planted in my mind, but I was determined to establish a stable relationship if at all possible. I reminded myself that everyone has faults, and I was prepared to accept Roena's just as I expected her to accept mine. About four days after we arrived in Acapulco, I called my secretary at the office to see if everything was running smoothly. During that telephone conversation, my secretary told me she had received a call that some of Roena's checks had bounced. I told her to call any people she knew who had received bad checks to tell them we would take care of it on our return. I told Roena about the conversation. She pulled out the bags, began packing, and made immediate reservations for home. Her actions were somewhat abrupt, but I assumed they were reasonable in light of her worry about her bank account. It was only a matter of minutes before she turned unreasonable. On the way to the airport, she turned to me with a cold look on her face which I was to see many times in the future.

"Fire her!" Her voice was just as cold as her look.

I asked her what she was talking about.

"Your secretary," she replied. "Fire her!"

I told her that my secretary had been with me for many years. She was competent, dedicated, and I had no intention of firing her.

"Your secretary knew that I had bouncing checks for two days," she said, "but she didn't call."

I tried to explain to Roena that my secretary had been concerned about ruining our honeymoon and had tried to spare us for a few days.

Roena's eyes narrowed and she said again, "Fire her."

I flatly refused and was determined that no one would exercise that type of control over me. However, Roena put such pressure on my secretary that it was not long before she resigned. The same tenacity and determination that under some circumstances could be admirable, under other circumstances were reprehensible.

For the next five and one-half years, Roena and I engaged in a power struggle over the operation of my office. The advantage alternated from side to side, but the tension grew steadily. Early in our marriage, I gave Roena an office near me so that she could handle the books. She wanted to take over more and more of the office management. I became as determined as she that the economics of the law practice was my domain. This difference finally resolved itself in 1971 when I took her office away and told her to find another activity to keep herself busy. I told her she had to refrain from interfering with my law practice. It was one of the few times in all the while that I knew her that a look of disbelief and hurt came into her eyes. It was a defeat from which she never recovered.

She possessed a talent for investigation! The same traits that sometimes made her difficult to live with, when channeled into an investigatory project, were magnificent. She was intrigued with the law and desperately wanted to be part of it. I learned that when I discussed cases with her, she was often brilliant in her analytical ability and almost psychic in her probing. She wanted to help, so I decided to utilize her talents and train her to be an investigator. In some of the cases that I handled while Roena and I were together, her investigation became an integral and important part. I have mentioned her involvement in the Noguchi hearing. I had never seen Roena so excited, so involved, so effective. She used her incredible capacity for recall in immediately finding the spot in any transcript that we were looking for. She was so effective and her performance so phenomenal that at the same time they were calling me "The Meat Grinder," they were referring to Roena as "The Computer."

Roena's courage was unbelievable. She displayed it many times in many ways. Although she weighed less than one hundred pounds, there was no physical danger she would not face. She had a burning conviction that she could accomplish anything.

In our first apartment, we had a young maid to whom Roena was very attached. The custodian of the building was a big burly man weighing more than two hundred pounds who was an ex-marine and who claimed that he had killed men in the service with his bare hands. Everyone was somewhat frightened of him. This man apparently fell in love with our maid. One day, when he thought Roena and I were out, he tried to break into our apartment to embrace the object of his love. He had no concept of what was to come. Roena had just arrived home and raced out after the man. She pushed him by his neck against a car and began screaming at him. He was petrified. She told him if he opened his mouth, she would kill him, and he apparently believed her. Finally, Roena's rage subsided. She backed away, and he ran down the street. From a distance, he turned back and yelled at Roena that he was going to kill her. By then, the owner of the apartment house was on the street. He fired the man on the spot.

The custodian was furious. We began to get telephone calls from him in the middle of the night. Sometimes, he would threaten to come and kill Roena. Sometimes he would say he was going to throw acid in her face. I thought Roena was getting worried; in fact, she was getting angry. One night Roena and I were in bed, shortly after midnight, when the telephone rang. I picked up the telephone and the ex-custodian began yelling. Roena took the telephone from me and I heard her tell him, in that icy cold tone I had come to recognize, "Let me tell you something, buddy. I'm going to get up right now, put on a robe, and I'm going outside alone. I am going to walk three blocks south to Pico, across the street, and walk back again. I give you my word I will be unarmed. Come and get me. If you're not big enough, bring your friends. There's just one thing I want you to know, if any one of you comes close to me, I'll kill you."

She slammed the receiver down and went into the closet and put on a robe. She was heading for the door when I tried to stop her.

"You stay out of it," she said.

I told her I would call the police. She said that if I did, she would divorce me. As she was going out the door, I said, "For Christ's sake, Roena, what in the hell do you think you're doing?"

She turned around, looked at me, and said, "I'm going to kill him."

She then went out and walked up and down the street for a half-hour. I was concerned for her safety, but even more concerned about what I saw in her face. Deep down I knew she wanted the man to come, and I really believed that he would have come out of it second best.

There were many things about Roena that defied logic. At

times, she was very difficult to interpret; I don't know whether she was psychic or just sensitive. I remember the terrible night Robert F. Kennedy was shot, an event that later was to become so important to me. I was supporting Robert Kennedy for the presidency of the United States. I was sitting in bed, watching the primary election results on television. Roena, lying beside me, had been asleep for over an hour. As I watched Kennedy make his victory speech, I was very elated that he had won the California primary. He finished his speech and was led out of the room. Only moments later, there was pandemonium on the television screen. Robert Kennedy had been shot. I was upset and agitated and wanted to tell Roena. I woke her up.

"Roena," I said. "Bobby Kennedy has been shot."

"I know," she said, and simply turned over and went back to sleep. It was another Roena puzzle. Did she really know, or was it another example of her just being super-cool?

Sometimes it was very difficult to understand Roena. I remember once in particular, because she had been so pleased with me. I think on occasion she did things just to test my reaction. We had just returned from a visit to Coronado, where we had relaxed and enjoyed the sun. We got back to Los Angeles on a Sunday night; the following evening, we were at a restaurant having dinner. As we talked, a doctor friend of Roena's whom I had met, walked into the restaurant, saw us, and rushed over to our table.

"Godfrey," he asked, "how did you like Africa?"

I looked at Roena, looked back over at the doctor, and answered his question with a question. "Who wouldn't like Africa?"

He left. I started to ask Roena why she had said we were in Africa when we had only been in the San Diego area. But before I could speak, I realized that Roena was looking at me with great tenderness and love.

"Godfrey," she said, you're learning."

The Noguchi case was not the only one in which Roena

was impressive. I was retained by a young USC cinema student who was charged with the first-degree murder of his girlfriend. Let's call him Roberto Gutierrez. A client had asked me to see Roberto in jail. There was no question that he needed representation. Roena's interest was immediate. Something about the case fascinated her. She was convinced from the start that Roberto had been insane when he killed his girlfriend and, therefore, was innocent. She almost identified with his acts. Whatever the psychiatric explanation, she wanted to investigate the case. By that time I had confidence in her ability. I told her that from the standpoint of ascertaining the facts, the investigation was in her hands.

Roberto had been a brilliant student at USC. He was a bright and sensitive young filmmaker and had already won significant awards for the motion pictures he had produced, written, and directed while still an undergraduate. He was tall and broodingly handsome. Everyone who knew him predicted that he had a glorious future in the motion picture industry. To Roena, this was not just a case. To her, Roberto Gutierrez became a cause.

Roberto had brutally killed his girlfriend. He had stabbed her repeatedly, then took his knife and cut her eyes out. Roena started with those facts and worked backwards in uncovering all of the materials which finally led to the successful conclusion of the case.

She worked at a feverish pitch, throwing herself totally into the investigation. She was determined that she would prove Roberto was insane and, therefore, not guilty by reason of insanity. During those months, there was no other topic of conversation in our home, and Roena had no other interests.

She discovered that Roberto had experimented with LSD for many months and that he had had numerous bad trips. More importantly, although he had been off the drug for months, he would occasionally experience flashbacks. In other words, although he was no longer taking the drug, he was still periodically experiencing its effects. We, of course, obtained our own psychiatrist to examine Roberto and report to me. Roena concentrated on the lay witnesses and put together the factual summary that led to Roberto's acquittal. Roena quickly concluded that Roberto had a Jesus Christ complex, and she set out to document it. I was able to get permission for her to visit Roberto in jail in her role as my investigator. One of the difficulties we encountered as the case progressed was that Roberto fell in love with Roena. He often urged her to "leave Godfrey and come with me." She would report these conversations to me. The situation began to concern her. She told me that she sometimes felt that when he eventually got out, he would come to get her. It seemed to me that she had tuned in to a channel of insanity and, frighteningly, understood it.

She documented his life as far back as he could remember. His mother had called him Bobby throughout his life. She was a very domineering woman. He felt that his mother would not let him develop and wanted to smother him. He had had an incestuous relationship with her and suffered great guilt feelings because of that. As Roberto grew older, he tried to break away from his mother and developed a hatred of being called Bobby. He insisted that everyone call him Roberto. His girlfriend always called him Roberto.

The day of the killing, Roberto was feeling strange, apparently having a flashback. On the grounds at USC, the people he was talking to seemed, in his disturbed mind, to grow larger in front of his eyes. He noticed a strange odor. He was agitated and upset and decided to go see his girlfriend.

He drove to Glendale, where she lived. She attempted to comfort him. For some inexplicable reason, on this one occasion, she called him Bobby. When he heard this name, which he associated with his mother, he began to feel that he was in the presence of his mother. He had thought that he was free of his mother's domination, but now he believed she was here again, as strong as ever, looming above him, calling him Bobby. He decided that his mother would not dominate him again, not this time. He would stop her before she began. He decided that he would kill her and she would be reborn younger and less domineering. The woman he believed to be his mother looked over at him, "Bobby, everything is all right."

She seemed to grow larger as she looked at him. He decided to stop her from dominating him once and for all. He pulled a knife from his pocket and stabbed her repeatedly, to try and stop her from growing, to stop her from calling him Bobby. She kept looking at him and he couldn't stand it; he cut out her eyes so he wouldn't see that look again.

Roena assembled all of the data and, as the court date approached, I had a compelling argument that Roberto was insane. This was one of those cases where the groundwork and preparation were so complete and so thorough that there was little doubt about the results. Roberto was found not guilty by reason of insanity and sent to an institution for the criminally insane. There he was treated and about a year and a half later released. They say he is cured. He calls me occasionally and he always seems all right. My first call came from him when he heard that Roena had died; he wanted to tell me how sorry he was.

Roena was never the same after the Gutierrez case. She began to worry about insanity. A few times I woke up in the middle of the night to see Roena lying beside me, with her eyes wide open. When I would express concern, she would say, "I'm afraid that I am going insane."

Sometimes, during the long sleepless nights, we would begin to talk about Roberto. She felt some kinship, some apprehension, and I think some danger. The fear of going insane became very real to Roena, and she began taking more and more barbiturates so that she could sleep. She would go from doctor to doctor, and until the end I had no hint as to the number of sleeping pills she was taking. After Roena and I had attended the Muhammad Ali fight with Phillip Spector, we flew to Carmel for a long Fourth of July holiday. Roena seemed to be looking forward to our five days at the Highland Inn with great anticipation.

The Highland Inn is known as a honeymoon hotel, and Roena was almost coquettish. It was an uneventful flight to Carmel; we had a lovely suite with a wood-burning fireplace which Roena loved so much. We were getting along better than we had in months, and we spent our first three days in sightseeing, sunning, having romantic dinners, and making love. The morning of the fourth day, I awoke and thought that Roena was still sleeping. I called room service and ordered breakfast for the two of us. After breakfast arrived, I started to awaken Roena. Within moments, I was on the telephone for the Fire Department; they arrived almost immediately. The first fireman to approach her shouted, "Oh my God, she isn't breathing."

They brought in oxygen and their resuscitating equipment, and Roena was rushed to Monterey Community Hospital. There she lingered in a coma and on the Fourth of July, 1972, it was all over.

There was an empty bottle of sleeping pills beside her. The Coroner of Monterey County was called. It was his conclusion that she had died by an accidental overdose of sleeping pills. I suppose I will never know whether it was accidental or intentional.

Chapter Nine

MURDER TRIALS have a tendency to be more sensational than others. It is certainly understandable, when the issue is the loss of life, that there is often a great deal of public attention. For this reason, highly celebrated trials often get the lion's share of publicity. There are very few persons who have not heard of James Earle Ray, Sirhan Sirhan, or Charles Manson.

Murder and the death penalty are not the only controversial subjects, however. You can start an argument almost anywhere by expressing a strong opinion one way or the other about abortion. That subject is one that is periodically on center stage. For many years all abortions, except those necessary to save the life of the mother, were illegal. Many doctors have languished in prison for an act that they believed to be in the best interest of their patient and society. By the same token, charlatans have flourished over the years and amassed fortunes, performing illegal abortions in out-of-the-way places. Fortunately, things have changed and the law now takes a much more enlightened view. Today the lives of thousands of women are not being needlessly lost, because abortions are now legally available to them.

One of the men responsible for the evolution of the law has been a client of mine for twenty-five years. He is a tall good-looking man, who has dedicated his life to one goal, based on his unwavering belief that abortion is not only proper, but moral and necessary. He is a psychologist and the inventor of a flexible cannula to be used in vacuum aspiration, a modern method of abortion. His name is Harvey Karman.

I met him under bizarre circumstances in about 1953 when he was accused of performing an abortion on a woman in a hotel room. She died. He was prosecuted and served a term in prison; shortly after his release, he came back to see me.

If I had expected to find a young man, contrite and determined to change his ways, I would have been in error. In prison, Harvey conducted group therapy sessions for his fellow inmates and became somewhat of a prison reformer. He had a lot of time to think and had solidified many of his own thoughts. He came back to society convinced that it was his mission in life to make a safe, cheap, and nontraumatic abortion available to any woman who desired it. In those days, his dream was practically unthinkable. Today it is a reality. Although he was a psychologist, Karman studied this narrow field of medicine; he may have become one of the world's authorities on abortion and its technique. When he subsequently invented the flexible plastic cannula, he was applauded by many in the field. With Karman's cannula, and the proper vacuum device, an abortion can be accomplished with very little risk or pain. A dedicated operator can make a living performing such abortions for less than $50. It may have been a medical breakthrough, but the law looked at it differently.

Karman was to be arrested many times in the years after his release from prison, but he was never again sentenced to serve time. For years I would see this good-looking and personable man walk into my office, smile from ear to ear, and say: "Well, Godfrey, you'll have to do it one more time."

He seemed to have an almost religious belief that if he came to me he would never go back to prison again. So far, I have not let him down.

In about 1969, Harvey became the center of a police crackdown on abortionists. He was arrested time and time again, sometimes under amusing circumstances. One homicide veteran of the Los Angeles Police Department, assigned to the abortion squad, loved to knock on his door and say, "Well, Harvey, here I am again."

Harvey would not stop performing abortions and the police would not stop arresting him. I was caught between those two adversaries.

Once, I became very irritated at Harvey. He had been arrested and I rushed down to arrange for his release. After making those arrangements, I was leaving the police building and was suddenly confronted by a battery of cameras and a horde of newsmen. They asked me, point-blank, whether Karman had been performing abortions. Because I was his lawyer and because I felt a reply was required, I simply stated that I was satisfied that there would be no evidence indicating that Karman had performed even one abortion.

That night while I was watching the news, a television commentator suddenly caught my attention. He was saying that there seemed to be a difference of opinion between Harvey Karman and his attorney, Godfrey Isaac. They then switched to my interview in which I had said, categorically, that Karman had performed no abortions. Then they showed Harvey being interviewed about an hour later.

"Dr. Karman," he was asked, "have you ever performed any abortions?"

"Yes," he replied, with a note of pride, "about 5,000 of them."

I could have strangled him at that moment, but instead I had to laugh. Here he was, as always, the dedicated abortionist. The fact that his statement, in those days, could have put him in state prison never deterred him for one moment. I had a grudging respect for his honesty in the face of possible disaster.

Eventually all of Karman's charges were joined together and I commenced a multi-year effort to delay the trial. It was my goal to wait until the United States Supreme Court finally determined that the laws making abortion illegal were unconstitutional. Unfortunately, the cases were disposed of before the decision I had anticipated was made by the Supreme Court, but I had been able to maneuver all of the actions into one simple plea, resulting in straight probation.

Karman went on to become internationally recognized as an abortion expert and has become notable in many foreign countries such as Bangladesh and Pakistan. It has always seemed bizarre to me that for the same act he was called a criminal in California and a hero in Bangladesh.

Another case that intrigued me involved Lloyd Bell, a movie producer. He was a pleasant, attractive man, married to a lovely, intelligent woman. Together, they had dreams of producing some of Hollywood's great motion pictures. Leslie Bell was running a talent agency for nightclub acts, and they were both excited about their new endeavors. They lived in Phoenix, Arizona, and often drove back and forth to Hollywood as they continued to take care of business in both states.

What was scheduled to be a pleasant ride from Arizona one day turned into a nightmare. As Lloyd was driving his car on the long stretch of road from Phoenix to Indio, California, suddenly there was an accident, and a child was dead. As long as there are automobiles and highways, there will be accidents, but this one resulted in a manslaughter charge against Lloyd Bell. The police believed that Lloyd had been drinking before taking to the highway and that the child's death was a result of his being under the influence of alcohol. He needed a lawyer and he came to me.

The basic facts were not really in issue. Lloyd had been driving the car, an accident had occurred, and he had been drinking. I believed him to be an honest and forthright man. He told me that he had had a few drinks, but that he truly believed they had not affected him; I accepted his statements and determined that I would find a way to prevent his being convicted of manslaughter.

Although Lloyd had been driving and had a high level of alcohol in his bloodstream, I had to show that it had not been a proximate cause of the accident. I drove along the highway where the accident had happened. As I was driving, I remembered having read an article describing "highway hypnosis." It rang a bell with me and from that moment on, I was sure that I could prove that any inattention on Bell's part was caused by highway hypnosis and not excess drinking. It sometimes happens that you hit on an idea and instantly know it will work. That was my feeling with the Bell case. The decision was made, the Bells agreed, and what remained was preparing a case that would be persuasive to a Riverside County jury, sitting in Indio, California, consisting of twelve persons who had probably spent their lifetimes driving those very roads and who may never have had an accident. I felt I could do it.

I found some experts who would testify on the effect of highway hypnosis. On certain roads, such as desert roads, there are long stretches of straight and unvarying pavement. The regular and monotonous thump-thump of the wheels going over dividing strips, the endless procession of roadside posts, the glare of the sun, perhaps music on the car radio— all those factors can combine to literally hypnotize the driver. Essentially, the experts would verify that a person driving down the highway into the glare of the sun and with the conditions on the day of the accident could become hypnotized and cross the double line or even run off the highway. I felt it was important, however, to have a demonstration for the jury to illustrate this position, to show them, tangibly, what I was claiming. I decided on what I needed. Through Lloyd Bell, I arranged for a camera crew to work under the supervision of the director of the picture that Bell was producing. I instructed that a camera was to be attached to the left front fender of a station wagon at eye level to illustrate for the jury exactly what a driver would see on that specific stretch of highway. We ran the car along the desert highway at a steady speed, filming just what a driver would see as he drove along that road in the sunlight. After the filming I had Bell arrange for a screening so that I could look at the best ten minutes of the film. During the screening, I was satisfied that any jury looking at that film would believe in the theory of highway hypnosis.

Indio is a small city located in the desert. I was concerned whether the judge would be sophisticated enough to allow me to show the picture. I anticipated that the prosecutor would vociferously object. During the trial of Lloyd Bell for manslaughter, when it came time for the defense, I requested permission of the court to set up a screen and bring in a projector. Outside the presence of the jury, the judge asked for what purpose. As I anticipated, the prosecutor objected and said the whole thing was a trick and that he was there to see that I didn't get away with any such Hollywood flimflam The judge seemed to be leaning toward the position of the prosecutor.

At that point, I turned to the bench and informed the court that the investigating officer who was sitting with the prosecutor was very familiar with the highway. I offered to screen the film for the officer and I told the court that if the officer was willing to testify under oath that my film was not a fair representation, I would withdraw the offer. After looking at the film, the officer turned to the judge and said he recognized the area that we had photographed and was satisfied it was the stretch of highway where the accident occurred.

We showed the film to the jury. As I anticipated, they appeared almost hypnotized themselves. With the sun flashing on the windshield and the lines on the road and the cactus beside it speeding by at sixty-five miles per hour, it was easy to believe that highway hypnosis was at fault. The jury deliberated and found Lloyd Bell innocent of the charge of manslaughter. The case reinforced my belief that demonstration can be a lawyer's most persuasive tool.

The Bell case was won by a motion picture, but I have had several cases which I thought would have made good motion pictures. One that comes to mind is the Gerald Howard case. While I was trying the case in Georgia, I had the feeling that I was in the midst of a movie, because the basic plot seemed familiar.

A national industrial firm hired me to go to Statesboro, Georgia, where they had a plant. The manager of their plant was being held in jail and had been charged with murder in the first degree. The president of the company and I flew to Savannah, Georgia, where another corporate executive drove us to Statesboro. As we drove those last few miles, we all discussed what effect it would have on the outcome of the trial in this rural community that Gerald Howard was to be defended by a "big city lawyer." I insisted that we hire a local lawyer to sit at the counsel table. I wanted the jury to see one of their own sitting at the counsel table with Howard.

Howard was basically a decent man who was stunned to find himself suddenly torn from small-town respectability and charged with murder. He must have felt as if he had entered the Twilight Zone.

One night, a few weeks before, he and his wife were awakened in their sleep at about 3:00 A.M. when their sixteen-year-old daughter, Karen, burst into their bedroom; she was weeping, scratched, and, with her clothing torn, saying that she had been raped. Karen's boyfriend arrived shortly after Karen, reporting that he had been looking for her. She had disappeared from a roadhouse where they had been having a beer with a few friends. They all sat around the kitchen table considering alternatives while Karen told them her story and the name of the man who had assaulted her. When she finished, the two men, Gerald and Billy Lee, looked at each other.

"Mr. Howard," Billy Lee said, "we have to go and see this man."

They discussed it a while; then it was agreed that Gerald and Billy Lee would go find the rapist and that they would take Karen with them. Gerald got his gun, and the three of them piled into his Datsun sportscar in search of Karen's assailant. They found him. Billy Lee reached into the back of the car, picked up Gerald's gun, and headed toward the truck. The man whom Karen had accused of raping her was sleeping in the cab of his truck. His name was Daryl Smith. In a matter of moments, Billy Lee had shot him dead. When Gerald heard the shots, he gunned the car, made a U-turn, picked up Billy Lee, and returned to his home. By the time I arrived, Gerald Howard and Billy Lee had been indicted for first-degree murder; the trial was set for several days later.

When I got to Statesboro, I went to the jail to interview Gerald. The only place I could talk to him was on the bunk in his cell. Neither of us could sit up straight, because the ceiling was so low. He was beside himself. He told me that he had never intended to harm Daryl Smith, the victim. He was terrified when he heard Billy Lee's shots. He was shaking and frightened when I saw him. He had visions of the electric chair.

My local colleague, a bright young lawyer, and I quickly prepared the case for trial. It was agreed that he would pick the jury since he knew most of the townspeople. We would share the cross-examination of prosecution witnesses, and I would make the closing argument. I learned that the attorney for Billy Lee was a local judge who had taken a leave of absence from the local court to defend Billy Lee. I got the impression that this case was considered a major event in the area.

It was my first experience as a lawyer in the deep South, and it was hard to get used to the folksy way that cases were handled. Underneath the grits-and-cornpone manner of the prosecutor, however, I observed a very keen legal mind at work. The judge had a Southern drawl you could slice with a knife, but he did not have to take a backseat to any judge I had ever met. He knew the law, he ruled decisively, and he was one hell of a jurist. It was a strange setting for me, but by the time the trial began, I knew that the lawyers were sharp and the judge was able.

The courtroom was like a setting from an old movie. There were people jammed in front of the doors before court opened. Excitement about the case ran high. The townspeople came to see that justice was done. I discovered that one of the attractions that brought the people to the courthouse in midsummer was the Hollywood lawyer who was going to appear. This was disturbing to me; I considered it a negative image in that community, but the die was cast.

The first day of the trial was extraordinary. The judge, bright and smart as he was, quoted scripture from the bench. The jurors were all men, and they stared at me with open curiosity. The prosecutor was friendly and folksy, but there was steel determination beneath his friendly attitude. We began to pick a jury. Not only was it all male, but it was all white. More alarming to me, it was all rural. During the questioning of the jury to determine whether each juror was impartial, I was not surprised to find that almost all of the jurors knew all of the principals and even knew the dead man. In fact, the victim's widow was seated on the judge's side of the courtroom divider, where only lawyers are permitted, and she nodded to the jurors as they entered the box. My first motion to the judge was to ask that she be instructed to sit back with the rest of the audience. If there is anything that the defense does not need in a murder trial, it is the widow seated close to the jury and right behind the prosecutor.

Before taking testimony, I asked the court to allow the two

defendants to have separate trials. I argued that it was the only fair way to try my client. The judge ruled against me, which wasn't too surprising, but his words were shocking to me. He said, "Mr. Isaac, your client saw fit to drive the getaway car for Billy Lee, and if he can drive Billy Lee away from the killin' I see no reason why he cannot be tried with him."

Hearing the judge describe Gerald as the driver of the getaway car nearly congealed my blood.

After the opening statements, the district attorney stressed certain basic points that he considered important. He hammered away at his theme that nobody knew whether Karen had been raped or not. It seemed to me that that would be a major element and, every night after court, I worked with Karen on her testimony. I was satisfied that she was being honest, but her reputation was marginal in that small town and I was concerned. She was a likable, sensible girl, and I spent some time with her mother discussing what she should wear to the courtroom.

Part of the testimony was scientific. The prosecutor emphasized the fact that there had been no physical examination of Karen to determine the presence of sperm. The moment that Karen's mother heard she had been raped, she insisted that Karen take a shower and a Lysol douche. If there had been any evidence of that type, it had been swirled away. I was surprised to find that Daryl had been married and living with his wife. I knew that the fact of his marriage had nothing to do with whether or not he was a rapist, but I had no way of ascertaining whether the jury knew that. Throughout the trial, in my cross-examination and in my direct examination, when I put Karen and her father on the stand, I was deliberately low-key. This environment was no place for a power play.

Gerald insisted on the stand that he had no intention of killing Daryl and had not driven to Daryl's truck to kill the man. He testified that he did not know that Billy Lee was going to shoot Daryl. The prosecutor asked Gerald why he got his gun and drove Billy Lee to Daryl's truck. Gerald's answer was a classic. He was asked the question many times, and each time he replied, "I don't know."

My younger Georgia colleague thought the answer fatal to our case. I was concerned, but made a mental note to try to turn it to our advantage.

After all the evidence was in, the district attorney made his argument. As I listened my stomach sank a few inches. He was so good, so powerful, and so effective that I could hardly believe it. His argument was brilliant. He paced up and down in front of the jury and, in essence, this is what he told them:

Well, you all know me. I've been the district attorney here for years. I've known most of you since we were kids, and I know your wives and kids. And you know you can believe what I'm goin' to tell you. Did you know that this is the second trial of this case? I can see my good friend, the Hollywood lawyer, making a note on that. He's gonna tell you this is the first trial, but he is wrong. The first trial took place in Gerald Howard's kitchen the night that Karen came home and told her parents that she was raped. Now maybe she was raped and maybe she weren't. I don't know, and neither do you. But that's what she came home and told her parents and her boyfriend, Billy Lee. And you know what those folks did? They had themselves a trial. You see this judge sitting here? There weren't no judge in Gerald Howard's kitchen. You folks look at each other. You are a jury of twelve folks here. There weren't no jury the night that Daryl was executed. You see that lawyer over there? He's from Hollywood, California, and he's good. Ain't that something? All the way from Hollywood, California, just for this here trial. Sure weren't no lawyers present the night they killed Daryl. How about that? No judge, no jury, no lawyers, and you know somethin' else? . . .There weren't no appeal either. Those folks, Gerald, Billy Lee, and Karen, they had themselves some kind of trial. Yes, they sat around that kitchen table and they had themselves a trial. And you know what they did? They done found Daryl

Smith guilty, and then you know what they did? They passed judgment and they sentenced him to death. There was no lawyer to speak for Daryl. He wasn't even there to speak for himself. There were no rules of evidence, and there weren't no defense. Yes, sir, they just sentenced him to death, and then you know what they did? They went right out and executed him. Yes, sure, they just got in their little old sportscar and they went right out and executed him. Is that the kind of justice we want here in Georgia? Is that the kind of trial you want to see here? I think not. These two men are guilty of murder. We have to show people that they can't take the law into their own hands here in Georgia. These two men committed cold-blooded murder when they executed that boy that night.

It was one of the few times I felt that maybe a situation was absolutely hopeless. The prosecutor had been brilliant. His argument appealed to both the intellect and the viscera, and part of me felt, "Dammit, he's right."

Next, Billy Lee's lawyer addressed the jury. He was eloquent and brief. I could not believe what I was hearing. His theme was that it was all over for the men of the South unless they protected their womenfolk. He told the jury that they must understand that men must protect their women from attacks from other men. It seemed to me that he was admitting that Gerald and Billy Lee had gone out and deliberately killed Daryl. At that point I felt all was lost.

I was momentarily stunned from the remarks of Billy Lee's lawyer, but I found myself striding toward the jury box. For some reason, I stopped and returned to the counsel table and sat down. I arose and this time approached the jury box slowly. I knew that I was being somewhat theatrical but all types of emotion were bubbling up within me. I was determined to win, and at that moment felt that I was in a culture I did not understand. It was at this point that I walked in front of the jury box and looked each juror squarely in the eye. I was not conscious of the passage of time. After I had

looked at every juror, I headed back for counsel table without
having said a word.

I turned around and I could almost feel my shoulders
slumping. I addressed the jury. My first words were simply,
"I'm scared." Then, I went on. "I'm scared because I am
concerned that I may seem strange to you. I'm scared that my
speech may seem different. We have accents from opposite
ends of the country. Somehow, I feel deep within me, that
when it comes to the essentials, however, we are alike. I have
confidence that if you do detect any differences between us,
you will not allow that to interfere with that sense of justice
that is so deeply rooted in the South."

I went on in that vein, and the entire atmosphere seemed to
begin to change. I looked at each juror as a friend, and I
could feel the response in them. Then I conversationally
began to discuss the case with the jury. I complimented the
district attorney, and I quietly explained to the jury that their
district attorney was maybe the best prosecutor I had ever
heard. I explained to them how clever his argument had been
and how much I admired him for its content and delivery. I
told them what an emotional impact the district attorney's
argument had made on me and how I was sure it would sway
anyone who was not bright enough and smart enough to
analyze the facts that were really important. Then I discussed
the case with them. I particularly spoke of Gerald Howard's
statement that when asked why he put his gun in the car and
drove to Daryl's truck, he had replied, "I don't know."

I used his answer over and over as my theme to explain his
innocence. I said the reason he went out was because he was a
father and the only answer to why he did it was, "I don't
know." Then, I shared the fact with the jury that I did not
know how to swim. I told them that I lived quite near the
Pacific Ocean and may well be the last living male adult in
California who did not know how to swim. I told them that I
have a daughter, the same age as Karen, and I told them we
like to go to the beach. I told them that if, on my return to

Los Angeles, I was waiting on the sand for her and she was in the ocean where the water was deep and began to scream for help, I would rush to her aid and would die. I said that I could not leave her out in the ocean drowning and not go to her, even though it meant my death. I said I would do it because I was her father. If someone asked me why I had to die, I could only answer, "I don't know."

I likened Gerald Howard going out to see the man who raped his daughter to my plunging into the Pacific Ocean. I suggested that probably most of them were fathers, and I wondered how many times they had done something or made some comment to their children and when asked why, could only answer, "I don't know." I suggested that Gerald's answers showed he was innocent. I told the jury that I was sure that they would come in with that same conclusion.

The district attorney gave his closing argument and appeared totally confident. The jury retired for less than two hours. They returned and found Billy Lee guilty of manslaughter. Their verdict was that Gerald Howard was innocent. Billy Lee was sentenced to ten years in the state prison. Gerald went back to work.

One of my most exciting criminal cases was not a murder trial. The facts of the case resulted in both a criminal and a civil trial. It was (and still is) one of the most stimulating cases I have ever been involved with.

Dr. Oswald Dawkins is a physician in Los Angeles specializing in anesthesiology. Dawkins is not only a respected professional, he is an exceptional human being and a magnificent man. He was brought up in Jamaica, received his medical training in Canada, and was on the staff of Cedars of Lebanon Hospital in Los Angeles. Dr. Dawkins was in his mid-forties, a relatively small and compact man and an accomplished runner. He is a senior athlete who participates in track meets all over the world; at one time or another, he has held two world records.

On April 17, 1973, Dawkins had a particularly difficult day

in surgery and was working under extreme nervous tension. When he left the hospital he went to his home nearby and changed into track clothes. From there, he went to the running track at Los Angeles City College where he often practiced sprints and worked out.

He descended into the field from street level and proceeded to warm up by running around the track. In the midst of his warmup, he began to hear sounds and finally a scream. He looked across the field and saw a tall, heavyset black man molesting a white woman. Dawkins was concerned and decided that he should render assistance to the woman. As he ran toward the skirmish, the assailant saw him approaching, let go of the woman, and ran off through the field. The woman appeared injured and dragged herself up a flight of stairs to the street. Dawkins followed her with the intention of rendering medical aid. He attempted to attract her attention, but as he did so, she ran even faster up the stairs and darted away into the dimly lit streets. She was never seen nor heard from again, and she never made her presence known to the police, nor to the court, nor to me.

Dawkins shrugged his shoulders and resumed his running. He ran several laps and was concentrating on his running. Meanwhile up above, several people had seen a black man dragging a white woman down into the field, and they had heard her screams. One of them lived nearby and had the improbable name of Boom Boom Buttram. Boom Boom called the police and waited there at the top of the stairs leading down to the track for their arrival. When the officers arrived, Boom Boom met them on the street and immediately described the man he had seen.

He told the officers that the man was black. He stated that the man wore a "heavy woolen turtleneck sweater, of a dark color, a rolled-up stocking cap, wool, appeared to be wool, of a dark color, dark pants, and probably either sneakers or track shoes." He later said that the shoes were white, he saw no stripe on the pants and they were a solid color.

After describing the assailant, the officers claimed that Boom Boom pointed out the man running around the track and identified him as the assailant. The officers later wrote in their police report that the assailant had never been out of Boom Boom's sight. One of the officers went down on the field with the intention of arresting or, at the very least, detaining the man who was running around the track. Dawkins saw the policeman and immediately trotted over to him, stopping about eight feet away. He greeted him by saying, "Hello, Officer."

The officer replied, "You have been pointed out."

"What for?" Dawkins asked.

With this, the police officer pulled out his baton, held it over his head, and reached for Dawkins. At the same moment, the second officer was on his way down the stairs. He arrived on the track just in time to see his partner gesturing with a nightstick. The second officer leaped forward and applied a bar armhold on Dawkins. In essence, this is done by using the forearm pressed against the Adam's apple for the purpose of subduing the victim, by cutting off his air supply. Dawkins instinctively reached for the arm that was cutting off his breath; at that moment, Dawkins believed that the officers were trying to kill him. The officers threw Dawkins to the ground, one of them sitting on his chest and the other on his legs. As he lay beneath them, one of the officers pulled out his sap and struck Dawkins on the side of his head and shoulder, at which time Dawkins slipped into semiconsciousness. Dawkins heard one of the officers say, "You black son-of-a-bitch . . . This will teach you to attack white girls."

Now that Dawkins was subdued, the police officers pulled him to his feet and half dragged him across the field and up the stairs. Dawkins tried to tell the officers who he was, that he was a doctor, that he had not done anything. Finally, in desperation, he even told them he knew Alan Cranston, who was a senator from California.

The officers ignored his protestations. Upon arriving at the top of the stairs, Morris Moses, a sometime running companion of Dawkins and a man who had seen much of what occurred, told the policemen that they had the wrong man. The officers refused to listen. Moses, too, heard the officers call Dawkins a black son-of-a-bitch.

Dawkins was then placed in the back seat of a police car while the officers conferred with each other and with other officers who were arriving. It was at this point that some of the officers at least began to listen to Dawkins. They checked and verified that he was indeed on the staff of Cedars of Lebanon. I have always believed that at this moment they knew they had made an error. Had they admitted it and apologized to Dawkins, the incident would have been over. That was not their course of action. Some of the officers were stubborn and went right ahead with their criminal procedures. They drove Dawkins to a police station and booked him. He remained there until he was bailed out.

Dawkins had sustained minor injuries to his head and throat. Those would heal quickly. What may never heal is the feeling of deep humiliation and racial dehumanization that Dawkins sustained. He had been brought in up Jamaica and had never experienced blatant racial prejudice before. He was a believer in law and order, and never expected to be mistreated at the hands of the police. He sustained a deep psychological wound and it altered his attitudes.

When he returned to the hospital, facing trial on the charge of resisting arrest, he wanted proper representation and asked his colleagues for a recommendation. He spoke with a pathologist there, Dr. Victor Rosen, who had testified so brilliantly years before in the Noguchi hearing. Dr. Rosen remembered his participation on behalf of Noguchi and told Dawkins to get Dr. Noguchi's lawyer. "Get Godfrey Isaac."

Dawkins came to me. We have been fighting his battle continuously from then until now. It still continues. Dawkins and I have become friends, and my respect for him has grown over the years. He is gentle, charming, and decent, and his home is always warm and cheerful.

The criminal action was tried in the Municipal Court of the

Los Angeles Judicial District. I decided to try the case with a
jury, since some judges are known to favor the police. The
assistant city attorney chosen to try the case was young, but
able. From speaking with the prosecutor, I learned that he
intended to vigorously try the matter to infer that Dawkins
was the attempted rapist, and he had every intention of
winning. Undoubtedly, the young prosecutor was aware that
if he lost the case, a civil action against the city would
certainly follow. During the trial, which lasted four days, my
adversary, although keeping within the bounds of propriety,
bordered on the ferocious. He hammered away at Dawkins'
guilt. Not only did the two officers testify, but Boom Boom
Buttram became the prosecution's star witness.

On cross-examination of Boom Boom, he repeated the
description that he had given the police officers of the assailant. He was most positive about the fact that the assailant
wore a heavy woolen turtleneck sweater, a dark cap, solid
color pants, and white shoes. The jury was attentive and
surprised to learn that Dawkins was wearing a blue track suit,
with a prominent white stripe down its side. They learned
that Dawkins was not wearing a turtleneck sweater, that
Dawkins' cap was bright yellow, and his shoes were red. I put
Dawkins' clothing into evidence; it was hanging in the
courtroom for the jury to see. The plain truth was evident.
The only part of the description that Boom Boom gave the
police that fit my client was that he was black.

Up until the time that Dawkins took the stand, I felt that
we had a sure winner. There is no room for overconfidence in
a courtroom, however, because something occurred that I had
not anticipated. On direct examination, Dawkins was superb.
He looked and sounded good. Then this very young and able
and very energetic prosecutor got his turn with the witness. As
I am sure he planned to do, he got under Dawkins' hide by
intimating that Dawkins was the would-be rapist and by
asking questions that Dawkins resented. Dawkins' attitude
changed, his eyes blazed, and his answers were tinged with

hostility. The court had to repeatedly admonish him to just answer the questions. Somewhere within Dawkins' wounded feelings, rage was being released, and it was being directed toward the city attorney. In short, he lost his temper. After his testimony, arguments were given, and the jury retired for deliberation.

I took Dawkins downstairs to the cafeteria. I was livid. I gave him a tongue lashing and told him that he had destroyed everything I had tried to build. I felt he had screwed up a terrific defense that I had presented for him. Suddenly, I realized that I was, momentarily, as angry at my friend, Oswald Dawkins, as he had been at the prosecutor. I calmed down and quietly said, "Ozzie, I think you've blown it, but after all, it is your case."

The jury returned and the verdict was read. I have to confess that I could not have been more in error in berating my client. It was a unanimous verdict of innocence. Several of the women jurors ran to embrace Dawkins, hugging and kissing him. The jurors were as incensed at the police as Dawkins had been. The jurors told Dawkins that he should sue the police and make them pay. In speaking with them afterward, I discovered that Dawkins' rage and hostility on the witness stand convinced the jury that he was innocent. Several told me that nobody would get that mad at being arrested if they were guilty. Dawkins' anger had the ring of truth, and the jury responded with a fast verdict in his favor. I had learned yet another lesson. Honest emotion is recognizable. Somehow juries seem to have the ability to separate the sham from the real.

It was now time to turn our attention to the civil action. I filed a lawsuit against the City of Los Angeles and the two police officers for wrongful arrest and assault and battery. In Los Angeles County, it takes years after you file before you get to trial. That period is useful for taking depositions, asking questions, and utilizing other discovery techniques. Mostly though, the two or three years or more between filing a lawsuit and trial are simply frustrating. As time progresses, witnesses move, forget what they saw, or just plain become disinterested. In this instance, however, it gave me an opportunity to get to know Ozzie Dawkins better. We have exchanged visits to each other's homes and developed a great mutual respect. He has introduced me to Jamaican foods and drinks, and I now can recognize a really good strawberry rum punch.

The better I have come to know Dawkins, the more I realize how the night of his arrest had truly been a turning point in his life. He began to identify much more with the black community and to consider their problems his problems. He learned in a few short hours what generations of blacks in this country have fought against. He tasted prejudice and bigotry, and he did not like them. He decided to apply for a staff position at Martin Luther King Hospital, which is primarily a black institution. The Ozzie Dawkins after the incident is a different man than he had been before.

Because of the change in his attitude, the civil suit became very important to him. He is essentially a private man and was not looking forward to public exposure. The potential money verdict was not a major motivation. He wanted a forum, a place once again to relate his story about police prejudice and bigotry. He has an abiding feeling that the world must know what happened to one innocent black man in the hopes that it will prevent the same thing from happening to other blacks, or for that matter, anyone. He had learned that bigotry can seek you out, can find its victims anywhere.

One incident stands out among the various pretrial procedures prior to the civil trial. The city sent a notice that it desired to take the deposition of Dawkins, and we were instructed to appear at the city attorney's offices. Assistant City Attorney William Eaton had been assigned to take the deposition. During the deposition, it was not difficult to get the impression that to Eaton, no one with a black face was to be trusted. At the conclusion of the deposition, Dawkins and I were standing in the hall. Eaton came over to us, pointedly said good-bye to me, and totally ignored Dawkins. It was as if Dawkins was not even there. Dawkins and I exchanged looks as we walked away from the city attorney's office, and Ozzie Dawkins said to me, "Now I know why this suit is important."

Eaton's attitude fired the fuel of our desire to win the case. Dawkins interpreted Eaton's attitude as one more example of official bigotry.

Not only had Eaton added insult to injury by his attitude towards Dawkins, but he managed to aggravate me too. He knew that I was a friend of his boss, City Attorney Burt Pines, a young and rising political star in Los Angeles. He spent a great deal of time during our conferences in running Pines down. I finally asked him why it was, if he disliked his superior so much, that he stayed in the office, but I never got a satisfactory reply. Eaton expressed a determination to win the case that I felt went beyond his professional duty, and he despised the thought of Dawkins receiving any money.

Shortly before the trial, the law required a Mandatory Settlement Conference before a Superior Court Judge. The judge listened to our respective positions and strongly suggested that we settle the case. The court suggested a tentative figure and instructed Eaton to call his office. Eaton did so and came back with an offer of a few hundred dollars and a knowing grin on his face. It was clear no settlement was possible, and a trial date was set.

We went to trial before an elderly jurist from a prominent Los Angeles family. Judge George Dockweiler is a sensitive and thoughtful man and one of the most experienced judges on the bench. He called us into chambers before the trial began. He too listened to our respective positions, and he also suggested a settlement.

Eaton was unavailable for the trial; a young, aggressive city attorney, Tom Hokinson, had been chosen to try the case. He launched into an attack, and it was clear once and for all that the case could not be settled. The judge told Hokinson that he was making a big mistake in not settling the case, but Hokinson was adamant. At this point, I decided to waive a jury and try the matter before Judge Dockweiler. He was intelligent and sympathetic, and I was willing to rely upon his judgment. He made an interesting observation, saying that in a case like this, he felt it was wise to have a jury, and he preferred that I proceed with the matter as a jury trial. I assured him that I would, and the trial began.

From the start, Hokinson's attitude amazed me. From his manner and presentation, it was clear that once again the city attorney's office was on the attack. I will never know what possessed them to repeatedly try to paint Dawkins as a criminal. I suppose their attitude is a necessary by-product of the adversary system. Hokinson was forceful and pounded away at our case. He kept raising his voice and shouting at my witness, but I felt that, in the end, the jury would resent it.

Dawkins was excellent on the stand, this time being more positive and less angry. Hokinson cross-examined him at length but apparently to little avail.

I presented our case simply, as clearly as I could, with little histrionics. It was when the city put on its defense that my emotions began to sizzle. I cross-examined the officers and Boom Boom Buttram with determination and, I suppose, with blood in my eye. The officers testified that Boom Boom pointed out the man running across the track and identified him as the assailant. During my cross-examination of Buttram, I asked a simple question, but I struck oil. I asked him whether he had pointed out Dawkins on the field to the officers.

"That's impossible, counselor," he answered. "You couldn't even see the field from where I was standing."

In asking him the question, I had hoped for an equivocal answer, but I got more than I had bargained for and have never stopped hammering that point home. The entire police rationale and their explanation of why they had arrested a

man who did not fit the description was that he had been
pointed out by Boom Boom Buttram. Now Buttram testified
under oath that he not only had not pointed out Dawkins, he
could not even see him. I then took on the police officers. In
the police report, they had recorded that Buttram had told
them that he had never lost sight of the assailant. I forced the
officer to admit that at the time he made that entry in the
police report, he knew it was false. I believed at this point that
victory was ours, but faced with this deception by the police
officers, I became even more emotional as we prepared for
final argument.

In his closing argument, Hokinson talked about the two
types of damages the law permits—compensatory, which could
be levied against both the city and the two individual policemen, and punitive or exemplary, which could only be assessed
against the officers. Our law only allowed these punitive
damages to be levied against the officers, because it held that
the city could not be punished in such a fashion.

Hokinson, flailing his arms like an old-school orator, began
talking about how these poor officers would have to pay any
punitive damages out of their own pockets. "And I don't
know," he went on, "whether we have enough evidence
concerning Officer Ellington and Officer Akesson, but I would
say that they are married men."

He went on, in his overwrought fashion, to hint that
Dawkins was, indeed, the rapist, and used other material the
city attorney's office had used, in vain, in the criminal trial. It
hadn't worked then and I wondered why on earth they
thought it would work now. But here it was all again, and I
could see that the jury wasn't buying.

My turn came and I immediately addressed the issue Hokinson had brought up about the two officers being married men,
and the whole question of punitive damages he had raised.

"Punitive damages, it's true," I said, "can only be directed
toward the officers. Whether they are married or not, I haven't
heard up until now. If counsel says so, well, I notice that they

don't wear wedding rings. I have a suggestion, and this is the only monetary suggestion that I have that this man called this man a black-son-of-a-bitch, and to show him once and for all I recommend one dollar punitive damages, and even with a wife, children, I imagine he can afford it. What I am asking for is one dollar punitive damages, because I believe there should be a statement that you can't call a man a black son-of-a-bitch and you can't do what was done.''

In reading that transcript from my closing argument, it is clear that I hadn't rehearsed it. I skip from one thought to another, and it is hodgepodge English at best. But it was effective in court, because I was so impassioned, and I ended up almost shouting. No, not almost—I was shouting. I wanted them to come up with a dollar bill, to pay Dr. Oswald Dawkins that dollar bill so they would learn that black people are human, and that just because they were in police uniforms they had no right to call people names or assault them merely on the basis of their color.

That was the only time I mentioned monetary amounts in my entire closing argument. I stressed that justice was important, not money—except for that symbolic one dollar. I said that the important thing was Dawkins and what was done to him, and I wound up with these words, (which the city attorney's office would later claim went "beyond the limits of fair comment upon the evidence"):

". . . to them [the policemen] he looked like garbage. To them he smelled like garbage. To them he was treated like garbage. I think I am going to close. Give him back his manhood. This is not garbage. This is a man.''

Maybe it was a little theatrical, but it did the trick. When I sat down, the court was graveyard-still for a few, dramatic seconds. Then I could hear everybody exhale at once, in a kind of unified release. I could tell I had touched them all.

Again, the jury didn't take too long to deliberate on the matter, and came back to the courtroom soon bearing a unanimous verdict. They had awarded Dawkins compensatory damages against the city in the amount of $100,000. And punitive damages against the two officers—of $5 each.

After the judge dismissed the jury, one of the ladies on the jury ran over to me with a big smile on her face. "Mr. Isaac," she said, "we all wanted to see your face when we awarded five dollars instead of the one dollar you asked for."

I have a feeling my face would have been something to see at that moment. The grin was probably so wide it might have bisected my ears.

That was not the end of the Dawkins case. The city attorney's office didn't give up. They immediately moved for a new trial, and part of their allegation was that my courtroom tactics had inflamed the jury and "served to arouse passion and prejudice in the minds of the jurors." Judge Dockweiler turned a deaf ear to that, but did say he felt the compensatory award had been a bit high; he suggested that $75,000 would have been more appropriate and advised the city to settle for that figure. The judge asked me if that would be acceptable to me and my client, and I said that, if it would save years of appeals and added expense for all of us, yes, we would settle for that. But the city, as I expected, turned that down. The judge denied their motion and upheld the award.

The matter was appealed to the District Court of Appeals and on to the California Supreme Court. It took a year before the matter was initially heard by the District Court of Appeals, and I knew the moment I walked in the courtroom, that things wouldn't go well. I could feel an atmosphere of animosity emanating from the bench. Seated there was Associate Justice Lynn Compton, who had been a chief deputy district attorney of Los Angeles County and had been chief counsel during the Sirhan trial. He radiated hatred; I could almost feel his dislike of me and my client. This was the judge who had written a scathing letter to the editor of the *Los Angeles Times,* attacking my efforts on Sirhan's behalf. It seemed obvious that he should have disqualified himself from the Dawkins' appeal, but he did not do so. He seemed prejudiced strongly in favor of the city and the police, because of his previous affiliation with local government. Compton led his colleagues into reversing the judgment. The grounds: first, the verdict was excessive as a matter of law; second, the original trial court should have held the detention not the arrest of Dawkins valid as a matter of law; and third, I had confused the jury about compensatory and punitive damages. I disagreed, and that is when I prepared a petition to the Supreme Court to nullify the District Court of Appeals' ruling.

I didn't mince any words in my petition. I was so angry about this case that I wasn't about to pussyfoot. Two juries had found unanimously for Ozzie Dawkins and now, because of the appellate ruling, we were back to square one. So, right at the start of my petition, the first page of the brief, I wrote:

> The trial jurors and the trial judge clearly recognized that the detention and arrest of Dr. Oswald Dawkins was not reasonable. The only direct similarity between Dr. Dawkins and a reported assailant is that both of them were black. Bigotry is never reasonable. Division Two of the Second Appellate District of the Court of Appeal of the State of California either ignored this, or endorsed bigotry in this state.

When a copy of my petition brief reached the city attorney's office, I got a phone call from the latest young assistant to be assigned to the case. He was laughing. He said as soon as he read it, he knew who had written it. It sounded like me.

"But I think you've blown it," he went on. "The Supreme Court will never respond to that kind of thing, an emotional appeal such as that."

I thought of offering to make a small wager with him that they would respond, but decided against it. I would have won, because the word came quickly that the Supreme Court had accepted the petition, meaning that they had agreed to hear the matter.

What that did, in effect, was to nullify completely the

decision of Compton and the Court of Appeals. So it was back to court again and, on January 9, 1978, the Supreme Court of the State of California, with Chief Justice Rose Bird presiding, began to hear the Dawkins case.

Deputy City Attorney Daniel U. Smith began matters, but he had barely said three words when several of the justices— California has a seven-person Supreme Court—started in on him. Justice Bird was one of them, and I was very curious to see her in action. Since she had been appointed by Gov. Jerry Brown, there had been much controversy surrounding her and questions concerning her competency. I very rapidly reached the conclusion that she knew exactly what she was doing and had a fine grasp of the law and was, without a doubt, a legal force to be reckoned with. She and the other justices began zinging questions at Smith in an attempt, I felt, to test his reasoning powers. I knew him to be a very experienced and capable attorney, but in this case, on that day, he soon became flustered and went on the defensive. For some reason, the Dawkins case had been a tough one for all four of the city attorneys who had appeared.

Smith struggled, and he grew reckless in his frustration. He made a sweeping, all-inclusive gesture, taking in the entire court—which had a black justice, Wiley Manuel, as one of its most distinguished members—and he said, "It's not my fault Dr. Dawkins was black." The remark was so flagrantly inappropriate that you could see everyone—from justice to spectators—recoil in shocked surprise.

When it was my turn, I could feel the difference. The justices were gentle by comparison with the way they had treated Smith. I had the sensation of rapport with them from the start.

One justice, Stanley Mosk, the court's veteran, said he was troubled by the amount of compensatory damages that had been awarded. He said the physical injuries sustained by Dawkins had been relatively minor, which was true, and wondered how I justified the high monetary award in light of the slightness of the injuries.

"Justice Mosk," I said, "I can't justify it based on physical injury. But it's the invasion of Dr. Dawkins' psyche that brings me before this honorable court. Who can put a value on being taught that to be black is to be suspect? Who can set a figure on instilling fear in a human? How can we put a value on telling a man he's inferior? No, the verdict is not excessive. In fact, I'd put it somewhere between modest and inadequate."

Later, after the court adjourned, a city attorney from Long Beach, who happened to be in court that day, came over to me with a startled expression on his face. He reached for my hand, grasped it, and, shaking his head in amazement, he said, "Godfrey, I still can't believe what I just heard. That's the first time in all my years of practice that I have ever heard any lawyer give a jury argument in front of the Supreme Court."

In reflection, he was right. Ordinarily, when matters reach the Supreme Court, the arguments are dry as dust, deep discussions of law and procedural matters. I have never heard anyone else before an appellate tribunal get as emotional as I did that day, and perhaps never will. It was simply that the case had become something of a crusade with me. I felt so strongly about it, and about the injustice that had been done to Dawkins by the police originally and then by the Appeals Court, that whenever I had the chance I let it all pour out. Justice Mosk had given me that chance and I had told the court just how I felt, and from the look of the justices, they were not offended.

It was much later that I received the Supreme Court's opinion and realized that still another trial was yet to come. The justices split four to three in our favor, and that one vote is how close we came to being done. In any event, the majority of the court has spoken, and so on and on we go in the Dawkins matter.

Chapter Ten

In America, most of us have grown up watching our favorite football or baseball teams and believing that winning is important and to the victor belongs damn near everything. One of our perennial California politicians, Jesse Unruh, once was quoted as saying, "Winning may not be everything, but losing is nothing."

Every trial lawyer is aware that our clients want us to win. We are retained to get results. Nevertheless, some cases are won and some are lost. That is a by-product of the adversary system.

I have won many cases. I have lost some, too. Sometimes it is difficult to determine whether a particular result can be fairly labeled as winning or losing. An example of winning what you appear to be losing is illustrated by my defense of a man named Bernard Zeldin.

Zeldin is part of my Las Vegas experience. Beneath the glitter of the Las Vegas strip is a real city, composed of real

203

people. The place has fascinated me. I like to watch the action and I enjoy the big shows and the characters. From time to time I have had some legal business there. On one trip, I was there to confer with a client, a firm that manufactured prefabricated houses. Through that client I was introduced to Bernard Zeldin, a contractor who was involved in the prefab deal. At the time, our meeting was perfunctory, purely in connection with my representing the industrial firm, and I thought no more about it.

I happened to run into him again a year or so later. At that time he told me that he owned the Tam O'Shanter Motel, a fairly large motel complex on the Strip near the Sands Hotel.

A few more years went by before my next meeting with Zeldin. This was about 1974; my secretary told me that Bernard Zeldin from Las Vegas was on the phone.

"Godfrey," he said, "I need you."

There was no mistaking the quality of desperation in his voice. I admire a man who gets to the point—and there is hardly any point as sharp as "I need you."

"All right, Bernie," I said. "Tell me why you need me."

"I need you because I was just sentenced to Federal Prison today."

I was truly concerned, but a little miffed. It is hardly the time to tell a lawyer you need him after you've been convicted and sentenced. But he begged me to come to Las Vegas to talk about it. Maybe there was something I could do.

When I got there, he told me the story of his conviction. It was one of the strangest legal stories I had ever heard, and it got stranger. He said that after his conviction and sentence, his Las Vegas lawyer had said it would be cheaper for him to go to jail and serve one year than to hire a high-priced lawyer (that was me!) and appeal the conviction.

"That may be right," I said. "And I want to tell you going in that there are no guarantees. What you have to do is decide two things—do you want to go to jail, and if not, do you want to pursue every available avenue for relief?"

He blurted out, no, he certainly didn't want to go to prison
and he took my hand and asked me to help him, to keep him
out of jail—no matter what it cost. I took the case, and it
turned out I represented him for years, following his case
through appeal after appeal and on to the Supreme Court.

Throughout the appellate procedure, I was unable to win a
reversal of his conviction. My appeal brief was complimented
by the lawyers involved and others who read it. Before the
Ninth Circuit Court of Appeals, the justices who heard the
case were interested and seemed sympathetic, but they sustained Zeldin's conviction. I petitioned the United States
Supreme Court and won nothing there, or anywhere, except
for the important thing. Zeldin hired me to keep him out of
prison, and he never spent a day in a jail cell.

Meanwhile, Bernie's Tam O'Shanter Motel became my Las
Vegas headquarters, my home away from home when in
Nevada. He was always a gracious host, wining and dining
me and giving me the finest room his establishment had to
offer. Once, I brought a lady guest to Las Vegas for her first
visit to that incredible city. I wanted her initial exposure to
Las Vegas to be in one of the luxurious hotels, so I asked
Bernie if he could book us a room. He did, and we had a great
room at the Sands. I sensed, though, that I may have hurt his
feelings because we didn't stay at his hotel. So, from then on,
to this very day, I always stay at his place when I go to Las
Vegas.

Zeldin's case was, in a sense, almost an American tragedy.
He was a naive part of a scheme, and a victim of the schemer.
The schemer's name was Miro—he was called Mike—Mizera.
But, in a sense, it wasn't his fault, either. This time I would
have to say that the culprit was the system.

Zeldin, as a contractor, was approached about participating
in a deal to build houses. A very distinguished 76-year-old
architect, Adrian Wilson, owned some land that he thought
would be ideal for a housing tract. He asked Zeldin if he
would be interested in building the homes—provided they

could get the necessary changes in the zoning laws. Zeldin was interested. He knew Wilson to be a top-notch architect and a man of proven integrity.

The Clark County zoning laws were the rub. To change them, the Clark County commissioners had to vote on the matter. Wilson and Zeldin retained an experienced Las Vegas lawyer, a man who knew the ins and outs of dealing with the county commission, to guide them.

There were problems, however, and the lawyer withdrew. Then Mizera insinuated himself into the deal. He was a Las Vegas real estate broker who spoke with such a thick accent that people were never quite sure what he was saying. He also suffered from terrible migraine headaches; this fact may seem extraneous, but it eventually was a critical issue in the case. Mizera confused some commissioners, annoyed others, and still others called him a nut, and said his behavior was "spooky" and "kooky." And yet, when he approached Zeldin and Wilson and offered to help them through the maze of legal trickiness to help them get those zoning laws changed, they went along.

Clark County is a strange place, politically and legally. I imagine that it would almost have to be strange, to be regulating all that goes on in Las Vegas. One of the strangest of the strange is the double standard they have there on campaign contributions. Like all double standards, somebody gets the wrong end of the deal. They wink at some campaign contributions, but others cause them to throw up their hands in utter horror and scream "Bribery!" Apparently, it all depends on what words you use as you hand the money over. If you use the right words, you are a big man in Las Vegas, with influential and kindly friends on the Clark County Commission. But, if you're the wrong person or use the wrong words, you can go to jail and be labeled a briber.

While Mizera went on his merry way in his quest for zoning changes, he was not aware of something brewing in high places in the county. Nor, of course, were Zeldin and Wilson.

There was one commissioner named James G. Ryan, a color-ful politician known around Neveda as Sailor Ryan. For reasons which have no bearing on this story, the Nevada State Attorney General was gunning for Sailor Ryan. They had had him under surveillance for a long time.

Several times during the early months of 1972, Mike Mizera met with Sailor Ryan. He talked about getting the needed zoning changes on Wilson's land, so Wilson and Zeldin could build houses there. There was talk of a contribution—$10,000 was the figure Mizera mentioned—but nothing was estab-lished. Mizera was also talking to other commissioners. One of these was a man named Broadbent who acted also (this gets more involved as we go along) as an undercover agent for the Nevada State Attorney General's office. That's Nevada politics for you—a county commissioner is also a spy for the state. Broadbent had been instructed to assist in the plot to get something on Sailor Ryan. When Mizera began talking to all the commissioners, talking money as he talked zoning, Broad-bent figured this might be just what the attorney general was looking for. A wiretap on Mizera was established. Then Broadbent suggested to Mizera that the man he should talk to, the man who wielded the biggest influence in zoning matters, was Sailor Ryan.

At first, Broadbent said he would introduce the legislation needed to change the zoning laws for Mizera. Then he said no, he couldn't. Mizera said he had to do something, because his headaches were getting worse. Broadbent said he should go and talk to Ryan. So Mizera did, and apparently offered him $5,000 to sponsor the zoning change bill in the commission.

Wilson and Zeldin were caught in the net the attorney general had rigged to get Ryan. Mizera, who had done it all, wriggled free. The headaches were such a tangible thing in his life, that he was easy prey. Agents of the state attorney general cornered him one day, told him they knew everything, told him he'd go to jail for ten years and there would be no medication for his headaches. The poor man was terrified. He clutched his aching head and said he'd do anything, only don't send him where he couldn't get medication for his headaches.

"Let me talk to my lawyer," he pleaded, with the last shred of resistance he could mutter.

They crowded around him, and they said no, he couldn't talk to his lawyer, and anyhow, it wouldn't do him any good. "Your lawyer is going to sell you down the river," one of them said to him.

"I have to go home," Mizera said. "My head is killing me."

"If you so much as say a word to your lawyer," another said, grabbing his arm so he couldn't move, "the deal is off."

"What deal?"

"Why, the deal we're going to make with you so you'll be able to get medicine for your head."

The deal was that they wanted to get Ryan. If Mizera confessed, they'd let him off the hook. But he had to wear a concealed mike and get Ryan to incriminate himself.

The conversation between Mizera and the state attorney general's agents is replete with governmental falsehoods. Mizera said he wanted to be sure that Zeldin and Wilson were OK. The agents assured him they had no interest in either Zeldin or Wilson; they just wanted to nail Ryan. That was pure nonsense. When the time came, the investigators caught them all—except Mizera, who was allowed to turn state's evidence.

Mizera went through with what he had been instructed to do, contacting Ryan, giving him the $5,000. Later, the commission met and by a 3-to-2 vote, approved the zoning changes. Ryan's yes vote was decisive. He was arrested.

Ryan, Zeldin, and Wilson all went to trial and were convicted. It was after the conviction that Zeldin called me. The more I heard about it, the more testimony I read, the more facts I learned—the more I became convinced this was an improper conviction, brought about by deception and unlawful state acts. Only Mizera escaped conviction.

Worse than Mizera's treachery were the actions of the government agents and government officials. Some of them lied and cheated, threatened and bullied, maneuvered and bludgeoned—and they prevailed. They used all manner of dirty tricks to gain their objective, which was to catch Sailor Ryan and anybody who had the misfortune to be near him at the time.

I resent what those government men did. I believe government agents should be held to a high standard of integrity. There sometimes is a fine line between the good guys and the bad guys. There are times when "good guys" use tactics that are as bad, or worse, than those of the "bad guys." The cops and detectives have the law on their side, and that is what makes what they do OK, but it should be unacceptable to society when they bend and twist and break the law just as the crooks do. In the Zeldin case, the good guys were really not good guys; the people on the government side did not live up to the oath of their office.

We lost at the Ninth Circuit Court of Appeals. I petitioned the United States Supreme Court for a writ of certiorari (review) and it was denied. I asked the United States District Court for Nevada to modify Zeldin's sentence, to reduce it from the year-and-a-day and $20,000 fine he had been given, to something somewhat less. The court initially turned me down.

It looked like, despite all my efforts, Bernie Zeldin would have to go to jail after all, and it looked as if we had "lost."

A few days before he was due to report to prison, I received a call from the clerk of the sentencing judge, Roger Foley. He asked me if Zeldin had paid his $20,000 fine yet.

"No, I don't think he has," I said.

"Well, there has been an indication that it might be a good idea if he did," the clerk said. That was all.

I sat at my desk and began to get excited. It sounded good to me. I had been practicing law for twenty-six years and had never had a clerk call me to say anything like that. It seemed to me as if the paying of the fine might be preliminary to what I had been working for. The judge might be considering suspending the prison phase of the sentence. That seemed the only logical explanation for the clerk's telephone call.

I immediately called Zeldin. "Bernie," I said, "get your ass over to the bank right now; get $20,000 out and pay that damn fine."

"Wait a minute, Godfrey," he said.

"No, not even a minute." I told him what had happened, and what I thought it all meant.

"But we can't be sure about it, can we?"

"No, there are no guarantees about anything in this life. But I think that's what it means. Trust me, Bernie. Get the money and pay the fine."

I told him that, one way or another, the fine would have to be paid eventually, and it might as well be now, when it could conceivably do some good. My gut instinct, which is generally pretty reliable, told me this was the breakthrough I had been waiting for.

Zeldin was still hesitant. Times had been hard, and that was a lot of money to him. I insisted that it was a small price to pay to stay out of jail, and, anyhow, there was no way around it. It would have to be paid sooner or later. Finally, I just insisted, "Bernie, trust me. Pay the fine."

He did trust me. He went to the bank and borrowed the money. I waited, my stomach churning. I had forced the poor guy to borrow money on my hunch that the clerk's call was a clue. Suppose it wasn't? Suppose the clerk was just checking up on what fines were outstanding? Suppose it was just a routine, meaningless call? My instinct told me I was right, but I could be wrong. Zeldin called to say he had paid the fine.

I called the clerk and reported that fact, and the clerk said, noncommittally, "Thank you."

Within days I received a notice that the date for Bernard Zeldin to appear had been stayed. The judge had set no new date for him to begin serving his prison sentence.

I got excited all over. Why would the judge do that, if not as a prelude to suspending the sentence entirely? Bernie had been gloomily getting his affairs straightened out, prior to going to jail. Now at least I could tell him to hold everything, unpack, and wait a while.

Then, within a few more days, came the definite, final word that the prison sentence had been suspended.

So I lost every appeal—and yet won the most important phase of the battle as far as my client was concerned. He never went to jail.

Chapter Eleven

Much of law is hard work, tedious research in law libraries, and the constant search for precedents. The chance to engage in courtroom histrionics is hardly an everyday occurrence. I has never yet pulled a Perry Mason—at the last minute accusing a witness of being the killer, instead of my client, the accused. I think every trial lawyer secretly dreams of being Mr. Mason, but we all know that television shows are not real life.

Despite that, I have had my moments in the courtroom, moments of fun, excitement, and accomplishment. I have already mentioned a few that are part of local courtroom history—at least, they live in my own private annals. Building a replica of a men's room was one, and showing the jury a movie that virtually hypnotized them was another. There have been some others.

Back in 1955, I was retained by a dark-haired lady named Pauline Kent. She came to me, clutching a seventeen-month-old baby to her bosom, and told me that the father of the child was a wrestler known as Big Art Carnation. I never was quite sure whether he took the name from his habit of passing out carnations to his loyal fans, or whether he began passing out carnations because that was his name. Anyhow, Miss Kent claimed that he had given her a lot more than a flower; she said he had caused the birth of the boy she called Roger Allen Carnation. She wanted Big Art to put down his flower pots, come to court, and admit his fatherhood, and be forced to pay child support.

We got Big Art into court, and then I had that old problem of proving paternity. It is sometimes very difficult to prove. In this case, however, I had the assistance of Big Art's toes.

It was a funny trial all around. Big Art's lawyer had rounded up three other men, nonwrestlers all, who took the stand and testified that it was conceivable—if that is the correct word—that they might have been Roger Allen's daddy. The judge, A. A. Scott, called those witnesses "three dirty rats," which didn't help Big Art's case one bit.

Pauline told me there was a family trait among all Carnations and there was pretty strong proof that her son was a true Carnation, because he had inherited the trait. That involved the toes. In that family, the second toe is longer than the big toe. Very rare. She had showed me Roger Allen's toe, and lo and behold, the little nipper's second toes were longer than his big toes.

So, in court, I asked Big Art to take off his shoes and his socks. Everybody jumped up—his lawyer to object, Big Art to object—and the judge rapped his gavel, and then he ordered the toe display to proceed.

Carnation glowered at me, and I had visions of what he and his 300 pounds could do to me and my 145 pounds or so. Still, I stood my ground, and the huge man walked down in front of the bench and took off his shoes. Then I brought the child down, too, and took off his shoes, and had the two hold up their feet so the judge could study their toe structure. The kid thought it was a game of some kind and started to giggle, but Big Art didn't see the humor in it.

The judge looked at those tell-tale toes for a while, and that did the trick for my client. He awarded her $40 a month for support and he awarded me $250—hardly enough for either of us to retire, but remember, this was 1955 and the value of a dollar has changed considerably since then.

The case of the wrestler's toes got a lot of publicity at the time, with pictures of Big Art and little Roger Allen and close-ups of their feet. That publicity didn't hurt me a bit, although for a while my colleagues teased me about being "at the foot of my class" and "going after cases body and sole" and "representing heels" and other foot jokes.

The important thing was that my client won. The *Los Angeles Herald Examiner* carried a front page picture with the caption, "Tot's Toes Trip Wrestler." While I can appreciate courtroom histrionics, to me it has no value for its own sake and makes sense only if it does what it is supposed to do. That is, simply, if it advances the cause of your client by demonstrating a relevant fact. I've seen lawyers get tricky in court and lose. The purpose of anything that a lawyer does— whether it is a courtroom demonstration or just a brief—is to help his client win. So getting a wrestler to take off his shoes and socks in court is helpful—if it accomplishes something. In this case, it did.

From the foolish (but successful) to the serious (and equally successful) or from a wrestler's toes to an astronaut's aniseiko- nia. That's one of the joys of trial law; from day to day you can move into totally new environments.

It was a short while after the Noguchi case, and perhaps the notoriety attendant on that triumph made it happen, but I was visited in my office one day by Dr. William J. Thornton. He was a scientist and an astronaut, one of the Houston— N.A.S.A—type astronauts. There was still enough of the hero- worshiper in me so I was thrilled to meet him. He asked me if I would come back to Texas with him to represent him there.

They were just about to kick him out of the astronaut program and he wanted to stay in.

The problem was a physical one. For an astronaut to stay an astronaut, he must qualify as a pilot of the T-37 aircraft as well as the T-38. The latter ship is a high performance jet. Thornton had flown and had a good record as a pilot, but lately he had been having problems. There was, apparently, something wrong with his vision. Whenever he brought a plane in for a landing, he saw the landing strip as though it was leading upward, rather than the way it really was— absolutely level. Because of that eye abnormality, he was now unable to land a plane, and since that was a primary ingredient of the astronaut-training program, he was on the verge of being booted out. In fact, a board of three full colonels had been instructed to review his case and determine if his participation in the program should be terminated forthwith.

Thornton was devastated. He had invested a good part of his life in the program, but more than the wasted years, he was so gung ho about it that it was sad to talk to him. He had already added great expertise to the scientific aspect of space travel. I could almost see tears welling up in his eyes as he talked, as he told me what it meant to him to be an astronaut, how the termination would really destroy him. He had heard about me and had come to Los Angeles to plead with me to return to Texas with him and do something.

I was confident that I could accomplish something. But just what was the problem? Maybe he should let go. If there was something seriously wrong with his vision, perhaps, for his own good and the safety of his fellow astronauts and the overall good of the program, he should no longer be part of it. Moreover, even if I decided that his case was worth defending, how could I defend it? From what he told me, the result was practically a foregone conclusion. To be an astronaut, a man had to fly. He apparently could no longer fly. Therefore, he could no longer be an astronaut. It certainly seemed cut and dried.

Finally he told me something that made me think perhaps I could be effective in helping him without endangering anybody or risking the success of the program.

Bill Thornton was one of the ranking experts in aerospace medicine, as well as an aviator and a man of considerable other talents and interests. It was his knowledge of the new and burgeoning field of aerospace medicine, however, that fascinated me. He was tenacious in seeking the cause and cure of his trouble. He discovered that he had aniseikonia, a rare condition that is an ocular defect which distorts the vision.

"With one eye," he said, "I see the image as though it were one size. But, with the other eye, that same image is a different size. For some reason, the condition with me is particularly noticeable at the moment I am trying to land an airplane. The result is as though I was trying to land on an uphill runway."

Then, as a sort of afterthought, he added, "It's correctable with glasses, of course."

That put a different light on things. If it were correctable with glasses, why should he be denied the right to stay an astronaut? People with vision problems are permitted to fly a plane in civilian life provided they wear corrective lenses, so why shouldn't a man be allowed to land a plane in military life, if he wears corrective lenses?

I took the case. I went to San Antonio, and appeared for Thornton when his case came up for review. I had explored the matter in depth with Thornton and others, of course, and we brought along a box full of exhibits to strengthen our case. My old habit of presenting as much demonstrable evidence in court as I could was reasserting itself in the Texas sunshine.

I had several experts testify to the effect that Thornton's aniseikonia was correctable with glasses. Then, to prove my point in a graphic way, I had the members of the court—three full colonels—put on glasses that simulated the condition that was afflicting my client. When they had seen what it was and what it could do, I distributed the corrective lenses; they put the corrective glasses on over the glasses that simulated the problem. Immediately, their vision returned to normal.

I pointed out that that was exactly what happened to Thornton when he wore his corrective glasses. I argued that since the condition was so easily and totally rectified there was no reason Thornton should not be allowed to remain in the astronaut program.

Finally, the three members of the board voted unanimously to allow Bill Thornton to stay with the astronauts. Later, one of the officers who had led the fight to have Thornton terminated, came up to me and said, "You know, Isaac, you're responsible if this man crashes and plows a hole in the ground."

I would have been devastated if that had happened, but it didn't. As far as I know, Bill Thornton still flies—with his glasses on.

Thornton had his convictions, and I admired him. Another client I respected for being totally honest with himself was Joseph Kimball, the police chief of Beverly Hills.

Kimball was one of the new breed of cops—bright, modern, public-spirited. He had a tough row to hoe when he succeeded an old pro as head of the Beverly Hills force. His predecessor, a man named Clint Anderson, had been chief of police for years, and practically a legend in his own time. Legends are difficult acts to follow.

Kimball was a progressive man, thoughful and considerate. He did things that went contrary to police tradition. He wouldn't let his men use hollow-nose bullets in their guns. He said they were cruel, that they tore up the flesh too much. He made friends with the high school kids, he was compassionate toward ex-cons who were going straight, he cared about people forced into crime by poverty. He was a long way from the traditional cop.

As you might expect, some of the traditionalists quickly took a dislike to him. He had been in office a year when the Beverly Hills City Council voted, by a 3-2 margin, not to make his appointment permanent. This was pussyfooting on a grand scale; they wouldn't fire him, because he had too many friends, and yet they wouldn't give him a permanent position either, because he had too many enemies. Instead, they danced on a tightrope and agreed that they would not make his appointment permanent. They said they couldn't give him the job permanently, because his image wasn't good, because he hadn't inspired high morale among his men, because he was soft on the narcotics issue, because other chiefs in the Los Angeles area he had to work with didn't respect him.

At that hearing, a parade of Beverly Hills high school kids marched in, placards high, in defense of Joe Kimball. The councilmen had never seen anything like that. In addition, some of their friends' offspring were among the marchers. So they decided to shilly-shally their wishy-washy procrastination, and they voted to give Kimball another "probationary" year as police chief. They were, in effect, sweeping the problem under the rug for a year, by which time they hoped, somehow, it would go away.

I followed it all in the papers, and I was sympathetic toward Kimball, although I didn't know him well. He was a symbol of many things I admired. He was modern, intelligent, thoughtful, and he obviously had a different view of what a policeman's role should be.

That "probationary" year was just about up when Kimball called me. I had met him earlier, when he had attended the big dinner for me given by the Japanese-American organization during the Noguchi matter. Tom Bradley, now Los Angeles' mayor, but then a councilman, had come to that affair, and appeared along with Kimball as one of the speakers. Kimball now called me to ask my help. He said he thought he was about to be fired. Because of the success I had had with Noguchi, he wanted me to represent him if it turned out that he did get the sack.

I did some quiet probing and found that the council was still anti-Kimball and the margin was still 3-2. So I said to

Kimball that he'd be smart to cultivate a councilman named Jake Stuchen, who appeared ready to vote against Kimball. This was the one man on the majority who seemed to be the only possible switch. He was less convinced of Kimball's poor performance than the others.

"Joe," I said, "it can't hurt. Take Jake Stuchen out to dinner. Wine him and dine him. Make him feel important."

To Kimball's credit, he wouldn't do it.

"I won't have a job," he said, "if I have to kiss ass to keep it. I know who I am. I know what I can do."

It came to pass that the Beverly Hills City Council—in its infinite wisdom or stupidity, depending on which side you were on—did, in fact, fire Joseph Kimball. And that was when everything hit the fan. There were demonstrations and counter-demonstrations, letters to the editor for and letters to the editor against, speeches and parades and television interviews, and all kinds of furor. On Kimball's behalf, I brought suit against the city of Beverly Hills, filing a petition for writ of mandate to get his job back.

The suit was progressing toward the eventual trial date when Kimball came to see me one day.

"Godfrey," he said, "you can drop it."

"What do you mean, drop it?"

"Well, I've been offered another job. Security chief at the State University of New York at Stony Brooke. It's a damn good job. So let's just forget it, because even if I won and got my job back here, I don't want it any more."

So I contacted the Beverly Hills city attorney to see what I could do. I didn't want Kimball to leave under a cloud, so, without telling my client, I asked the Beverly Hills legal people if they would agree to a deal: they would reinstate Kimball and issue a statement that all the charges against him had been untrue and, after that, Kimball would resign. Thus, my client would not have the termination of his job by being fired on his record. Yet, Beverly Hills would be rid of the controversial chief and would have no unpleasant lawsuit to defend. Beverly Hills agreed to that arrangement.

Enthusiastically I told Kimball about it. He would be free to go to New York and take his new job, and the record would officially show that he had resigned to accept his new post. Nowhere in his personnel file would there be anything about his having been fired.

"The hell with that," said Kimball. "And the hell with them, too. They fired me and everyone knows it, so let them live with it. I know I can live with it, because I know that I've done nothing to be ashamed of."

So that deal was never consummated. Joe Kimball was fired, and then hired by his new employer. He left with his head high and his eyes clear. He simply refused to dicker with people he felt had treated him unfairly. He went on to a fine career in the college security field.

Joe Kimball and Suzy Crandall are certainly two entirely different types, yet in their different ways they had their principles and they stuck to them. From a lawyer's standpoint, that made them both good people to defend. It is always easier for a lawyer to fight for people who stand up for their own beliefs.

Suzy Crandall's principles were more earthy than Kimball's. With her, it was both her refusal to be bullied and not wanting to play false with the man she loved.

It all began with my secretary. She said she had a friend who needed legal help. The friend had mentioned to my secretary that he required a good criminal lawyer, and he was right. Harold Herman was his name—or at least that's what we will call him. When he came to see me he told a somewhat sordid tale. Harold owned a furniture store on Western Avenue, a section of Los Angeles which is hardly elegant. Every city has a street like Western Avenue—old and rundown, full of second-hand furniture stores and used record stores and thrift shops. Harold said that he was the apparent target of a very tenacious arson investigator for the Los Angeles Fire Department.

When he said that, I immediately assumed that he was suspected of hiring a torch to burn down his store for the insurance benefits. That is the usual story of arson. This was, as it turned out, something quite different.

Harold was accompanied by Suzy Crandall when he came to see me. Suzy was something. She was blonde and perky, very sexy, very showy. She dressed and made herself up in the most flashy, flamboyant way. You had to turn around to look at Suzy when you saw her, and most people would immediately leap to the wrong conclusion. Under the harsh makeup and the gaudy garb was a decent sort of girl.

"Mr. Isaac," Harold said, "this arson cop thinks that I paid Suzy and her ex-husband $5,000 to burn down my competitor's store."

It turned out his competitor's store, across the street from Harold's on Western Avenue, had burned down. The fire department investigators considered it suspicious in origin. They figured out that the owner had no motive—not enough insurance to make it worth his while—so they decided that only Harold stood to gain from the fire. They thought that his romance with Suzy, plus the fact that she still saw her ex-husband, and other evidence, pointed to the fact that Harold financed the fire, and that Suzy and her ex actually set it.

Harold, who was in love with Suzy, asked me if I would represent Suzy. I said I would, and he gave me a retainer. It seemed to me, from what I learned and from what Clyde Duber dug up, that the fire department people were fishing. They seemed to have no solid evidence, so I felt pretty certain I could get them to drop the case without it ever going as far as an arrest or a trial.

The fire department people asked to see me, and I was sure they were going to say the matter was dropped. Not this time. Instead, they told me they had no quarrel with Suzy, but they were after Harold. They said they were sure Harold had been the brains behind the fire, and that if Suzy would testify against him, they would let her go. The ex-husband was out of it, because they admitted they had no evidence against him. It was now just Suzy and Harold, and they wanted to know if I would go along with their proposition.

The whole thing had me on the horns of a pretty sharp legal dilemma. I was, technically, Suzy's counsel. Harold, however, had hired me, and it was Harold who paid me the retainer fee. I could now get my client—Suzy—off if she would point the finger at Harold—who had paid me. The two could conceivably wind up in conflict, and I had some obligation to both of them.

I called Harold, and I told him that he had to understand something. Even though he had paid me, my primary responsibility was to Suzy. I said it was possible that, in representing her, I might have to do something that would hurt him. "Unless you understand and accept that, Harold," I said, "I'm going to return your money and withdraw from the case."

"I love Suzy, Mr. Isaac," he said. "All I really care about is that she doesn't get hurt, so you do what you have to do, OK?"

"OK, Harold," I said. "But I'm going to speak to Suzy about this, too, and tell her the same thing I told you."

Then I called Suzy in. I laid it on the line to Suzy, explaining that there was some conflict between her position and Harold's, and that, as her attorney, it could happen that in helping her I'd, unfortunately, have to hurt him. She looked at me with those solemn blue eyes as I told her I would do what I felt was right for her, no matter who else it hurt.

"Do you understand what I'm telling you, Suzy?"

"Yes, Godfrey," she answered.

"All right, then. If it's OK with you, then we'll keep going. But if you don't like it, then I'll withdraw and I'll give Harold back his money. It's up to you."

"I want you to be my lawyer," she said. "But please do what you can to see that Harold doesn't get hurt, will you?"

Then I fully explained to her about the offer and its ramifications. "Suzy, let me stress to you what the fire department people told me," I said. "They said that if you testified that it was Harold who was behind that fire, they would grant you immunity. Now immunity means that you can never be prosecuted for that crime. In other words, if you will tell them it was Harold who masterminded the fire, you're home free."

She turned pale. "The hell with them," she said. "I won't do that. I won't say that. In the first place, it isn't true. Neither Harold nor I had anything to do with that damn fire. In the second place, even if it were true, I sure wouldn't go for a deal like that. I'm not even about to testify against Harold, because I love Harold. Who do they think they are?"

I almost felt like standing up and cheering. Mostly, I try to stay aloof from my clients' emotions and not get involved with them, because one of a lawyer's best tools is his unclouded judgment. Nothing clouds judgment as much as emotional entanglements. I always try to keep in my mind that I am a professional, not a participant. But Suzy touched me, with the sincerity of her statement. This girl, whom you would notice immediately if you saw her in the street, was willing to stand up for the man she loved. Yet, he was no great catch for her when you come down to it; he was a married man fooling around with a flashy blonde. Despite all that, the two of them illustrated that all love affairs are not necessarily sanctified by marriage. They truly loved each other, and their love was a wondrous thing—capable of going through fire, but, hopefully, not setting a blaze.

So I stayed on the case. I told the fire department officials it was no deal. They were furious, because I think they realized the deal was their best chance to get a conviction in the case. They kept hoping that Suzy would rat on Harold, or Harold would implicate Suzy, or something like that. As it turned out, there was not a rat in the cast.

The district attorney proceeded against Suzy. The first court appearance was, as the law requires, the preliminary hearing. This is a procedure to determine if there is sufficient evidence against a person to constitute probable cause for which to bind him over to superior court on felony charges.

When the day arrived for Suzy's preliminary hearing, I insisted that Harold stay far, far away from the courtroom. He was so emotionally involved that he just might do something rash if he were there. I didn't trust his emotions, and there was not a thing in the world to be gained by his presence.

"Harold," I said, "stay away. Don't come near the courtroom. Is that understood?"

"Absolutely. I won't come near the place."

As the proceedings began, I took a cautious look around and was gratified to find he was absent. However, during a recess, as Suzy and I stood in the hallway, my eye caught a sudden movement in the telephone booth. I snapped my head around and saw something, or somebody, duck down below the level of the glass in the booth door. There was no question who it was. In that brief flash, I recognized the top of Harold's head as it tried desperately to avoid my eyes. I walked over to the booth, furious with him for disobeying my instructions. I jerked the door open, fully prepared to give Harold hell—but there he was, cowering on the floor, looking up at me with big, brown, guilty eyes, so sad and so pleading. Instead of bawling him out, I just started to laugh and shoved the door shut.

When I rejoined Suzy she gestured to the booth. "Godfrey," she said, "was that—?"

I just nodded.

The hearing resumed, and the prosecution had a surprise witness. He was a tall, slim, good-looking young man. He said he had been a fellow student of Suzy's, when they were both attending an art school. Suzy looked at me and nodded; he was telling the truth. So far. Then he began weaving a tale that she whispered to me was mostly untrue.

The two of them, Suzy and the witness, had flirted between classes at school, and whenever they met in the school hallways. Nothing to it, however. Just two healthy and attractive young people trying out their lures on one another. The witness said he had often asked Suzy to go out with him. She had said no every time. Suzy signaled to me that that too was untrue. She was in love with Harold and, by her standards, she was a one-man woman. So she had constantly turned down his requests for dates.

Then, the witness went on, one day Suzy called him at home and said she wanted to come to his house. Bingo! He told her to come on over. She arrived in a few minutes.

He said she seemed very agitated. Agitated and upset. Furthermore, he told the court that she was obviously in a romantic mood. He asked her why the sudden change, why when she had rebuffed him for so long was she now ready, willing, and eager.

"I'm mad at Harold," she said, according to the witness' testimony.

He asked her why. She told him, he went on, that Harold had earlier promised to take her with him to San Francisco for the weekend, a trip that she had been looking forward to for a long time. When the weekend arrived, Harold had, instead, taken his wife to San Francisco and just left her all alone back home.

"I am really pissed about that," she said, the witness testified.

Then, according to the witness, she went on to say, "Do you know what Harold made me do?" She then told him that Harold had made her and her ex-husband burn down a store across the street and had paid them $5,000 to do the job.

There it was, the most damaging possible evidence against my client. In legal terms, that amounted to a confession, and it was obvious that the judge was impressed by it. In cross-examination, I brought out the strong fact that the witness had never gone to the police with his story. I argued that was because he hadn't believed her story. There was a curious secondary feature to his testimony. Sometime after that alleged conversation with Suzy, the witness' home burned down. Fire department investigators found evidence that gasoline had been used, and they believed it to be arson. They questioned the witness. Did he have any idea who might have started the fire? No, he told them, not the slightest. But, then, later he remembered Suzy's story, and felt he should tell the fire department people. There was never any claim that Suzy might be connected with this second blaze; it was simply that the fire triggered in the witness the memory of Suzy's story.

It was this alleged confession that led to the prosecution of Suzy. Legally, she alone had confessed. The fact that she had implicated Harold and her ex-husband in that confession was hearsay and, hence, not admissible. So only Suzy could be effectively prosecuted because of what she told that witness.

When Suzy and I conferred, she told me that she had continually repulsed the witness' sexual overtures. She felt that the story—which she insisted was totally false—was his attempt at retaliation, getting back at her for turning him down. It seemed to me that he was going to great lengths to retaliate, but Suzy swore to me that she had never said what he testified she said. I had to cross-examine him and hoped to discredit him if I was to save Suzy from being bound over for trial. I could tell he was a pretty cool customer on the stand, so I knew the cross-examination would be a difficult one. It was.

I led him through it all again. Then we reached the point where I had to ask him why he had made such statements if they weren't true. That brought me, naturally, to questions about the alleged sexual relations in his house.

Point-blank, I asked him if he had had sexual relations with Suzy. He gave me a surprising answer. "I didn't have sex with her," he said, "but she had sex with me."

What the hell did that mean? One of the cardinal rules of cross-examination is never ask "Why" even if you don't understand and never ask for clarification. No such questions such as, "What do you mean by that?" That way lies disaster. But, this one time, I went against everything I knew to be safe and secure, and I asked him what he meant by his reply.

He looked me square in the eye and, in a calm and serene voice, he said, "Well, what I mean is that she gave me a magnificent blow job, if you know what I mean."

I knew what he meant, but I didn't want to hear any more about it in court. At the witness table, Suzy turned all shades of red, and sputtered her denial incoherently. The spectators buzzed. The judge pounded his gavel. The prosecutor was trying hard to hide an amused chuckle. I was standing there weighing the effect of it all.

I dropped the subject and moved on to other matters, but I knew the damage was done. The judge bound Suzy over for trial. I asked for, and got, a jury trial. I felt that she would have no chance if there was only a judge to decide her fate. A judge would probably convict her. But, if there was a jury, and a jury that was roughly evenly divided between men and women, she might stand a chance. The problem wouldn't be the evidence about her fire-setting—I was sure that was so weak it could be beaten—but, rather, her sexual activities. Today there would be less prejudice in the relating of sexual goings-on. In those days, however, it was different. The fact that she was going around openly with a married man would be horrifying to most people. The idea of a "blow job" would have been totally outrageous to a jury. Just the idea of that would have almost automatically convicted her in the minds of a lot of people back then. Our only hope would be to present a different view of Suzy Crandall, and to deny all the allegations that her sexual appetites were in any way incriminating.

My concern was that if the jurors thought she was kinky, they might easily jump to the next conclusion—that she would be capable of doing anything, even setting a fire.

I tried to avoid any sort of trial, however, by approaching the prosecutors and suggesting a settlement. In those days, it was still acceptable to sentence-bargain, as well as plea-bargain. The first people I talked to—the deputies assigned to the case—were willing to bargain. I think they were concerned about the case, anyway, so they would have been glad to make a deal. But the senior deputy district attorney sent down an edict—the only deal he would accept would be a plea of guilty to arson. It was either that or a full-scale prosecution, he decreed. That didn't seem like much of a compromise to me, so I turned it down. I had in mind a misdemeanor and straight probation. I would not settle for less. It was lucky for Suzy that I didn't.

I knew that in this case my client's appearance would be a significant factor. If Suzy came into court in her usual manner—dress cut low to reveal a great deal of bosom, and with a slit in the skirt to flash her legs, wild hairdo, scarlet lipstick, and nail polish—the jury would take one look at her and immediately think "hooker." That was no way to help our cause. I had to turn flashy, sexy Suzy into shy, demure Suzy. Appearance, in a jury trial, is quite important.

What she needed was primarily a wardrobe from a standard, middle-class department store. So I sent Suzy and Harold off to the May Company, which is as standard and middle-class as you can get, with orders to come back with a selection of clothes purchased on approval. The approval would be mine. They did, bringing home boxes and boxes of dresses, and Suzy modeled them all for me. I picked out a handful. Then I sent her out to have her hair toned down and suggested some bland-colored lipstick and nail polish. It was Pygmalion in reverse—I wanted to take this bird of paradise and make her into a sparrow.

She came to court dressed like a proper young lady about to go to church on Sunday.

The trial was hard-fought. The prosecution had prepared its witnesses carefully, and they all played their parts to perfection. But they turned out to be nothing more than a group of bit players. Suzy was the star of this production. She took the stand and was superb.

It was another of those occasions when I wished there had been an award for the Best Performance by a Witness, some Oscar or Emmy or Tony for her work on the witness stand. Suzy followed my instructions to the letter. She reacted expertly under relentless cross-examination. She was demure, sincere, bright, responsible—and, above all, she made a great appearance. The jury, to a man (and woman), fell in love with her.

She denied having sex with that important witness. She admitted having a romance with Harold, and did it with the proper air—a mixture of sorrow (for breaking up a home), and pride (for being in love and being loved). She said, yes, she loved him. But, no, she didn't start a fire. And, no matter how much she loved someone, she would never set a fire or do anything that loathsome. The jury believed her and set her free.

There was a tragic postscript to this case. Not long after the trial was over, as Suzy and Harold were still floating and enjoying the sense of release that always accompanies the happy end of a criminal case, tragedy struck.

A man came in Harold's store and was obviously disturbed. Harold asked him to leave, and he went. Ten minutes later he came back (driving a brand-new Cadillac). He came into the store with a rifle and pointed it at Harold. Harold reached out and grabbed the muzzle of the weapon, but the man pulled the trigger and blew Harold's brains out.

Chapter Twelve

THE MAJORITY OF LAWYERS are qualified; most judges are skillful, dedicated, and judicious. The occasional exceptions to the rule come about because we are all human. Sometimes lawyers act like jerks and judges leave something to be desired. However, although we tend to notice the less desirable practitioners, they are a minority.

The really good lawyers and judges deserve special notice. In the case of George Ollendorf both the judge and opposing counsel were outstanding. George was the administrator of a hospital. He got caught up in a plot that was bigger than he was. He was a little fish trapped in a very large net.

The mastermind was an Orange County doctor named Louis Cella. Cella was a gung-ho Democrat and, in fact, one of the largest contributors to the California Democratic party. As it turned out, however, most, if not all, of the money that Cella turned over to his party had come from state medical funds, not from his own pocket. Ultimately, he was discovered, as most (but not all) crooks are discovered, and he was indicted on 127 counts of state felonies and 44 counts of federal felonies. The broom that swept him up also swept up a bunch of others who had believed in Cella and worked for him, including George Ollendorf.

Ollendorf is a very sensitive and honorable man. I don't believe he was aware at the beginning that anything illegal was going on. He just went along with whatever Cella said. Now, he was in a spot where he could go to jail for 1,000 years, give or take a decade, because of all the counts against him.

"If you can promise me I'll live that long," Ollendorf said to me when I told him how much time he might get sentenced to, "I'll plead guilty."

All the defendants were tried together, before Judge William Matthew Byrne, in Federal District Court in Los Angeles. Most of the other lawyers seemed to feel there was nothing to worry about. They had all given lip service to the belief that nobody would be convicted. It seemed to me, however, that the evidence against the defendants would be strong in court and a conviction was inevitable.

I felt, along with the other attorneys, that the best shot would be to suppress certain evidence. So we made such a motion. The evidence and arguments, pro and con, on the motion to suppress took ten days. In those ten days, I came to have a tremendous respect for Judge Byrne. He was very bright, tough but fair, intellectual, and street-wise. He was ahead of the majority of judges in having those qualities. In fact, I concluded that he was a great example of what a judge should be. I felt he would deny the motion, ultimately, because, while it would have helped my client, it really was not justified by the facts. As predicted, he did deny it when the arguments were in and done.

I went to my chief adversary, Assistant U.S. Attorney Stephen Wilson, another man I had come to regard highly. He was also tough, bright, and fair. I told him that I would like to resolve this matter privately between the two of us.

"Fine, Godfrey," Steve Wilson said. "That's OK with us. As a matter of fact, you're the only lawyer on your side who really concerns us. Frankly, we'd love to have you out of the case."

Eventually, we made a deal. Ollendorf pleaded guilty to a much lesser number of charges and was sentenced to a year in prison; he was finally released after serving only six months. On the state charges in Orange County, I made another bargain in which Ollendorf pleaded guilty to a few charges and got off with unsupervised probation. All the other defendants were convicted in both the state and federal cases, and some served considerably more time.

In this case, I think everybody involved acted with high motivation. I think George Ollendorf, my client, was lucky in having dedicated people determining his fate—not only me, but also Judge Byrne and prosecutor Wilson. That's the way it should work.

I am experienced in family law and divorce matters, having handled them for years. I rarely find those cases enjoyable, because there is generally so much emotion involved; often I have had to deal with the pure, undiluted hatred of one spouse for the other. From time to time, however, there have been divorce cases in which a certain amount of levity, or at least amusement, cropped up.

In one of the divorce cases years ago, a very interesting judge figured prominently.

My client was a gentlemen I'll call Thomas Wood. Fifteen years ago or so, he came to me saying he needed a divorce lawyer. His problem, he explained, was that his wife of ten years was suing him for divorce—"and we've never even lived together."

That was a stunner.

"Let me understand you correctly, Mr. Wood," I said. "You and Mrs. Wood have been married for ten years, and yet you have never lived together?"

"Yeah, that's right."

"How is that possible?"

He shrugged it off as one of those things. They had gotten married, he said, but then they had gone off on their separate ways, their separate lives, and just stayed married because it was the path of least resistance. He said he had lived with his mother all those years. Now, the wife wanted a divorce, and he wanted help in sorting it all out.

That, as usually happens, was just one side of the story. His wife had a different tale to tell. They had not only been married for ten years, in her version, but they had been together every night of those ten years. When I confronted my client with her words, he vehemently denied it.

"She lies," he said. "I've never lived with her."

The battle raged. He produced witnesses who attested to his story, that they had never, ever lived together. She had witnesses who told a completely contradictory story and swore that they had, in fact, been living together and been lovey-dovey for a decade.

The lady then produced her trump witness, a person who said that my client had just brought his new girlfriend a fur coat. This was supposed to be evidence that he was denying the fact that he had lived with his wife so he could continue dallying with his new lady. My client denied that he had bought anybody a fur coat, and said the idea that he had another girlfriend was preposterous.

When we got to court, the opposition subpoenaed the alleged girlfriend, and ordered her to appear in court—and to bring the controversial coat with her. She duly appeared, coat and all, and the coat became an exhibit in the case. When it was examined, it proved to have the young lady's initials on it, with my client's last initial—a big, fancy "W"—just below hers.

My adversary bellowed to the judge, a jurist named Wong, "Your honor, do you see that? That initial 'W' in the coat. Now just what do you think the letter 'W' stands for?"

I should have thought twice, but I didn't.

"Your honor," I said, "it seemes obvious to me that the initial 'W' stands for Wong."

There was a moment of silence, and then the laughter began, and Judge Wong laughed louder than anybody else. He went very easy on my client, too. To this day, wherever I see Judge Wong, he gives me a broad wink, pulls back his jacket, as though to exhibit his initials, and starts laughing. Some other judges might have resented my wisecrack, but Wong, fortunately for me, was amused.

Divorces are generally accompanied by some attempt at reconciling the two parties. The American Bar Association believes it is the duty of a divorce lawyer to attempt to bring the couple back together again. I disagree with that as a definite rule.

My feeling is that attorneys, generally, are not trained in the behaviorial sciences. They could, therefore, conceivably work to reconcile husbands and wives who should not be reconciled. The attorneys in those cases have not been able to recognize the signs of definite, positive, and destructive hatred. I know of cases where husbands and wives, on the brink of divorce, have been persuaded to reconcile—and have ended up killing each other. Or, if not literal murder, have committed emotional mayhem. Or have had another child, in an effort to solidify the reconciliation, and merely postponed the inevitable and, in the process, created a child who may very well grow up unhappy and disturbed.

I don't believe that it serves a useful, healthy purpose for attorneys to attempt reconciliations when they don't know what they are doing. I do, however, feel that an attorney has an ethical duty to determine if his client has made an irrevocable decision and is serious about the divorce, or is merely going about the action in an attempt to gain his spouse's attention. That often happens. In effect, the person is saying, "Hey, you're ignoring me, and so I'm filing for divorce—now you'll look at me and listen to me." He is using the divorce action simply to make his spouse notice him and his wants. If we are sure our client is in earnest about wanting a divorce, then we should go ahead and file the action and not try to live his life for him.

In Los Angeles County, moreover, there is a reconciliation mechanism. Every morning, as court convenes, it is announced that the county maintains conciliation facilities for anyone who wishes to avail themselves of them. If either party in any action before the court that day expresses a desire to see a counselor, the judge will then order both parties, plus their attorneys, to immediately go and speak to the counselor. I have heard that this procedure has produced some positive results; men and women on the brink of a divorce decide to give their marriages one last shot, consult counselors, and it works. The system does seem to produce some reconciliations—although I don't believe there are any statistics to show how long these reconciliations last.

Therefore, for the reasons noted, I try to stay out of reconciliation work in divorce cases. In some other instances, however, I do try to do more than merely handle the legal aspects. A lawyer can be and often must be a practical psychologist, as well as a barrister. In one recent case, my adversary and I got together and worked out a settlement that took a conscientious and sincere effort on both sides.

This case is an example of how the law should work. Both lawyers and the court had one paramount interest, and that was the well-being and future security of a human being. In this instance we all seemed to be advocates for substantial justice.

"Mr. Isaac," said a woman's voice on the telephone, "my name is Beverly Ramsdale and I want to see you about an injury my daughter suffered recently."

I was reluctant, because I don't ordinarily handle accident and injury work. My first reaction was to back away, but, out of politeness, I let Mrs. Ramsdale tell me her story. The more I listened, the more intrigued I became. The claim was against the County of Los Angeles and their attorneys were quite familiar to me. We have gone around on many cases, and I think they appreciate me as a tough and effective adversary. So I asked Mrs. Ramsdale to come in and see me so we could talk further.

She came in with her husband, Larry. She explained that Larry wasn't the father of her daughter, Pamela; he was her stepfather.

Pamela Ramsdale was thirteen. Beverly showed me her picture—a bright-looking, pretty, clear-eyed, blonde California girl. She had freckles and an engaging smile. Beverly told me she was an athletic child, outgoing, cheerful, well-liked.

Beverly used the present tense as she described her daughter. And yet, when she told me what had happened, I wondered about her choice of tenses. She could very well have used the past, because little Pam was lying on a hospital bed at that time, pretty much a vegetable. She was no longer athletic, certainly. No longer cheerful. No longer intelligent. Yet Beverly kept saying, "Pam is very athletic. She is a cheerful girl." I became very well acquainted with Beverly's attitude, which was basically that one way or another, she was going to restore her daughter to her previous condition. She was not going to admit defeat, ever.

Still, the facts were these: At the moment, Pamela Ramsdale was in a coma, unable to speak, to recognize anyone, to say or do or sense anything. Furthermore, the doctors held out little hope that she would ever recover.

I asked the question point-blank. "Mrs. Ramsdale, what are the chances that Pamela will recover?"

"Oh, she will," Beverly Ramsdale said. There was never a doubt in her mind. By the sheer strength of her will, by her maternal determination, she would make Pamela well again.

Pamela and her younger brother had been enrolled in a summer program sponsored by the county. It was a wonderful idea, that program; it was called "High on Life." The idea was to help pre-teens become exhilarated by something other than drugs. In this case, the alternative offered was life itself, with the emphasis on natural things—the outdoors, sports, nature. The goal of the program was to keep the kids away from the world of dope, to show them that they could get high on other sources of excitement. If the kids got "High on Life," then they would not have the need or desire to get high on such things as drugs.

It was a magnificent theory—but, despite its lofty intentions, the program ruined Pamela Ramsdale.

One morning, the county workers who were running the program in Lancaster, northwest of Los Angeles, decided they would take their young charges on a bike ride. They told the children to bring their bikes with them. It was a warm morning in August of 1975, and all the kids had their bikes and their lunches. They wore their excitement like badges.

Pamela and her brother were there, with the others. In all, there were fifty-four children in the group.

The route ended at a park, with a pool, and the plan was that the fifty-four kids would ride to the park, then spend the balance of the day picnicking in the park and swimming in the pool. What none of the county employees in charge of the outing had taken into consideration was that a moderately strong wind had blown up. The Lancaster area is pretty much desert country, and the winds blow strongly across the California deserts.

There was another problem. None of the supervisory workers had bothered to ride the route themselves. They were unaware that there was a pretty steep hill that the bikers would have to descend en route from the starting point to the park and pool. One would think that a careful survey of the route would have been a prerequisite where children were concerned, to determine if the route was indeed safe. There had been no such survey.

They set off on a ride that some would never finish—their faces were radiant and shining, their eyes glowing with happiness.

The wind began to blow harder as they pedaled off toward the hill. Some of the county employees rode along with them. The first kids went down the hill, and it was a thrilling descent—so steep they flew along, with the wind making it seem ever more dangerous and exciting.

They all laughed, their faces turning pink from the triple thrills—the bike ride, the steep descent, the wind. The grown-ups laughed along with them, and apparently nobody recognized the inherent danger in the situation. As the group rode down, there were a few accidents. Minor tumbles, scraped knees, bruised elbows.

Then two kids took serious falls and the supervisory employees called an ambulance for them. Pamela Ramsdale was one of the last still to go down the hill. The wind was blowing very strongly by now. Despite those two fairly serious accidents and despite the fact that the wind was nearly a gale, nobody thought to suggest that the children walk their bikes down the hill. As Pamela reached the top of the hill, one of the adults was next to her. They paused there, and they watched as an ambulance carted away those two injured youngsters.

They had a lot of fun at the park in Lancaster. The fact that two of their number had been hurt didn't seem to put much of a damper on their high spirits. It had been a great adventure, particularly that hell-for-leather ride down the hill. Only one of the children seemed unhappy. That was Pamela's brother. He kept looking for his sister. Finally, the last of the riders appeared, but still Pamela was missing, so he went to a supervisor.

"My sister isn't here," he said.

The supervisor looked around.

"She'll be here soon," he said. "Why don't you go in the pool and swim for a while?"

The boy dutifully went for a swim, but kept looking for Pamela. She didn't appear. After another fifteen or twenty minutes, he again went to the supervisor, fighting back tears this time, because he was scared. Pamela was his big sister and she wouldn't just leave him. He knew that something must have happened to her, or she'd be there.

Almost reluctantly, the supervisory personnel sent out a search team to look for Pamela Ramsdale. They retraced the path of the bike ride, and came to the fateful hill. At first they saw nothing, but then they found her—or what was left of her. She was off the edge of the hill, in a ravine, her bike crumpled, her body still and inert. She was totally unconscious, lying in the hot desert sun. Literally, the sun had been cooking her brain. Pamela was rushed to a hospital where she lay in a deep coma.

They went back over the course of the ride, and realized, from the spot where she had landed, that the wind must have lifted her and her bike in the air, flung her 30 or 40 feet into the ravine. There she had been for perhaps an hour. By the time she reached the hospital, her temperature was 107 degrees. She had been fried by the sun.

That was the Ramsdales' story. As they talked, my mind (as it usually does) considered all the possible defenses the county might advance. There was assumption of risk—had the parents and the child assumed the risk of injury by the action of allowing her to go on the ride? Was the county a guarantor that nothing would happen to a child in its care? Was the wind an act of God?

Those were all possible defenses. Yet, from the start, I was certain this was a case that could be won. Further, this was a case that should yield substantial monetary compensation to Beverly and Pamela Ramsdale, because it seemed to me to be a clear-cut case of official negligence. I didn't see much doubt that we would be able to collect, but I did foresee a potential source of concern.

With any case in which a child is injured, the greatest care should be taken to see that, in any award to the child, his or her future, long-range interests are protected. There are three possible happenings which must be considered—if the child does not recover, but is bedridden or in some manner handicapped forever, sufficient funds must be available for maintenance; if the child dies from the accident, the parents should be recompensed as much as possible; if the child recovers, there should be funds to see to his or her future and to be handy in case of any possible relapse.

With Pamela Ramsdale, that was always my only concern. I must admit that, talking to her doctors, I held out little hope for any recovery. I kept that thought to myself, however, because her mother was absolutely positive there would be a recovery—and a complete one, at that. And, after months of lying there, in a coma, one day Pamela moved slightly, stirred, and opened her eyes. That was the beginning of a battle that is still going on, as Beverly, with her great strength and great belief, forces her daughter back to health. That first day made Beverly jubilant, of course. The doctors were cautious in their diagnoses and prognoses, and told Beverly not to become too optimistic. Beverly worked with Pamela night and day. She said she wanted her to come home, to their little house on the Lancaster desert, where she could maintain a total vigilance by the girl's bedside. I couldn't see how it would be possible for Pamela ever to go home, ever to be free of hospital and institutional care, but I was wrong. Eventually, Pamela did go home again.

We filed a claim against the county which, as a matter of course, was rejected. So we filed our lawsuit. Then Los Angeles County assigned a deputy county counsel, Charles Tackett, to represent their interests in the matter. Tackett was one of their senior attorneys and had a reputation as being one of their best. He was experienced, aggressive, tough. Chuck Tackett had a formidable legal mind and would be a difficult adversary. As it turned out, he was everything a public official and a lawyer should be.

When he was assigned to the case, he called me. "Godfrey," he said, "I've been wanting for years to have a case with you on the other side. And now they've given me one that I can't possibly win."

I said I agreed with him, and I added that it shaped up as a long and complicated legal battle, but one which, I was sure, would ultimately provide a substantial recovery for my client.

I started taking depositions from the county employees who were involved in that tragic bicycle ride. I must admit that I wasn't totally objective. I had fallen under the spell of that pretty little girl in the hospital bed, and thinking of how her life had been ruined through neglect made me downright mad. I know, of course, that accidents happen, but even if they had simply counted noses and gone off to find Pamela as soon as they realized she was missing, the damage would have been substantially less. It had been negligence, I felt, and that was what made me angry. Also, there was the hill itself. Any respectable, responsible group would have sent an adult riding down that hill first, and they would have immediately ordered the kids to walk their bikes down. As I got testimony from those people, I felt that they were ashamed—that they knew, through the wisdom of hindsight, that they had been wrong, that they wished they had it all to do over again, that they had no rational defense for their actions.

Chuck Tackett knew it all, as well as I did. He was the kind of attorney that governments—local, state, or federal—ought to have, but rarely do. He himself took his bike, stuck it in his car, went out to that hill, and rode down. I went there, too, but I didn't ride a bike. I went there with the Ramsdales and we rode up and down in my car. Then I got out and walked up and down. I concluded that, even without a wind, it was too dangerous for anyone to ride down—so think how it would be for a child in a blowing, gusty wind.

Tackett asked to meet with me, and we sat down and discussed it. We tried to find a way to resolve the matter without costing the county a fortune in trial costs. His interest, as mine, was to see that Pamela Ramsdale got the benefit of whatever settlement we could work out. Tackett went with me to see Pamela, lying in her bed. By this time, she had gone home, and had more and more periods of consciousness, and, with Beverly constantly at her side, was even trying to talk and to walk. She spoke very slowly and every step caused her to stumble and almost fall, but she was trying and she was progressing. I had seen her before, so I knew how far she had come. But it was the first time for Tackett, and all he could see was how far she had yet to go.

He almost cried. We left and he headed directly for the nearest pub and belted one down quickly.

As we drove back to Los Angeles from Lancaster that day, we began discussions that eventually led to a settlement which has drawn praise from the county and from the judge we appeared before. That first day, we agreed on certain principles, which we stuck to. Later it was merely a question of details and amounts of money.

The basic principle was that there should be lengthy protection for Pamela, so that she would be taken care of and never have to become dependent on welfare. We also agreed on another principle, namely that Beverly Ramsdale should receive some compensation, too, so she would be able to spend more time with her daughter. Both Tackett and I recognized the fact that Beverly was the best therapist Pamela could ever have, and she would take the child further and faster than anyone else.

After some days of discussion, we agreed on figures. Beverly Ramsdale was to get $150,000 outright. That was to be her money to use as she wished. Tackett and I knew that she would use it, almost entirely, for Pamela's well-being. Next, I was to get $150,000 for attorney's fees and costs. Pamela was to get $22,500 for 30 years, or a total of $675,000. At the end of those 30 years, there would be another $300,000 as a lump sum payment. It was a total package of $1,275,000, which is the second largest settlement with Los Angeles County in its history.

The way Tackett and I worked it out, however, it would only cost the county $600,000. They would immediately pay out $300,000—$150,000 to Beverly and another $150,000 to me—and then buy a $300,000, 7½ percent tax-free bond. The interest would give Pamela her annual stipend of $22,500 and the lump payment would be there at the end of the bond's life, 30 years. We added a stipulation that, should anything happen to Pamela, that money would go to her heirs. Tackett had thought up the bond idea as a means of holding down the county's expenses, and it was acceptable to me. We shook hands on the deal, both pleased.

I went to the Ramsdales and explained the arrangement. I said that it was entirely possible that, if we went to court, the award might be higher. I said that I recommended they accept the settlement. I said that the court proceedings might drag on for years. Furthermore, I knew of no settlement where a minor got 30 years of protection—and then a lump sum of $300,000.

"You think it over," I said, putting my papers back in my briefcase and preparing to leave.

"We'll take it," Beverly said, without a moment's hesitation.

"Wonderful!" I said. "But most people would want to sleep on it, at least. Why did you accept so fast?"

"Well, that way I can get the money right away," she said, "and I need the money right away to help Pam. I want to quit my job. I want to get a house with a pool, so she can swim every day. I want to get a lot of exercise equipment. That all costs money, and we can't do it by ourselves. But we can, if we accept that settlement."

She said, as she said so often, that she knew that one day Pam would be perfectly normal. The quicker they got to it, she reasoned, the quicker that day would come.

So they took the settlement. I think it was a good one.

There were certain other provisions that benefited Pam and her family, too. She was granted free medical care in all county facilities for the rest of her life, and that, in time, could amount to a sizeable additional sum. The county also waived all claims to monies it might have believed were previously due it for medical services to Pamela, easing some of Beverly Ramsdale's concerns.

We had to go to court for official approval of the deal Chuck Tackett and I had hammered out. We were all there—Tackett, me, Beverly, and Pam Ramsdale. Tackett and I each explained the settlement to the judge. He looked over all the paperwork and then looked at us and said that both of us were to be congratulated. "This is the best settlement of its kind I have ever seen," he said.

Then he asked me if it would be all right with me if he showed it to the other judges, as an illustration of what could be done when two attorneys of goodwill worked together for the benefit of everyone concerned. Of course, I agreed.

For all of us, that day in court was a warm and pleasant experience. There was no acrimony. Both attorneys felt good, felt as though they had won. The judge was smiling, the bailiffs and court stenographers were smiling, the Ramsdales were smiling. I have rarely had a moment in any courtroom that was so completely happy. Even Pamela, still confined to a wheelchair, seemed to be radiating hope.

The doctors are still pessimistic, but I suppose that's the nature of their profession. They can't promise miracles, even if they think a miracle may happen. They are dealing with people, and people grasp at straws and then resent it if the straws break. So Pamela's doctors didn't want to hold out any false hopes and, instead, adopted a pessimistic posture. In the long run, I imagine that's better than being too optimistic. Still, I have a hunch that Pam will recover—I'm betting on her strength and her mother's determination.

Tacket reported to me that one official called him up and said, "Tackett, what the hell did Godfrey Isaac do to deserve $150,000?"

Tacket answered: "Twenty years of effective law practice, including cases like Noguchi and Sirhan."

The bureaucrat didn't argue any more.

Eventually, the money was forthcoming. But the waiting put a strain on the Ramsdale's marriage. Beverly and Larry split, and the money might have been one of the reasons.

I call Beverly up once in a while to find out how Pamela is doing. Every time I call, she reports improvement. It makes all the work seem worthwhile.

Chapter Thirteen

IN 1973, there came that blight on American political life known as Watergate. As the sordid mess was uncovered, I watched and listened from the sidelines and felt that I should have a part in it. It was, after all, history, and everyone would like to be a part of an historical event. Furthermore, this particular historical event concerned lawyers—lawyers perpetrated it, lawyers covered it up, lawyers defended the perpetrators and the cover-uppers—and so I kept thinking that somehow I should have a legal hand in the unfolding scandal.

It might not have happened, had I not been invited to speak in Europe in the spring of 1973. Cyril Wecht, the coroner of Allegheny County in Pennsylvania—I had met him during the Noguchi case—invited me to join him in speaking to a group in Brussels, Belgium. That invitation took me to Europe and, since I was over on that side of the world, I figured I might as well stop off on the way home and visit friends in New York and Washington. One of those friends was Judah Best, a brilliant lawyer and an old friend. Later, Best would become known as the chief counsel for Spiro Agnew. Best's firm—Dickstein, Shapiro and Galligan—had recently changed its name to Colson and Shapiro. The Colson, of course, was Charles (Chuck) Colson, former special counsel to President Richard Nixon.

I didn't meet Colson on that trip. I merely had an old-fashioned friendly chat with Best. Later, when Colson got in so much trouble as a result of Watergate, Best thought of me when Colson needed representation in California.

Among other transgressions he was accused of, as the Watergate mess proliferated, was his involvement in the break-in at the office of Dr. Fielding, who had been Daniel Ellsberg's psychiatrist. Best called and asked me if I'd like to represent Colson in California. As I mentioned, I wanted to have a part in the Watergate affair. At one time some friends suggested me for the special prosecutor, which eventually went to Leon Jaworski. Best's call interested me immensely.

Jud Best's prime concern was that someone who knew Los Angeles procedures had to take Colson before the Los Angeles County Grand Jury, which was probing the Fielding break-in. Could I do that? Yes, I said. We didn't discuss anything specific and neither of us even mentioned the matter of money. Best was simply anxious to have somebody capable with his partner as he faced the grand jury. So he asked and I agreed, and that was that.

David Shapiro, another partner in the Washington firm, flew out with Colson. Best joined us. My first meeting with Colson was in his hotel room. I was very curious to meet one of the actors in the most publicized drama of our time. I liked him immediately—friendly, obviously intelligent, cooperative. I had heard that he was brighter than anybody else in the Nixon adminstration, and my initial impression was that that assessment could very easily be true.

We talked. The immediate issue was the Fielding break-in, and I asked Colson every question I could think of. He answered them all with what I felt was great sincerity and complete honesty. I concluded, from what Colson told me, that he was innocent of this crime. Now it was his turn to quiz me. He was naturally curious about the procedures before the Los Angeles County Grand Jury, and he, Shapiro, and Best fired questions at me on what he might expect.

At that time, the district attorney of Los Angeles County was Joseph Busch. Busch had been a classmate of mine at Loyola, and we had remained friends. Colson, Shapiro, and Best knew of that relationship, and, of course, felt more secure because of it.

While the three of them listened, I called Busch. I told my old friend that I was representing Chuck Colson, that I was satisfied he was innocent, and that I would be accompanying him when he kept his date with the grand jury. I think Colson was impressed with the informal tone I used. I gathered that such informality was rare in Washington, and had been unheard of in the Nixon inner circle.

When the day arrived for Colson to appear before the grand jury, I picked him up at his hotel and drove downtown to the courthouse building. I knew there would be a big press delegation there, so I parked across the street in an attempt to outwit them. It is hard to outwit newspapermen, and that ploy didn't succeed either. They spotted us and ran toward us. We tried to fight our way through the reporters and radio and TV newsmen, as we battled our way to the door. Because of my relatively small size, I was shunted aside in the crush. By the time the mob scene arrived at the door, I had been elbowed to the rear. At the door, a sheriff was screening everybody, admitting only those people with press passes or people he knew to be part of the proceedings. He didn't know me.

"Sorry, sir," he said, barring the door adequately. "You can't go in there."

"But I . . . "

He was pushing me away when Colson, my client, came to my rescue.

"That's my lawyer, sheriff," he said.

The sheriff apologetically let me pass. I had lost a little aplomb, but it didn't take me long to get it back. We went upstairs, and were standing in the corridor outside the courtroom, when Joe Busch sauntered up. He put his arm around me and I introduced him to Colson.

"Good morning," Busch said to Colson. "How did you get this cocksucker as your lawyer?"

I didn't know how Busch's rather inelegant greeting would go over with the man from Washington, the intimate of a president. But Colson beamed. Later, he said to me that as soon as he heard Busch say that, it bolstered his confidence.

"When he said what he did," Colson told me, "I realized that the two of you had to be very close friends. And with my lawyer and the DA so buddy-buddy, I knew everything would turn out OK."

Attorneys are not allowed to be present in the grand jury room. When Colson was called in to testify, I paced outside for what seemed like hours, talking to Jud Best and wondering what was happening inside. A few times, Colson came out to consult with us, to ask our opinion and advice on a piece of testimony, or how he should handle a question he had been asked. Hopefully, he took our advice on those matters.

When the session was finally over, Joe Busch came over to me and said, "Godfrey, why don't you bring Colson up to my office and we'll have some coffee and cookies."

We went up to Busch's office for coffee and cookies. Colson told me that he was a little concerned about what was going to happen to him in Los Angeles, mostly out of unfamiliarity with Los Angeles procedures and personnel. He said that he knew Washington and knew what was what and who was who in Washington, but Los Angeles was alien territory to him. He said that when he found himself sitting informally in the district attorney's office, chatting over a tray of coffee and cookies, he lost his concern. I could see the worry lifting from his shoulders. He unwound and was the charming man he could be when relaxed and at ease.

That night, four of us—Colson, Shapiro, Best, and I—had

dinner. Colson was effusive in his praise of me, of how my contacts had apparently eased the way, how he would have felt lost without me. He said he had seen well-oiled machines before, but nothing to compare to the smoothness of my operation.

"I can't thank you enough, Godfrey," he said. And then he turned to his partner, Shapiro, and he said, "David, write out a check for $5,000 for Godfrey."

Shapiro turned to me. "What do you think, Godfrey?" I was annoyed and I said so. "I'm pissed," I said.

"Why?" Colson asked, with genuine surprise.

"I'll tell you why. I'm not a bellboy you just hand a tip to. I'll set my own fee."

Colson thought that over; he laughed and then he said, "You're right. And from now on I want you on my team in Washington."

Judah Best was delighted but Shapiro wasn't. I think he felt I was moving in on him, encroaching on his area of leadership. That, of course, was the last thing I wanted to do.

In the next few months, I made many trips to Washington to consult with Colson. Usually, his chauffeur met me at the airport and drove me to wherever Colson was at the moment. Once, Colson was at the airport gate to meet me himself, and he wore a broad, very pleased smile.

"Hi, Godfrey," he said. Before I could answer, he said, "Guess what? Archibald Cox has been fired."

He was elated at that development because he felt (perhaps with some justification) that Cox had been out to get him. Thus, when Nixon sacked Cox, Colson felt (wrongly, obviously) that he would have clear sailing from then on.

I was working hard on Colson's defense and I think I would have contributed much to finding a way to hack him out of the legal woods, but I never got a chance to use my ideas. One very early morning, his phone call woke me up.

"Godfrey," he said, "I want you to hear it from me first. I have decided to plead guilty."

I was incredulous. Why? He had been so anxious to fight

the charges all along, so elated with the strategy we had discussed, so eager for a forum so he could plead his innocence. Why this drastic and unexpected about-face?

He told me, then, that he had been to a prayer meeting. He had suddenly realized that he had to plead guilty and that, if he did, "nothing bad will happen to me." So he changed his plea to guilty. Shapiro and some of the others felt that he would not get a jail term as a result of the guilty plea, but I believed they were wrong. I said he would go to jail because sending Watergate figures to jail was the in-thing that season—it was the time for jail sentences for political offenders. I was right. He was sent to jail.

After he had been sentenced and incarcerated, I went to his ex-law firm one morning to talk to Jud Best. Colson was in his old office. We talked a few minutes. He was assembling some Watergate material for possible testimony in other cases, and we simply exchanged a few pleasantries. I have only seen him once since that day.

That one time was in Fresno where I went to attend a bar association convention. I happened to see that he was in Fresno at the same time, also to make a speech. He was to be the featured speaker at a bible meeting. He had been *Born Again*, as he called his book, and was talking to the people about his conversion. I decided to go and hear his lecture, which was called "Morality in the Law." I stood in the back of the hall and listened as he spoke, and he was truly magnificent. He had great power and a great delivery and he knew how to speak sincerely better than almost any man I have ever heard. I remembered how he had once been frightened to death, cowering before that mysterious grand jury session, on the verge of tears as he faced those unknown terrors. Now he was strong, completely in control of himself, powerful.

I walked up to the front of the auditorium after his speech. He was autographing books for a long line of people, mostly women with stars in their eyes. They all looked up at him as though he were some kind of hero. His conversion had turned him from just another one of the Watergate gang to a figure to be revered and respected.

Finally, I got up to him, and I tugged at his sleeve. He turned around and saw me, and his face broke into a king-size smile.

"Godfrey!" he said, and threw his arms around me and hugged me. "How about this? It's sure a lot different from the old days, isn't it?"

He was right. It was a lot different. The villain had become a hero. But there were still many villains left over from the Watergate scandal. The tragedy, to many lawyers, was that so many of the villains were lawyers and, because of that, the legal profession had received a black eye. The law has had many black eyes lately—some of them deserved.

Some lawyers have abused their trust. They should be exposed and punished. However, most lawyers are dedicated and hardworking and when they or all of us are maligned in the public eye, I am always ready to spring to the defense of my colleagues. Some of the general attitude toward lawyers stems from jealousy. Most lawyers are dedicated professional men and appear to be financially well-off. This creates envy in many non-professionals, and envy breeds some hatred. To the envious, we make too much money, and whatever we do is suspect. To them, when we get in trouble, it is well deserved. If we do a good job, it is what is to be expected. If we do a poor job, it proves what they already know—how bad we are. Sometimes, it seems as if we just can't win.

Many people think that lawyers merely get up in court, talk a bit, and collect a large fee. The average person has no concept of the time or detail involved in getting ready for court. Preparing a case can be a back-breaking task and an emotional drain. The client only sees the end result. Well, he also sees the bill and generally concludes that he has been robbed. The bill usually falls far short of robbery and often is not only justified and a fair charge for the work involved, but is even less than it should be.

There is much to be done before a lawyer is ready to walk

into court and try a case. Every good lawyer wants to master the facts of the case and determine how best to present them to the judge or jury. This requires going to where the alleged crime occurred, studying the area, taking pictures from the most advantageous angles, making charts, and so on. This can be time-consuming.

The process of legal research is often a lengthy one. Reading, searching, seeking the cases that give an interpretation favorable to the client can take hours. It is not just any precedent that is being sought, it is one that can be advantageously used. Research can be exciting, but it can also be tiring, dull, and grinding. Often it goes on into the night; it can ruin your social life, and it can play havoc with a marriage. Probably that is why lawyers are notoriously poor marital risks, the long hours being grist for the mill of the suspicious wife.

We feel that we are entitled to be paid for our skill and knowledge. Often in our society, that is not the case. The process of successfully putting on a case and presenting evidence so that the appearance of the facts is accurate and persuasive requires unusual talents. The lawyer must be psychologically oriented, be innovative, analytical, and clever. These traits are in short supply, and those possessing them are entitled to be compensated. A lawyer must also be observant and selective. In most cases there are several possible witnesses who can be called to testify. If they have observed the same thing, you rarely want to use all of them, because their testimony would be cumulative and repetitious. The choice of which of the available witnesses to choose may determine the outcome of the case. That's where skill, experience, and just good old gut reaction makes the difference.

In these situations, I often start by having all of the witnesses quizzed by my investigators. I've had some great ones, and I consider their reports very seriously. In the final analysis, however, it is my judgment that is controlling, because I have the ultimate responsibility in the case. I have often read an investigator's report in which it is stated that the witness is sensational. Then, when I meet the witness I am stunned. Sensational? The same witness can be, in my opinion, a disaster area. He may have been glib and articulate to the investigator—that's what impressed him—but to me he exudes the air of a con man. I anticipate he will rub the jury the wrong way. He doesn't sound sincere and won't be believed.

Now comes another decision for the lawyer to make. Should I use that super-glib witness, knowing he will alienate the jury? Should I pass on him, even though his testimony is important? Should I try to change his personality, so that I can have the benefit of his testimony without the danger of his abrasiveness turning the jury off? Tough questions!

I have found that attempting to alter a witness' personality in a few days is dangerous. Vigorous cross-examination can strip that veneer away, with the result that you are worse off than if you had just let him alone. The witness then looks like a phony, and your entire presentation is suddenly suspect.

Sometimes an investigator may tell me that a potential witness is no good—a poor memory, wishy-washy, exudes weakness. When I meet him, I may feel that he comes across as sincere, despite those weaknesses. I often take a chance with a witness of that sort, if I believe he can be helped. I will work with such a witness, trying to build his confidence and self-assurance.

It is permissible to work with a witness and prepare him to testify. This entire area is a very sensitive one. A lawyer may be guilty of malpractice if he has a witness who is mistaken about a fact and the lawyer does not point that out. People who do not tell the truth are not always liars. A falsehood may be the result of a faulty memory, and it is the lawyer's duty to jog that memory. On the other hand, if a witness still believes he is correct after he is informed of a possible error in his proposed testimony, then you must not permit him to testify otherwise. It would be a criminal act to insist that a witness testify what you believe the fact is rather than what he recalls, even if he is in error. At that point, you either do not call him as a witness or you must allow him to testify based on his recollection. There is a fine line separating good faith from bad intent, and a lawyer is well advised scrupulously to stay on the right side of that line.

When I was first starting my practice, there was a gimmick among criminal lawyers called "the lecture." Most used it, and it worked. For example, a client would come in and say that he had been accused of embezzlement.

"Here is what happened," he would begin, but the lawyer would hold up one hand and interrupt him.

"First," the lawyer would say, "let me explain to you what the law says about embezzlement. Now, if the head of your firm told you to take some money home, say—how much are you accused of taking?"

"Ten thousand."

"Yes. If the head of your firm asked you to take ten thousand dollars home for safekeeping, because he was afraid that his secretary might be getting ready to steal it, then the fact that you took ten thousand home would not be a crime. On the other hand, if you took ten thousand dollars to bet on the horses, intending to repay it out of your winnings, then that is embezzlement. Now, Mr. Jones, tell me why you took that ten thousand dollars home?"

Usually, Mr. Jones would catch on and quickly recite a story about how his boss had asked him to take the $10,000 home for safekeeping.

"I see," the lawyer would say. "You may have been unwise in doing that, Mr. Jones, but you have committed no crime."

The point of "the lecture" is that the lawyer told the client what was a crime and what was not a crime, and he usually got back a story that placed the client in the ranks of the innocent. The technique is not often used any more. There was, however, an element of sense in it if it were not abused. It is the responsibility of the lawyer to explain to his client what the law states and what defenses there are to a particular offense. It is conceivable that a suspect may think he is guilty and, yet, be innocent under the law.

A classical example of this is found in the situation where two men get in a fight. One reaches into a drawer, pulls out a gun, and kills the other. What offense, if any, has been committed? The killer may be (1) guilty of murder in the first degree, (2) guilty of murder in the second degree, (3) guilty of manslaughter, or (4) innocent. If the man who pulled the gun believed the other was reaching for a knife to stab him and he was in danger of serious bodily harm, the shooting could be held to be in self-defense and the killing not a crime at all. If the shooting was negligent, the crime may have been manslaughter. If the shooting was intentional and there never was a knife, the offense could be first degree murder. If the shooting was in the heat of a fight, in the spur of the moment, it might be second degree murder. Was there premeditation? And on and on one could go in analyzing what occurred.

It is the duty of a defense lawyer to discuss these distinctions with his client. It may be extremely difficult to reconstruct what actually occurred. Who can tell, with absolute certainty, what went on in the minds of the participants during their brawl? Even witnesses, assuming there were any, might differ. Four people could have observed the fight and the final fatal shot, and you might get four conflicting reports. Depending on what can and cannot be proven to the satisfaction of a jury, that one act could lead the killer to be sentenced to death, to be imprisoned for life, to be imprisoned for a lesser term, or, if self-defense can be substantiated, to complete exoneration and freedom.

That is why the most often-asked question I hear from the lay public—"How can you defend a man you know is guilty?"—is really an unanswerable question. The asker presupposes that everything is black or white, that your client is necessarily guilty or innocent; the asker forgets that every person accused of a crime is entitled to be defended. In a large percentage of criminal cases, the same act can be interpreted in many different ways. An act which, on the surface, may seem heinous and indefensible, can be subject to an interpretation which makes it socially acceptable. A woman stabs a man who is trying to rape her. The stabbing is horrendous, but the circumstances render it socially acceptable. I know she is guilty of killing a human being, yet I can defend her because her crime was socially acceptable. Many crimes fall into that category—subject to interpretation. If you see a man strangling a child and you leap to the rescue and save the child, you are a hero, even if you had to kill the strangler. Yet, suppose it can be proved that you and the strangler had been mortal enemies for thirty years and you had been heard, on more than one occasion, to say that someday you were going to kill him? Then you are no longer a hero, but may be accused of premediated murder, even though ostensibly you performed a heroic act in the process. It can get very confusing at times.

When I am asked to take a case, I make the decision as to whether or not I will defend the accused based on my own standards within the framework of my professional responsibility. I've turned down many cases. It isn't the nature of the crime so much as the nature of the accused and the circumstances surrounding the act that are the deciding factors to me. I don't like people who are arrogant about what they've done, who boast about their deed and how they have gotten away with something. Let them find another lawyer, not me.

Once I defended a man who had done a terrible thing. He had apparently gotten drunk, then got in his car and gone for a drive. He slammed into the rear of another car, loaded with teenagers. The car caught fire and the passengers in the car he hit burned to death. Certainly, it was a multiple homicide. The man himself, though, was a gentle, sensitive, caring human being. He tortured himself over his guilt, felt ashamed and consumed with remorse. Irrespective of any guilt, I made the determination to defend him. Actually, I got him off—

there was insufficient evidence—which may have done him a disservice. Some time later, a free man, he killed himself. His guilt feelings were too much for him to bear. He judged himself, found himself guilty, and eventually executed himself. But I had been able to defend him with a clear conscience based on my belief that everyone is entitled to a defense and by my own standards of morality.

Our system provides that all persons are entitled to a defense. Sirhan Sirhan is a good example. I had, like all Americans, hated Sirhan for killing a brilliant and promising presidential candidate. Yet, I always felt that he was entitled to a defense, long before I met him. In California, we have a defense known as diminished capacity. It applies when a person is unable to form a meaningful intent to kill and, where applicable, reduces the crime of murder to manslaughter. Thus, even if you concede Sirhan killed Senator Kennedy, you could debate whether he suffered from diminished capacity. There was a triable issue at time of trial. Later, the possibility of a second gun raised even new issues. That was when I became involved. Obviously, Sirhan was entitled to pursue those legal avenues and needed a lawyer to do so. Everyone is entitled to a defense.

It is true that we lawyers believe in our system and the right of all those accused to counsel. It is equally true that none of us want people to be hurt, robbed, defrauded, or raped. These beliefs are not inconsistent. We recognize that we live in a society where crimes occur. We know that not all persons accused of crime are guilty. We believe in the rights of an accused and we work hard to protect them. I wish that all crime could be abolished, but this is a utopian dream. People will continue to commit crimes, and lawyers will continue to defend those people. This is part of our adversary system of justice. As aggravating as it must sometimes seem, our system is far superior to any other and reflects our American sense of justice.

Our talents should also be utilized to protect victims and

potential victims. Many believe that victims are the forgotten people of our system, and there is some truth in that. I do not believe in de-emphasizing the rights of an accused, but I am convinced that there must also be a vigorous effort to prevent the victimization of our people, and when they do become victims, they should have well-recognized rights.

Everyone agrees that there is too much crime. The streets are unsafe and the parks and alleys are worse. Even when we lock up our houses, they are often burglarized. Crime is increasing and law enforcement people seem unable to stem the tide. Who is to blame? What do we do?

The public cries for tougher laws, rigorous prosecution, stiffer sentences, vengeance. Many blame the courts and lenient judges. Legislators call for longer sentences and the death penalty. Every critic voices his solution, and the consensus is for harsher penalties.

I disagree. Long sentences breed crime; our prisons are training grounds for criminals. It is not the length of a sentence, but it is the certainty of punishment that is the most effective deterrent. I believe that probation should be rarely granted, and then only in unusual, meritorious cases. When a person commits a crime, he should know that he most probably will go to prison. Today, the offender often believes that even if convicted, he will never see the inside of a penitentiary. As a consequence, prison is not an effective deterrent to crime. The opposite will be true when incarceration can be speedily and definitely anticipated upon conviction, and for a shorter, more meaningful term.

Our judges are actually doing a good job based on the circumstances under which they function. Most jurists are dedicated and conscientious. They have the responsibility for sentencing, and that can be an awesome burden. It is easy to know how to sentence when one is merely a reader of headlines over coffee at the breakfast table. It is extremely difficult when one wears a black robe and looks into the eyes of a nineteen-year-old convicted of a serious crime. In my

view, it would be easier to sentence if the terms were shorter
and our institutions more effectively prepared to rehabilitate
the inmate and prepare him for a successful return to society.

I am opposed to capital punishment. The available studies
indicate that capital punishment is not an effective deterrent.
In fact, there is some indication that it actually may have the
opposite effect. Potential murderers may seek out states where
there is capital punishment as the setting for killing. Their
inner need for punishment and self-destructive drives can best
be fulfilled where, if caught, the state will put them to death.
In a recent highly publicized execution, the man sentenced to
death, Gary Gilmore, refused efforts to be saved and kept
insisting he wanted to die. This raises an inference that, had
there been no death penalty, his behavior may have been
different. He appeared to be seeking the ultimate punishment.

A powerful argument against capital punishment is the
imperfection of our judicial system. As good as it is, there are
still many mistakes that are made by the judges, juries, and
prosecutors. Generally, these errors can be rectified. Where a
mistake is made in a capital case, it cannot be corrected after
execution. If we put an innocent person to death, we are
taking a giant step backwards into the Dark Ages.

I am deeply troubled by the tendency of those with money
and better lawyers to escape the ultimate penalty. Many who
are poor or members of a minority are not so fortunate. How
can a system be allowed where life or death may hang on the
size of a defendant's purse or the color of his skin? Such a
condition erodes our respect for law and offends basic feelings
of decency.

I have always abhorred violence. If the decent, law-abiding
members of society have no better solution to a problem than
to kill people, I believe we are in serious trouble. Killing is
basically wrong. It is wrong for one human to take another's
life in a street or alley. It is wrong for society to solve its
problem the same way the criminal did. Certainly, as a well-
ordered society, we must have a better solution.

The whole question of the death penalty is one of the most emotional issues confronting our society. It generates much heat when discussed. People everywhere are interested and ready to discuss it—or argue about it. I am often asked my opinion and I am never reticent to expound on the subject. I have probably lost some friends over it. There is no question in my mind as to the sincerity of those who believe in capital punishment. I respect the views of those who disagree with me and can dispassionately express their reasons and state their position. However, too many proponents get very emotional and excitable, and it is impossible to have a real exchange of ideas. I believe the public is strongly in favor of the death penalty, but most have never really thought it out.

Law and life involve a never-ending balancing of equities. There are few absolutes to which we can cling forever without modification. We may have complete faith in the system, but continuing vigilance is necessary because of its changing nature.

Our civil rights are precious. They spell out the foundation of our country's jurisprudence. You do not need to be a historian to appreciate our Constitution and the Bill of Rights. I feel deeply about the brilliance of our founding fathers who wrote a document over 200 years ago that protects us all today just as it did then. The achievement in formulating that document was monumental.

Some feel that the Bill of Rights has only been used to protect criminals. Those accused of crime invoke its protection in court, but were it not for these protections, any one of us would be subject to arrest or unlawful search and seizure. We would not have the right to counsel or trial. In short, if not for our civil rights, we would all be vulnerable to arbitrary and discriminatory arrest and conviction.

To be effective, these rights must be available to everyone, including those who are accused. Otherwise, they would be meaningless. Our rights provide a mantle of freedom for each and every one of us.